Laura [illegible]nt in the open air

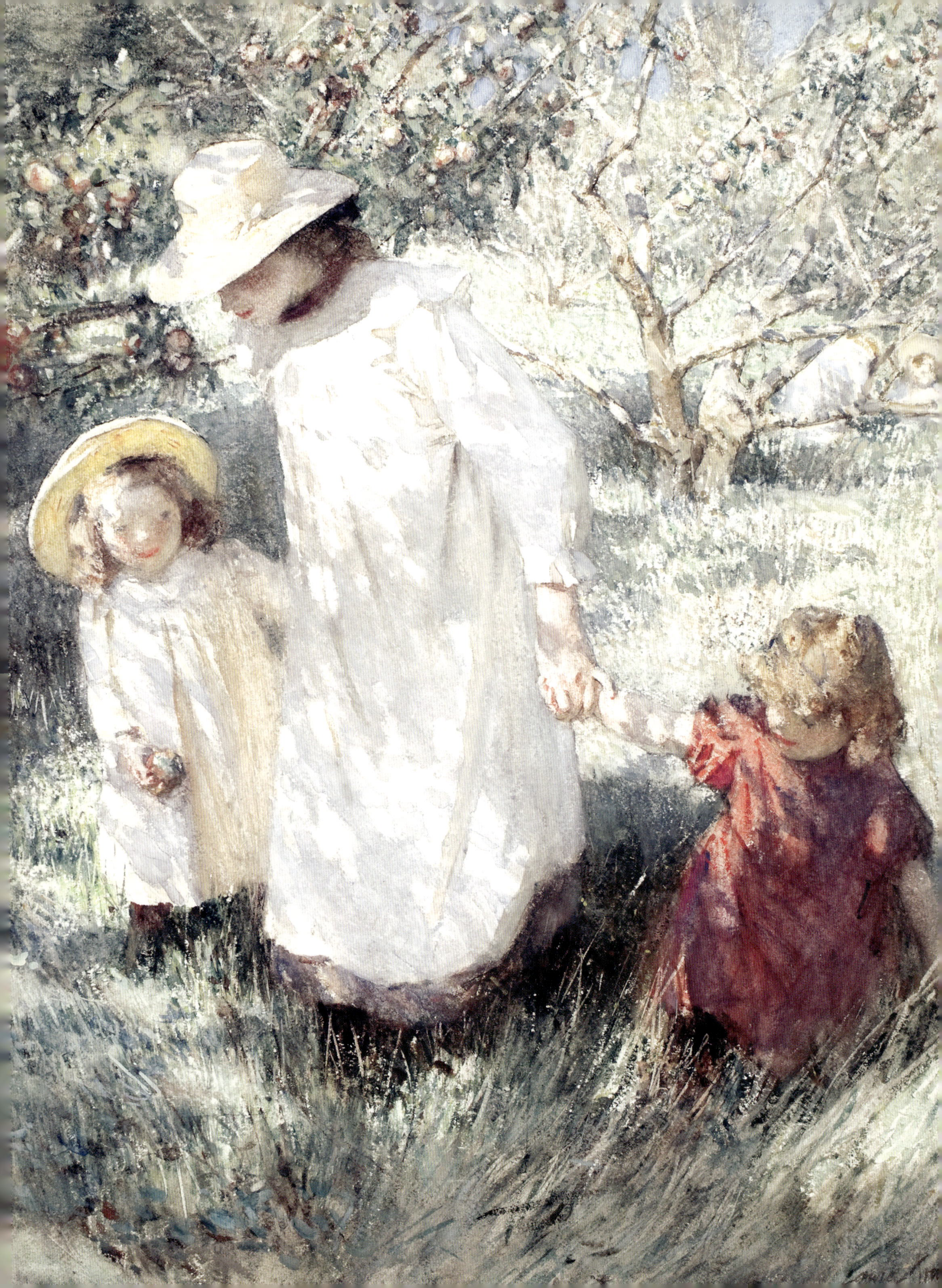

Laura Knight
in the open air

Elizabeth Knowles

Penlee House
Gallery & Museum
PENZANCE

Sansom & Company

Reprinted 2013
First published in 2012 by Sansom & Co Ltd.,
81G Pembroke Road, Bristol BS8 3EA
www.sansomandcompany.co.uk
info@sansomandcompany.co.uk

ISBN 978-1-906593-65-0

Produced in conjunction with an exhibition organised by
Penlee House Gallery & Museum, Penzance (16 June–8 September 2012)
and touring to Djanogly Art Gallery, Nottingham (22 September–4 November 2012)
and Worcester City Art Gallery (17 November 2012–10 February 2013)

Sponsored by MESSUM'S

British Library cataloguing-in-publication data:
A catalogue record for this book is available from the British Library.

Design and typesetting by E&P Design, Bath
Printed by Zenith Media, Tonypandy, Rhondda

Frontispiece: *In the Orchard*; watercolour
private collection; image courtesy The Fine Art Society

Contents

Foreword

Elizabeth Knowles's wide-ranging book, accompanying the touring exhibition organised by Penlee House Gallery & Museum, centering on Dame Laura Knight's work as a plein-air painter, offers insights into one of England's foremost female painters.

Knight's fascination with charged atmospheres and her determination to tackle her subject on site eventually drew her to the ballet and circus subjects, which, by 1929, had made her an artist of international renown. In March of that year, Knight went to St James's Palace to be made a Dame, becoming the first artist to be so honoured.

She managed to bring a wholehearted enthusiasm to her work that made it immediate and engaging, whether painted from the cliff tops at Lamorna, or sketched in a Ballets Russes dressing room. The sheer variety of subject matter she sketched, painted and even etched throughout her career gave her work a broad appeal.

Moreover, not many painters can claim her longevity; among female artists, only Georgia O'Keefe springs to mind. When she died aged 92, Knight had been at the forefront of British realism all the way from Staithes to Cornwall, and worked through two world wars. She painted and/or befriended, among others, Sir Alfred Munnings, T.E. Lawrence, George Bernard Shaw, Sergei Diaghilev and Anna Pavlova.

She remained throughout her long career focused on movement, temperament, time and energy, and their effects on people and places. Perhaps this is one reason why Dame Laura Knight remains such a fascinating figure in British art. She was always interested in what people did, rather than who they were.

David Messum

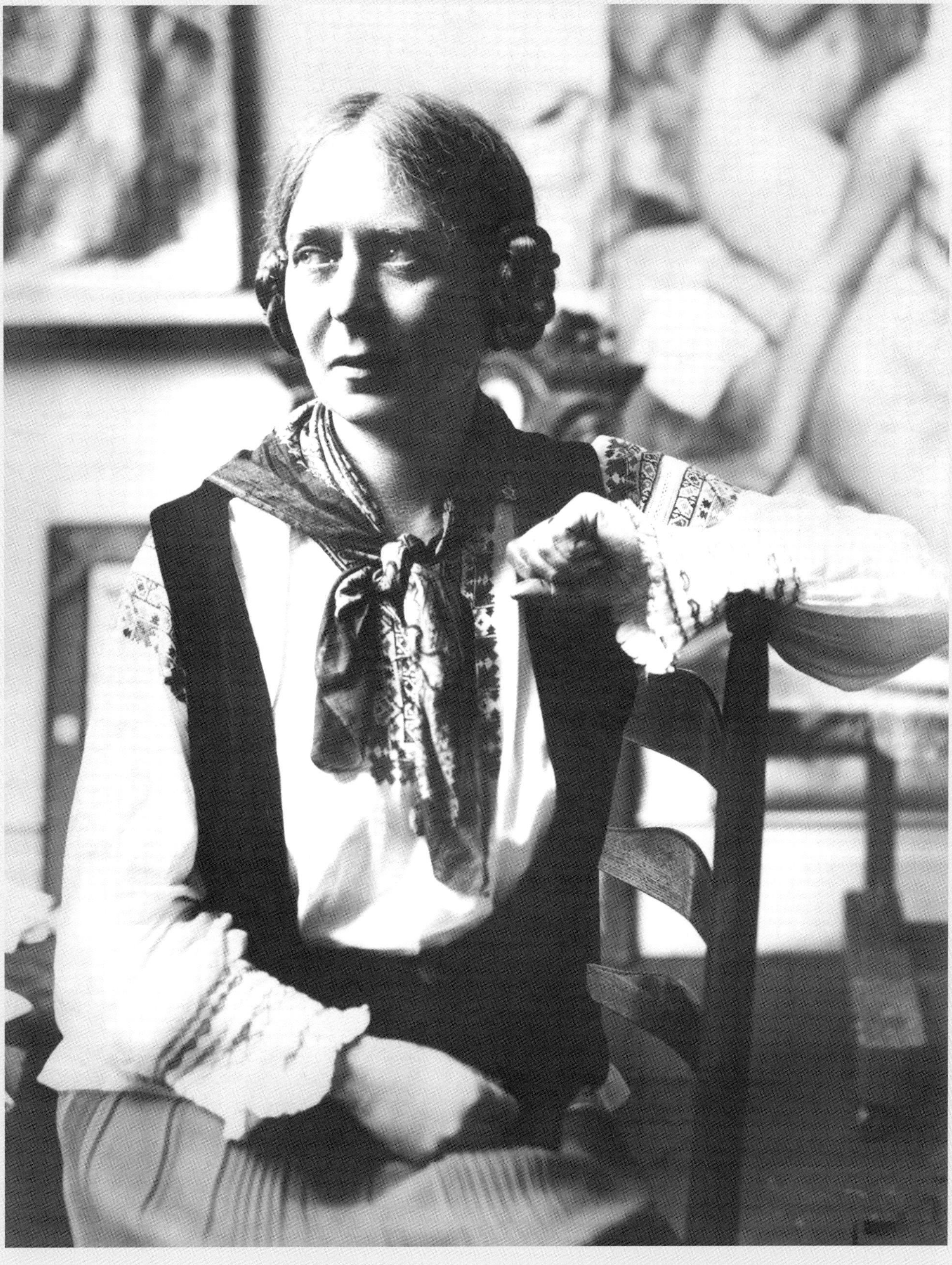

Laura Knight, 1 January 1923

Hulton Archive

Early days in Nottingham 1877–1894

Laura Knight's engagement with landscape began before she was twelve on sketching expeditions with her mother and lasted to the end of her life. From the first excitement of summertime trips out to green fields and woodlands beyond the limits of her home town, to the heartfelt love of peaceful farmlands she expressed towards the end of her life, Laura embraced the open air. Working directly from her subject was always her priority. Her long apprenticeship was a struggle to find pictorial expression in what was in front of her, or rather, what she placed in front of herself. She responded naturally to natural subjects but she drove herself to create and control her own subject matter within them. As a student she was bound by the conventions of her time and from their confines she developed her own language. In effect, she made them into her strengths by persistence. The way of working that she developed early on stood her in good stead right through her working life.

At her mother's knee, Laura learned to look and study and make pencil drawings. She was talented enough to go to art school where an academic regime kept her studying and drawing. Of course, she railed against the art school discipline and the slow pace of progress it imposed but she kept up the pressure on herself as she began to mature, endlessly drawing and studying her subjects before venturing to paint them. She was sustained by the belief that through rigorous study and practice good work could be achieved. In the event, it would not be until she was thirty and in Cornwall that the long years of study were finally left behind as she produced a series of paintings that expressed her true strength and maturity as an artist. Looking back on that time, Laura wrote 'I discovered the ecstasy of slinging paint without other thought or motive coming between. I am sure this extraordinary moment comes in the life of every artist: let the pencil or brush speak of its own accord to tell the little one can ever know.'[1]

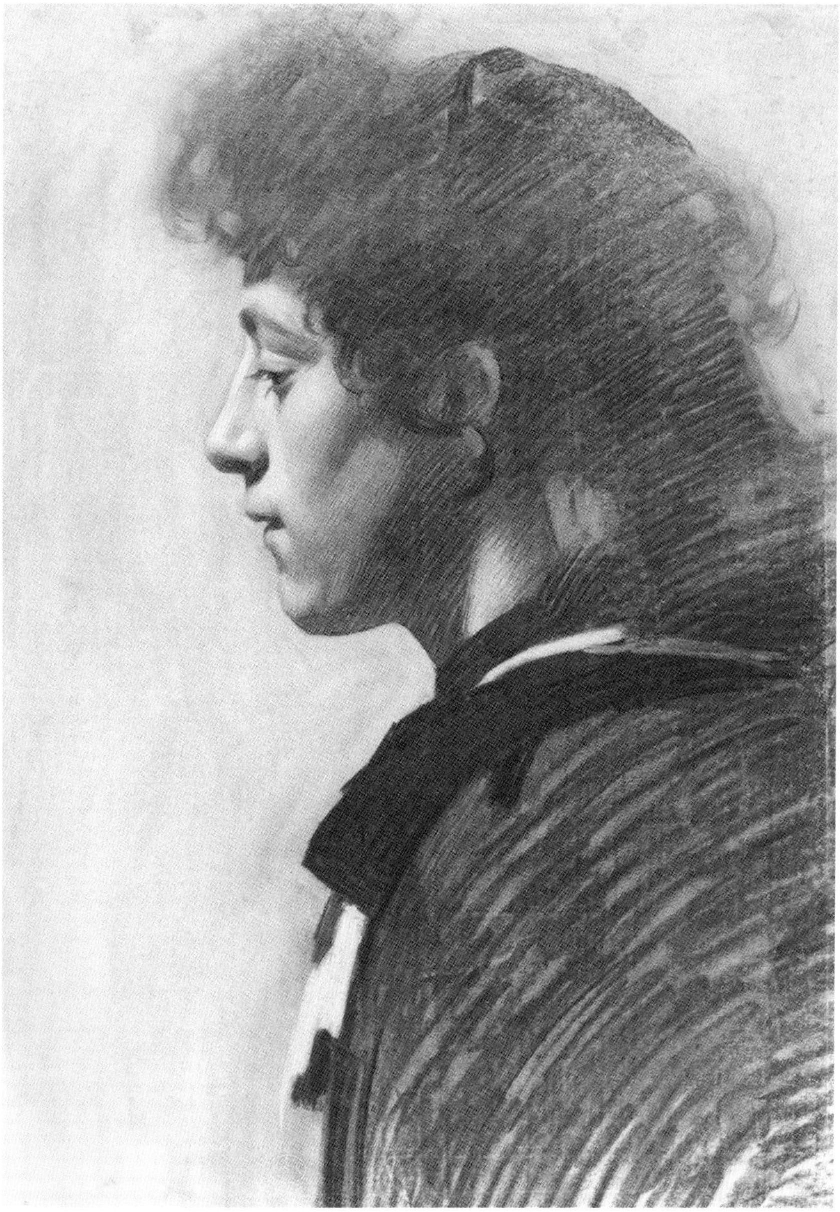

PORTRAIT STUDY – GIRL'S PROFILE

1896 | crayon and pencil

An art school study with a South Kensington label bearing a date of 1896 and giving Laura's age as 17

Nottingham City Museums and Galleries

In Laura's Cornwall paintings there is a balance of landscape and live models with light and air, wind and weather. The breezy freshness she achieves was the result of innumerable studies and sketches and then finally her canvas, painted out in the open air. She went to great lengths to arrange for working out of doors, finding it by far the most satisfactory way of working. In this she was following an important line for many of her contemporaries, who saw in various strands of the European late-nineteenth-century *plein air* tradition a way forward to the authentic, the real and the morally secure.

In this tradition, flowering in France in the early 1880s in the wake of the widely influential Barbizon School, it was generally accepted that artists should seek subjects, should travel to find a place to paint where particular subjects could be found, should seek to paint authentic subjects truthfully. Broadly speaking, this emphasis on a particular authenticity had grown out of Dutch and French *genre* painting of the 1860s to 1880s, in which the hard lives of working people on the land or at the coast were painted directly from life and in radical opposition to the Romantic, Symbolist and Neo-classical subjects that dominated Salon painting. Typically, in rural art colonies and most notably those in Brittany, poor country people were depicted in muddy, miserable scenes. The most humble cottage interiors or rural scenes were painted with respect and sometimes with religious overtones, as in Hubert von Herkomer's *Peasants Praying for a Successful Harvest* of 1877.

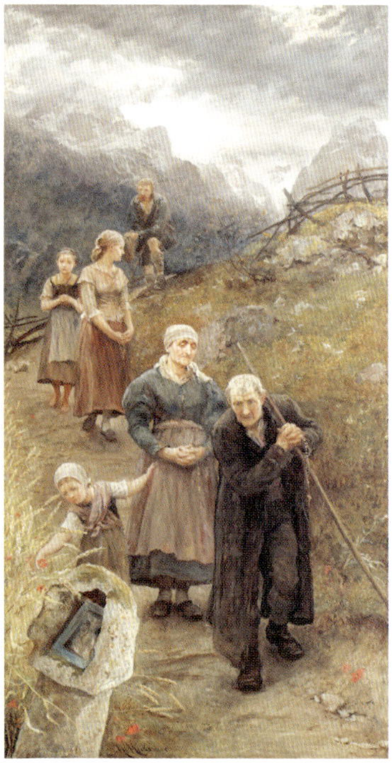

HUBERT VON HERKOMER
(1849–1914)
PEASANTS PRAYING FOR A SUCCESSFUL HARVEST
1877 | oil on canvas
Carmarthenshire Museums Service

At an early and impressionable stage, the hard lives of the fishing community at Staithes on the Yorkshire coast impressed the young Laura Johnson (as she was then) deeply and the more so because she was working to develop beyond the kind of conventionally picturesque or topographical landscape work her mother had made, and to paint figures. The small colony of artists working at Staithes gave Laura a sense of new directions and intensified her drive to raise the standard of her own work. She ceaselessly drew and made watercolour studies, and began to produce her first oil paintings. To find the right subject was paramount.

Laura had shown a talent for drawing from childhood. The landscapes she first drew were those her mother chose to take her pupils out to paint. These were generally well-known picturesque places like Wilford or Haddon Hall, popular with local artists. The paintings she first saw were those in Nottingham Castle's collection. In 1894, when she was seventeen, these included a showing of recent paintings from Cornwall and she particularly remembered seeing Frank Bramley's *A Hopeless Dawn*. By that time she was already committed to art and expecting to make it her life and livelihood. Much of the art she saw dealt with landscape as a rural idyll, often nostalgic for a country 'olden time', vaguely eighteenth century or medieval. There were in so-called high art powerful myths of the rural world and a life far removed from the reality of a city like Nottingham. Though Laura was used to using local children as models, it was not the local scene she chose to paint. She wanted subjects for a largely pre-ordered pictorial imagery, for an idea of art that was controlled in every respect. Through years of working from a still, carefully posed Art School model she had been taught that to control the subject, the composition and her technique was most important. She was bound by the need to find and arrange her subject – if she could do this, she felt, she might succeed as a painter.

Laura Johnson was born in Long Eaton near Nottingham on 4th August 1877. The family moved into a newly built semi-detached house in Noel Street in Nottingham when Laura was still a baby. The household included her mother, Charlotte Johnson and two older daughters, Charlotte Ellen (Nellie) and Evangeline Agnes (Sissie), but was presided over by Laura's grandmother Mrs Bates, called Big Grandma. There was also Mrs Bates' mother, Mrs Thir, known as Little Grandma. Charlotte's husband had left soon after Laura's birth and seems never to have been heard of again. For a time Charlotte's brother Arthur Peter Bates lived with them and tried to maintain as a going concern the lace-machine manufactory Mrs Bates had inherited from her husband. All through Laura's childhood times became more and more difficult. They were increasingly hard up and struggling to keep up appearances as they were forced to move down the scale of local rents. In two autobiographies,[2] Laura presents a vivid and fast-moving account of her early years, telling how they managed domestic life with less and less money and only occasional help from her aunt Mrs West, who ran a lace-making factory at St Quentin in northern France.

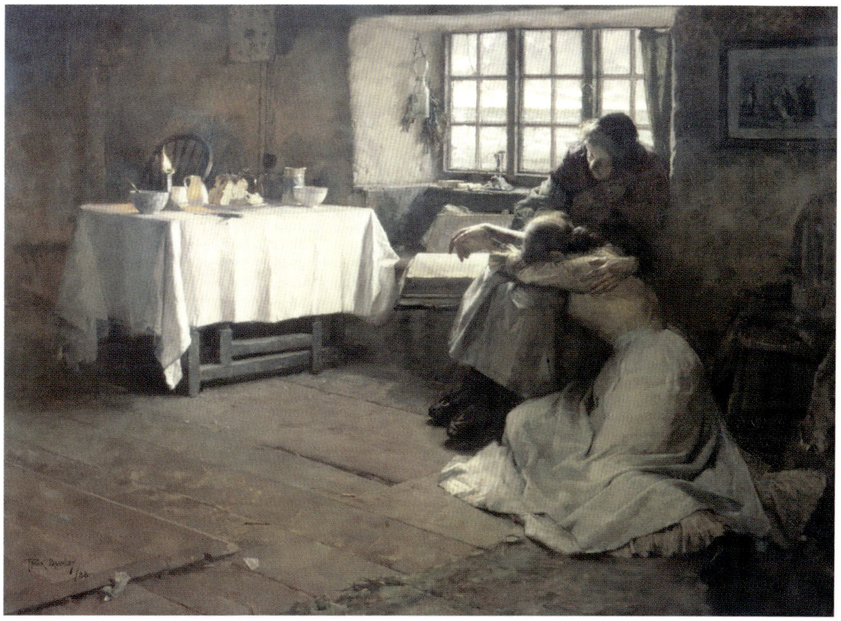

FRANK BRAMLEY (1857–1915)
A HOPELESS DAWN
1888 | oil on canvas | 123 x 167.6 cm
Tate, London 2012

Charlotte Johnson aspired to be a sufficiently professional artist to earn the family's keep. She was a teacher of drawing and watercolour painting to local girls. Though she seems to have suffered with ill health she worked to support the household as much as she could. She must have been delighted to find her youngest daughter showing a talent for drawing. It made a bond between Laura and her mother and imposed on Laura an obligation to do her best to earn money by her efforts.

Because Charlotte did some teaching at the Art School in Nottingham she was able to get Laura enrolled as an 'artisan student' paying no fees.[3] So from the age of thirteen Laura began serious study under a regime that dictated a very slow pace of development. It began with drawing casts and progressed to drawing from a live figure, though females were not permitted to work from nude models. Laura chafed against the discipline and found relief in summer holiday sketching trips in the countryside but nevertheless she was determined to do all that sheer hard work could do to succeed.

When her mother became seriously ill Laura took over her teaching, which involved presenting herself as a competent (and properly dressed) professional woman even though she was only fifteen at the time. At the Art School, she first admired from afar and then became friends with that talented student Harold Knight. Soon the foundations of their life-long contract of friendship and love were well established. Harold was born in 1874 into a well-to-do but far from harmonious or supportive family. He seems to have been very much at odds with his father (who was a successful architect), determined to be independent and to make a career as an artist. He won a scholarship that was supposed to pay for two years in Paris but spent less than one year there before the money ran out. Laura herself won a more modest scholarship and a gold medal in the nation-wide competition for students' work held by the South Kensington Museum (now the V&A). Her art school studies show how talented and skilled she was at drawing; she clearly felt far less comfortable with oil paint. She continued to give private lessons while she was a student and afterwards, using her facility with drawing and watercolour to earn money. By the time Harold went to Paris, Laura was adjusting to having left art school. The way she writes about the problem of seeing which way to turn[4] shows how much she relied upon Harold to find direction – not so much because he took it upon himself to guide her or make suggestions, but simply as she heard his talk and saw his work. She and Harold talked about the painters whose work they knew, like Arnesby Brown or George Clausen, about those they had heard of but never seen, like Gauguin or Van Gogh, and about what Harold had seen in Paris – Impressionism and *plein air* painting. There were no easy sources of images, apart from a few art magazines, most notably the *Studio*, of course, and Nottingham Castle Museum. The Castle had opened as a gallery in 1878 and was a fine example of those great municipal art galleries that were established in English industrial cities during the late nineteenth century. Besides the Castle there was also the Nottingham Society of Artists, whose first exhibition was in 1892.

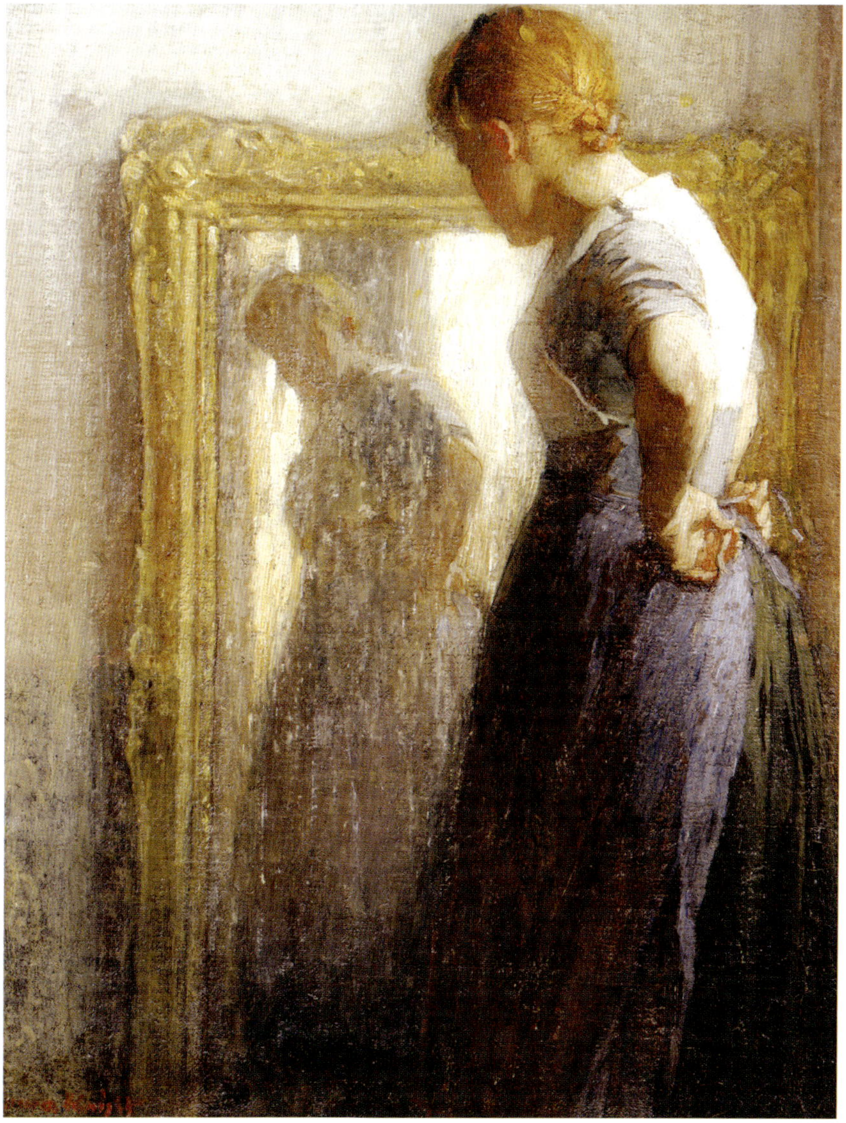

THE MIRROR
oil on canvas | 40.5 x 32.5 cm
private collection; courtesy David Messum

The Society provided a showcase for a wide range of ambitious local artists. Most importantly, there were the annual Royal Academy exhibitions that Harold and Laura travelled to London to see. Harold had a painting accepted at the Royal Academy in 1896, a modest domestic subject titled *While the Cat's Away…*, but he and Laura both knew they needed wider experience and fresh subjects. After bearing the deaths, in succession, of their sister Nellie, their mother Charlotte and both grandmothers, Laura and her sister Sissie had been left to live together and manage life on very little money. In 1894,[5] when their Aunt West came over from St Quentin and offered to take them away for a holiday, they went to Staithes on the Yorkshire coast. One of the art school tutors had already suggested that Harold and Laura should try painting there.

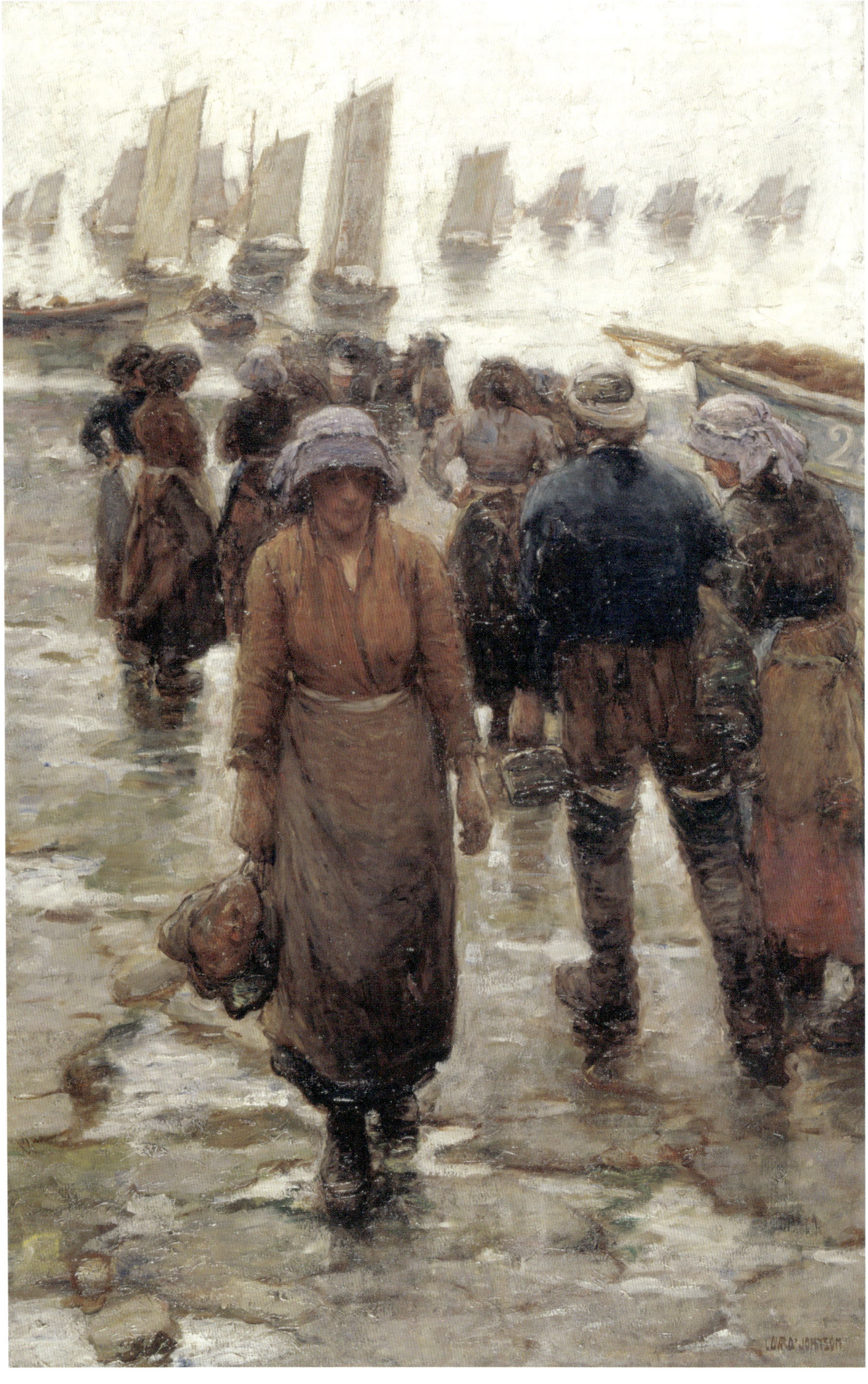
LAURA JOHNSON

Staithes and Laren 1895–1907

There had been a colony of artists at Staithes from the 1880s and though the first arrivals had dispersed, by the mid-1890s it was thriving and attracting plenty of new arrivals. Staithes was a small fishing village in a narrow cleft of the rocky north Yorkshire coast, between Saltburn-by-the-Sea and Whitby. The impression the place made on the young Laura Johnson was deep: it was 'life in the raw'[1] compared to the city she knew. 'As long as I can remember I had wanted to run wild in a broader life, away from factories, miles from houses in rows, dressed-up shops and the gentility of town…'[2] She felt the hard life of the people as much if not more than she responded to the look of the place and its landscape. Hers was not a detached view.[3] She drew the people in the hard conditions of their daily lives and felt all the drama of fear and tragedy as boats and men were lost. After their first visit in 1894, Harold and Laura returned to live and work at Staithes. Laura accompanied by her sister Sissie, and Harold sharing with other painters, found lodgings in nearby farms. Laura's studio was down in the village, 'just an empty room in a derelict house but from the window you could see all that went on.'[4] The life of the farming people up on the moors above the village was as much of a revelation to Laura as that of the fishing community itself. Besides the hardship and the poverty, both communities were bound by strong traditions that governed the division of labour between men and women, with codes of social conduct that the artists had necessarily to respect. Observing the women and children particularly, Laura found models for every-day domestic subjects, painted in low and shadowy tones. During her Staithes years, when she included an adult woman these were usually drawn from Sissie and she was probably the model for the small oil painting *The Mirror* of *c.*1900. Laura made studies, drawings and watercolours but in comparison to her later output, relatively few oil paintings. She was constrained by lack of money for expensive materials as much as by continuing insecurity about painting. The facility she showed in her polished art school drawings seems not to

THE FISHING FLEET
*c.*1900 | oil on canvas
122.3 x 81.5 cm
Bolton Museum and Art Gallery

have led to an equal facility with paint. It is interesting to note that she evidently recognised her prize-winning finished drawings as a dead end, in a painterly sense, and she concentrated her efforts on studies for paintings with which she wanted to express painterly values of a different kind.

Although Harold evidently felt comfortable in the congenial, bohemian company of the painters based around Staithes, it seems that Laura was less so. She was relatively reticent, as a young female among a group of male artists at that time; convention and deference to Harold's position dictated she should be discreet, though she certainly persisted with her work and expected to be taken seriously. The group included Harold's particular friends Fred Mayor and Harry Hopwood, and the Scottish painter Charles Mackie:[5] Mackie seems to have taken an interest in mentoring Laura, taking time and trouble to talk to her and suggest some colour theory.[6] He also suggested technical ways and means, as she was still convinced that there was something she had to *learn* in order to paint effectively – in other words, to make work that would be shown successfully and would sell. In fact, it is clear from the quiet, low-toned, intimate interiors with women and children she was painting, that she was beginning to find her way. In *Oil Paint and Grease Paint* she writes a quite lyrical description of seeing 'truly in my own way' in her Staithes subjects.[7] She began to develop more confidence with the theme of figures in a setting, out in the open air or in a cottage interior. The figures she drew and painted were mostly children and young women. As she had done in the streets of Nottingham, in Staithes Laura found children from very poor families who would sit for her for pennies. Having them as models gave her time to concentrate her study on them. At the same time Laura continued to find inspiration, if not successful subjects, in landscape. She made trips up to the moors near Roxby, a couple of miles inland: 'A switchback of a road ran on for ever between a land of waist-high heather, of broom and gorse that bloomed in the spring and summer. Larks sang perpetually in the sky...'[8] It is clear she relished wide-open spaces and the wind-blown weather of the high ground, though the moors may not have been resolved into successful subjects at this time. It was only much later, when she worked on the cliffs of Cornwall, that such spectacular open space was assimilated into her work.

In Staithes, Laura found difficulties with larger narrative themes and writes of a failed painting of people and boats on the beach, that it was 'beyond my powers...I had no funds to pay for models for the life-size figures; they had to be carried out from pencil notes and memory. It was painted afresh each year...Finally I cut it up to make a roaring fire in my studio stove'. But she goes on, 'Even though my studio was so often warmed by burning canvases and drawings, I do not regret all the experimental work done and destroyed. Staithes was too big a subject for an immature student, but working there I developed a visual memory which has stood me in good stead ever since.'[9]

Though Laura's work of this period is hard to find, at least two of her Staithes paintings have been identified, *Staithes*, a view from high on

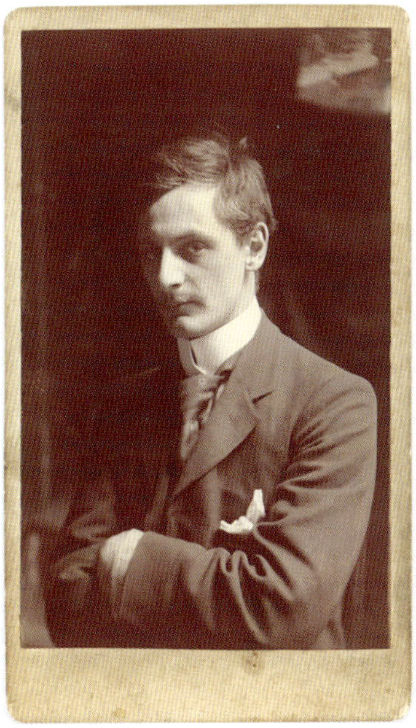

Harold Knight,
Nottingham, *c.*1900
private collection

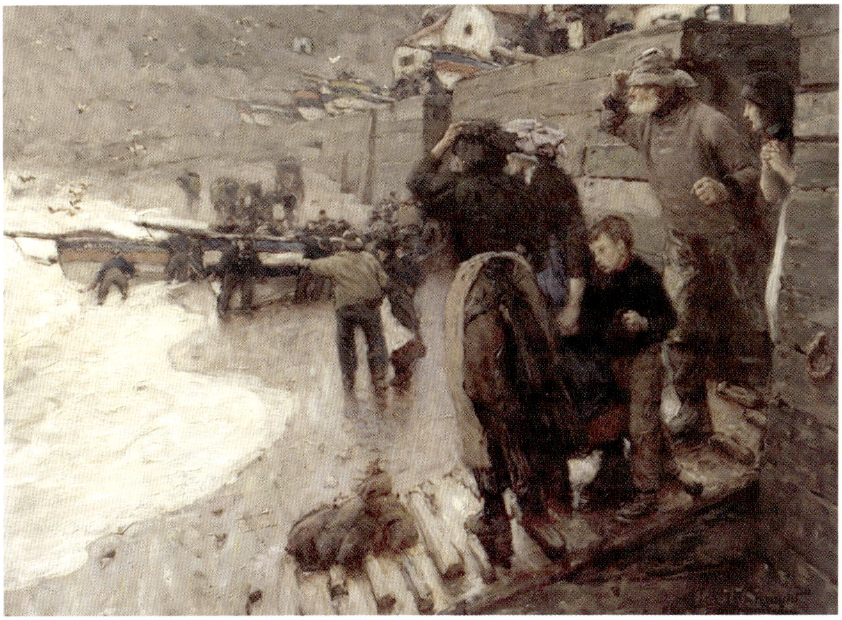

HAROLD KNIGHT
THE LAST COBLE
1900 | oil on canvas | 92.7 x 127.6 cm
Nottingham City Museums and Galleries

the cliffs looking down towards the village, and *The Fishing Fleet*, an evidently successful attempt at a larger Staithes theme. Both were probably painted about 1900. Harold's far more ambitious exhibition painting *The Last Coble* (shown at the RA in 1900) shows how he had found scope to develop through working at Staithes, although he did not pursue large-scale outdoor compositions in his later work.

It is telling that Laura writes of herself as a student in her early years at Staithes. Her habit of looking and studying through continual sketching was bound by notions of what was correct, or conventional, for the making of paintings. Her adherence to what she understood to be academic standards kept her in a programme aimed at the acquisition of skills. In effect, she thought all she had to do was to work hard. When some success was achieved, in other words when a painting sold, she was overjoyed. She attributes her early successes to hard work, not to her own innate qualities as a painter. Furthermore, she was equally thrilled when Harold sold a painting or received a good commission; to her it was a joint enterprise. Though she saw the work of other artists in Nottingham and London, and in the other studios at Staithes, her access to a wider range of current practice and ideas was severely limited. She listened to Harold and his friends talking about art, of course, but the debates she heard are likely to have been relatively parochial. She writes that they knew nothing of Slade School artists who dominated the New English Art Club, 'Augustus John, William Orpen, the Rothenstein brothers or McEvoy. We were strangers to the fight then taking place for the greater appreciation and expression of true aestheticism.'[10] That 'true aestheticism' was part of what Laura, looking back, saw as the key to her own eventual blossoming into maturity as a painter. In the 1890s and at the turn of the century, although developments in France beyond the influence of Bastien-Lepage – most notably Impressionism and Post-Impressionism – were little known in Britain, a number of artists were moving towards new, more direct ways of working in the open air. They included the Newlyn School, headed by Stanhope Forbes, Walter Langley and Norman Garstin, and the Glasgow Boys, among them James Guthrie and John Lavery when they showed in London in 1890. By 1900, the current of opposition to the Royal Academy tradition included New English Art Club artists like Wilson Steer, Henry Tonks and Fred Brown, who were working in the Wye Valley from 1900; Walter Sickert was painting in Venice and Dieppe. George Clausen was working in East Anglia and the Camden Town artists Charles Ginner, Robert Bevan and Spencer Gore were spending time in Devon. It is not known whether or not Harold and Laura saw it, but there was an important exhibition at the Whitechapel Art Gallery in 1902, in which paintings made in and around St Ives by Arnesby Brown, Louis Grier, Moffat Lindner, Julius Olsson and others were shown. Arnesby Brown, also from Nottingham and trained at the art school there but eleven years older than Laura, was best known for painting country life in East Anglia. The Newlyn School, having 'arrived' with paintings at the Royal Academy from the mid-1880s, was still highly acclaimed throughout the 1890s and into the early 1900s. Over the turn of the century, despite twenty years of widespread influences from French *plein air* painting, the Royal Academy tradition continued to be dominated by narrative, often mawkishly sentimental, quasi-Symbolist or historical work. It was also, however, the most important shop window for portrait painters like Harold Knight and Laura naturally hoped to be accepted there too. The Academy's selection process, for which a huge intake of work was whittled down by a selection committee of senior Academicians, underlined its controlling orthodoxy. Many aspiring artists still saw the Summer Exhibition – always a great public occasion – as the yardstick of their success and aimed their work accordingly. The first of Harold's paintings to be accepted was in the 1896 exhibition: *While the Cat's Away*, a modest domestic scene with a maid doing a little dance. He had a Staithes subject accepted in 1899, and then three in 1900, three in 1901 and another (a Scarborough subject) in 1902. Harold also had work shown at the Society of Oil Painters gallery in 1899-1900 and 1901, and he later became a member there. Laura showed there only once, with *Little Mother* in 1903.

Laura sent paintings for the Royal Academy Summer Exhibition without success until her *Mother and Child*, painted in 1902, was accepted in 1903. Between 1903 and 1907 she and Harold showed with the Nottingham Society of Artists in their annual exhibitions at the Exchange building. In 1903 Laura showed an oil painting titled *Mother and Child*, probably the one shown later that year at the RA, while Harold showed three portraits and a Scarborough subject. In 1904, Laura showed *The Road to the Farm* and *Mother and Children* while Harold showed another portrait. For both

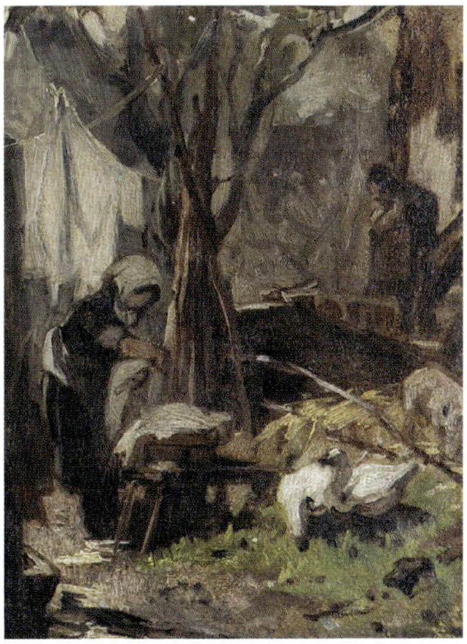

MATTHIJS MARIS (1839–1917)
WASHING DAY
oil on canvas on panel
23 x 16.8 cm
Dordrechts, Dordrechts Museum

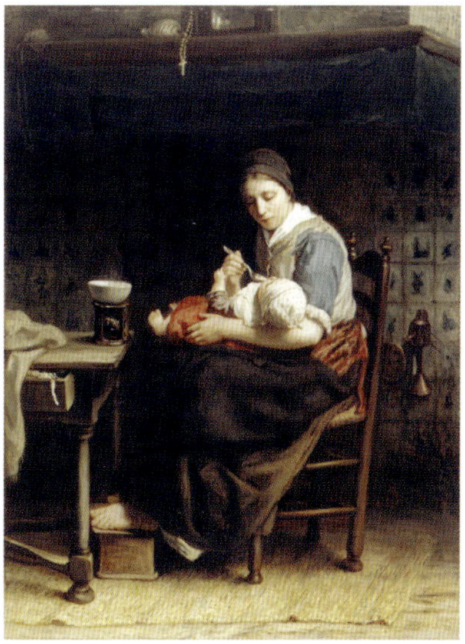

JOSEF IZRAELS (1824–1911)
THE COTTAGE MADONNA
oil on canvas | 99.7 x 134.6 cm
Detroit Institute of Arts, USA/bequest of Nell Ford Torrey/The Bridgeman Art Library

these years, their address was Belgrave Square, Harold's old lodgings. In the following three years their home address was given as Staithes while they divided their time between Yorkshire and Holland. They both showed genre subjects and in 1907, Laura's included *The Red Jacket* and *Dressing the Children*. She also sent in to the Spring Exhibitions at Nottingham Castle, where a number of her earliest Staithes paintings were shown. Despite the beginnings of an exhibiting career, Laura was not at ease with her own work, however: '...I knew my attitude to painting was wrong, and thought there might be some technical trick that would set it right – I fumbled and messed, wasting time, canvas and paper; if only someone could have said "go out and paint frankly what you see." Instead a wide detour was being made...'[11]

Laura Johnson and Harold Knight were married in 1903 and the following year they made their first trip to Holland, accompanying their friend Harry Hopwood. They had seen recent Dutch paintings in London, admiring particularly the work of Matthijs, one of the Maris brothers. They must also have seen the work of the most influential Dutch artist at the time, Josef Izraels while Newlyn paintings like Frank Bramley's *A Hopeless Dawn* had brought widespread attention to an English version of the new genre painting.

Harold had portrait commissions and his painting *The Last Coble* 1900 had been bought for Nottingham Castle Museum. Laura had her *Mother and Child* accepted for the 1903 Summer Exhibition and it was soon sold (to the Royal Academician Edward Stott). It seemed enough promise of

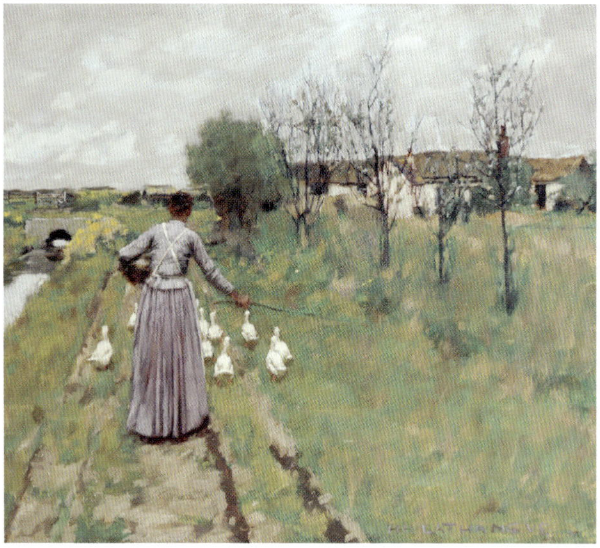

HENRY LA THANGUE (1859–1929)
LANDSCAPE STUDY
1889 | oil on canvas | 51 x 61 cm
Clifton Park Museum, Rotherham

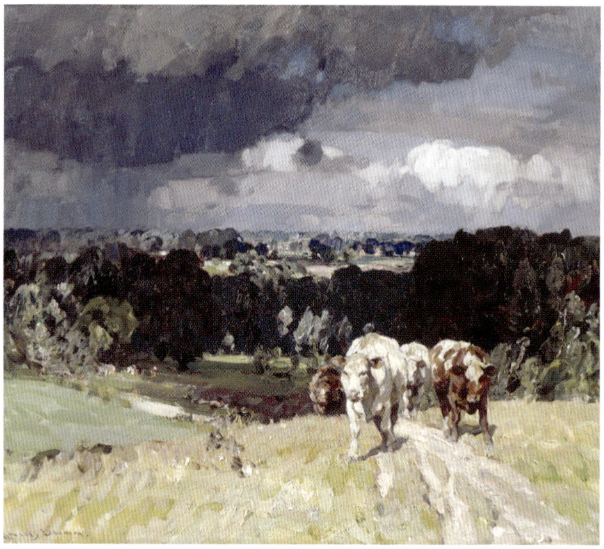

ARNESBY BROWN (1866–1955)
THE RAINCLOUD
*c.*1915 | oil on canvas | 63.5 x 76.5 cm

success to allow them to try Holland. The Knights had been based at Staithes, on and off, since Laura was eighteen and now, at twenty-seven and enjoying the new freedom of being a married woman alone with her husband, Laura was ready for new subjects and new landscapes.

Laura and Harold spent six weeks in Holland in 1904 and six months there in 1905. In Amsterdam they visited the Rijksmuseum and all the dealer galleries, absorbing Dutch painting from Rembrandt and Vermeer to the contemporaries. They travelled out to Laren, a village south-east of Amsterdam in the middle of fertile farming country. There a colony of artists assembled every summer, most of them followers of the Hague School artists who had been painting in remote and picturesque rural communities since the 1850s. There were French and American painters there, mostly young men, mostly far from serious in their outlook on life but always serious in their endless discussions about art. Their company contributed a great deal to broaden horizons for Laura and she saw Harold's usual seriousness and reserve soften under their influence.

Laren provided Laura with the means to take a step forward from her work at Staithes. Though the subjects are the same there is an increase of resolution in her paintings and apparently more confidence. The surviving paintings by Laura Knight of 1900 to 1906 are mostly of children, sometimes with an adult woman. Soft light models the form of heads and arms and the cloth of pinafore or skirt is carefully rendered. The figures merge into shadows in close interior settings painted in a range of soft earthy colours. There is a sense of care being taken, as in clean clothes and tidy hair, in the most humble domestic circumstances.

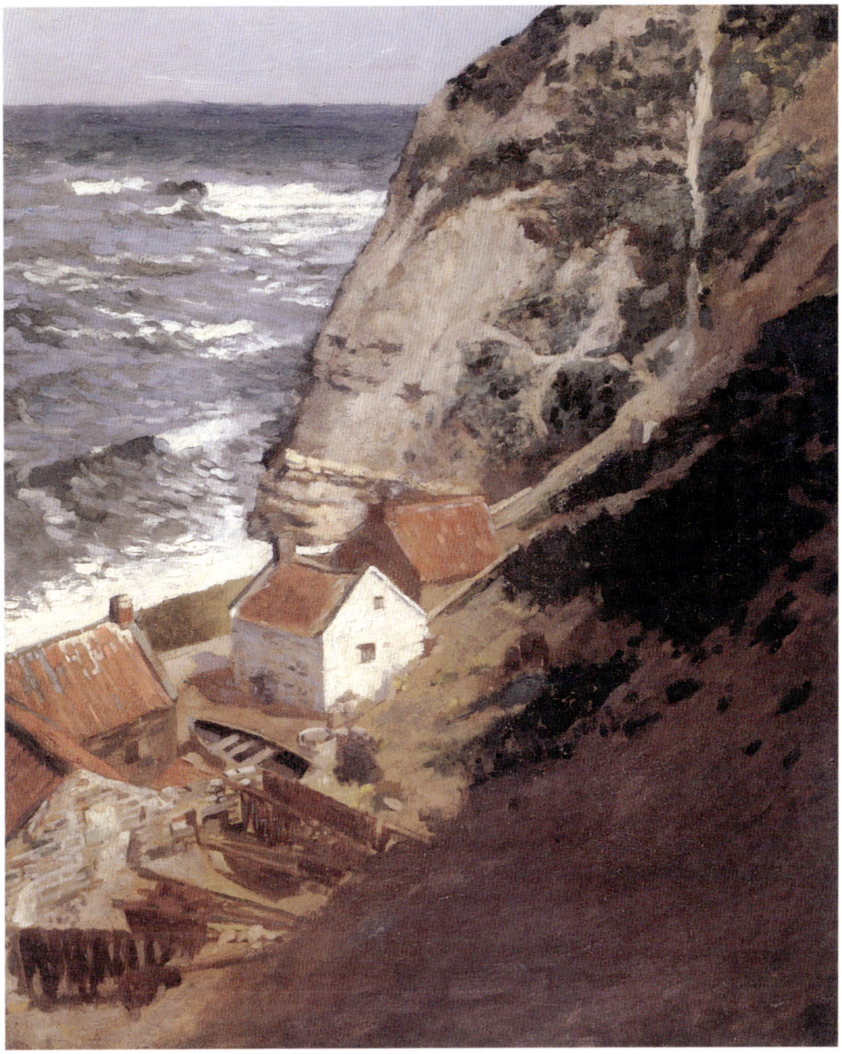

STAITHES

1900 | oil on canvas | 75 x 62.2 cm

private collection

Dressing the Children, arguably the culmination of this first chapter of her career, was painted in 1905-06. This may be the painting she was working on when she describes how she worked in the cottage of a very poor family in Staithes: 'I rented it by the week, using the mother and children as models. While working there I saw greater poverty and misery than it seemed possible for anyone to bear.'[12] The finished painting is a well-organised composition in which casual poses in the dim cottage interior are lit by a low window, producing a warm, intimate atmosphere.

In England, home for the Knights continued to be rented rooms and their studios at Staithes but they made a determined effort to find a London dealer who would take them on. Ernest Brown showed their work at the Leicester Galleries in June 1906 and did well enough with

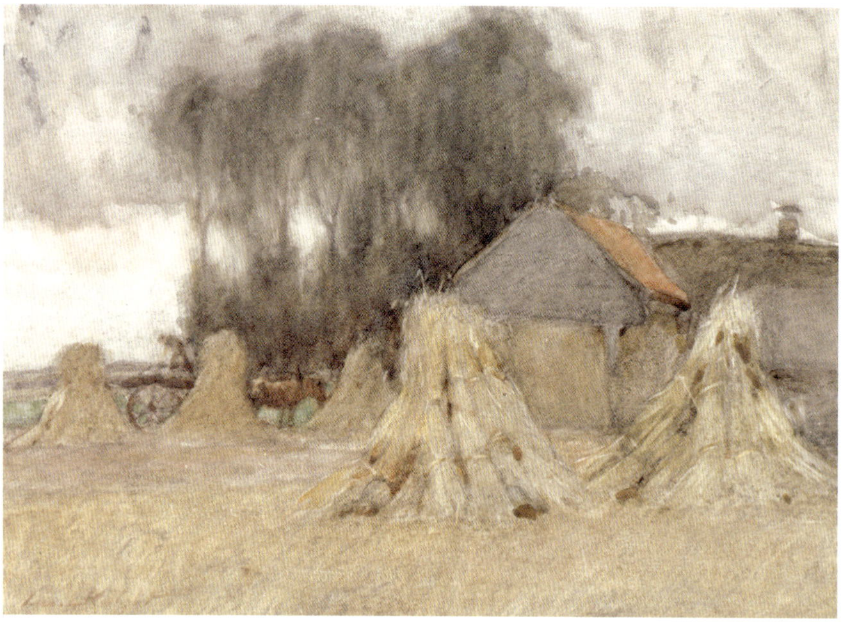

A CORNFIELD IN HOLLAND
1904 | watercolour | 25.3 x 35.6 cm
Laing Art Gallery, Newcastle/Tyne & Wear Archives & Museums

it to offer an exhibition for the following autumn. Messrs Ernest Brown & Phillips' Leicester Galleries was a highly respected dealership, showing a range of established artists such as Holman Hunt, Arthur Rackham, W Lee Hankey and Mortimer Menpes. In the Knights' exhibition 'Dutch Life and Landscape' Laura's work included *The Little Brother, Feeding the Goat* and *The Mirror,* all modest domestic subjects; Harold's included interiors and a couple of landscapes. In 1906–08 he was also showing regularly in the broader context of the Society of Oil Painters, always seeking portrait commissions. His watercolour portrait of Laura of this date is a delicately painted expression of the fashionable mood of the time.

Meanwhile, Harold's painting *A Cup of Tea* had been a success at the RA in 1905, being bought by Frank Dicksee for the Art Gallery at Brisbane, and Laura's *Dressing the Children* was a success in the 1906 Summer show. The RA that year was still dominated by history pictures, costume pieces and sweetened country scenes but it did include farming subjects by George Clausen, peasant subjects by La Thangue and Edward Stott, and fine landscapes by Arnesby Brown and Alfred East. These provided the context for Laura's constant study and her aspiration to succeed. The Knights made a third trip to Laren in 1906 and the winter of that year was the last they spent in Yorkshire. In 1907 they decided to move to Cornwall.

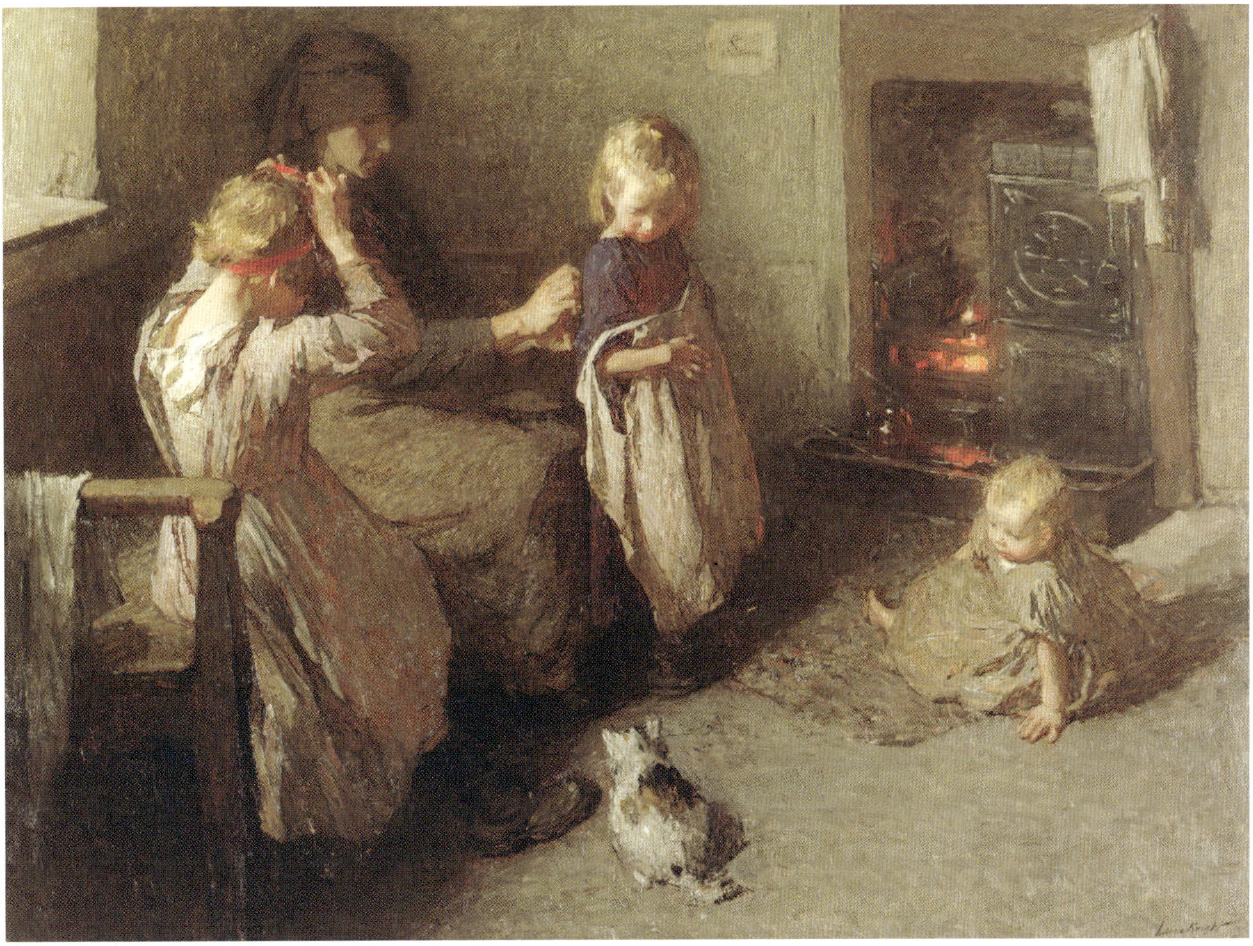

DRESSING THE CHILDREN
*c.*1906 | oil on canvas | 101.6 x 140.3 cm
Ferens Art Gallery, Hull Museums, UK/The Bridgeman Art Library

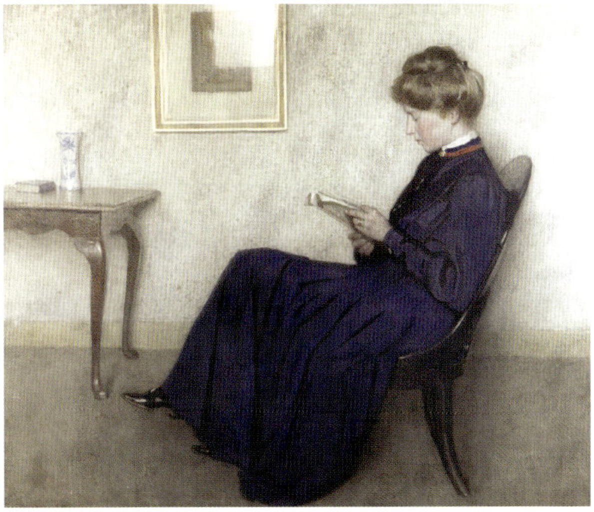

HAROLD KNIGHT
PORTRAIT OF LAURA KNIGHT
*c.*1907 | watercolour | 48.9 x 59 cm
Nottingham City Museums and Galleries

Cornwall 1907–1910

When Harold Knight arrived in Cornwall he could reasonably claim to be an established professional painter of portraits and domestic scenes, while Laura had yet to feel secure in her career. They had dates for their second exhibition together, in October 1907 at Ernest Brown and Phillips' Leicester Galleries. With this in prospect and some good sales of work made in Holland and Yorkshire, they laid plans for going to Cornwall that autumn. The show was titled 'Life and Landscapes by Harold and Laura Knight' and included paintings and watercolours. Laura showed *Children on the Beach* and scenes of babies, washing and back gardens; Harold's titles include *Staithes*, *Low Tide* and *The Sea Wall*. The exhibition was reasonably successful and it seems they left soon after the opening; they were certainly in Cornwall by late 1907 and both exhibited at the Newlyn Art Gallery in March 1908.

Laura, at thirty, felt more confident about the development of her work but wanted new subjects, or rather a renewal of what she knew she wanted to express. In and around Newlyn, the Knights found themselves in a very lively and sociable group of artists; there was an art school atmosphere around the central figure of Stanhope Forbes, whose School of Painting had been attracting new generations of in-comers since 1899. For Laura it was 'Student life in surroundings such as we had never dreamed of; a carefree life of sunlit pleasure, and leisurely study.'[1] The impact of this atmosphere on Laura was probably the most important turning point of her working life. As both autobiographies make plain, she responded by blossoming into the extraordinarily vivid and energetic personality she had been covering up since girlhood. Her childish love of theatre, dance, singing, parties and fun was revived. She saw herself as part of the sociable, competitive, energised group and to a degree it freed her from constraints she had felt it necessary to impose on herself. She began to understand that to be serious about painting did not presuppose a serious demeanour and conventional behaviour. The Knights were still

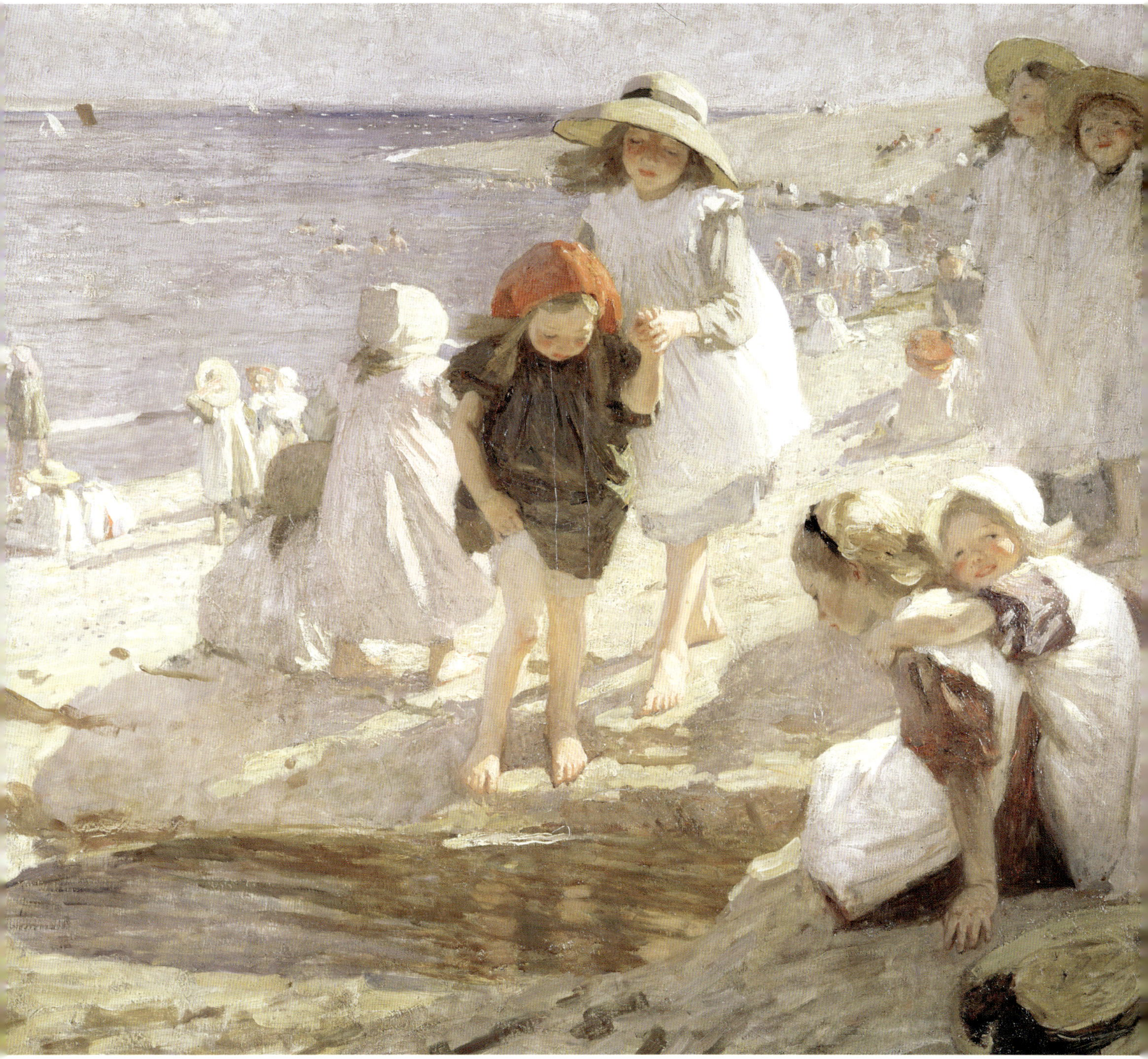

THE BEACH

1908 | oil on canvas | 127.7 x 153 cm

Laing Art Gallery, Newcastle/Tyne & Wear Archives & Museums

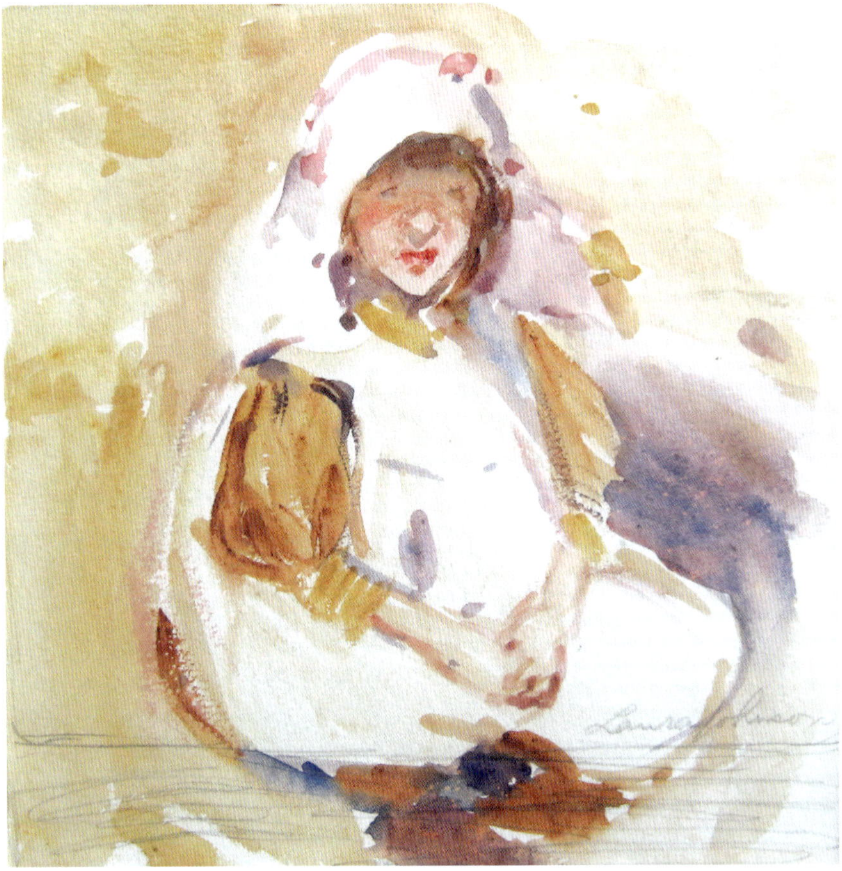

LITTLE GIRL ON A BEACH
watercolour | *c.*16 x 16 cm
private collection

not well off and needed to count their resources carefully but they were certainly able to be more relaxed than in the hard years in Nottingham, Staithes and Laren. They first took rooms in Newlyn village but soon moved up the hill to Penzer House, Mrs Beer's large double-fronted villa looking out eastwards over Newlyn rooftops and Mount's Bay. Laura, like other Newlyn artists, was adept at finding good food and improvising stylish clothes very cheaply from local sources, and, with many examples of profligate use of materials around her, she started to use canvasses and paint with much more freedom. In her first Newlyn studio she felt her work 'developed out of all recognition.'[2]

Laura Knight spent the summer of 1908 on the beach at Newlyn making studies for the large painting *The Beach*. As she says, the subject is set on a beach near Staithes,[3] though she worked from studies made in the open air at Newlyn and, significantly, the painting successfully expresses clear Cornish sunlight and breezy air. It takes Laura's primary concern with painting figures of children out from a dim cottage interior into the brilliant light. In this, her most ambitious work to date, figures of children are central and the seascape beyond is painted with less

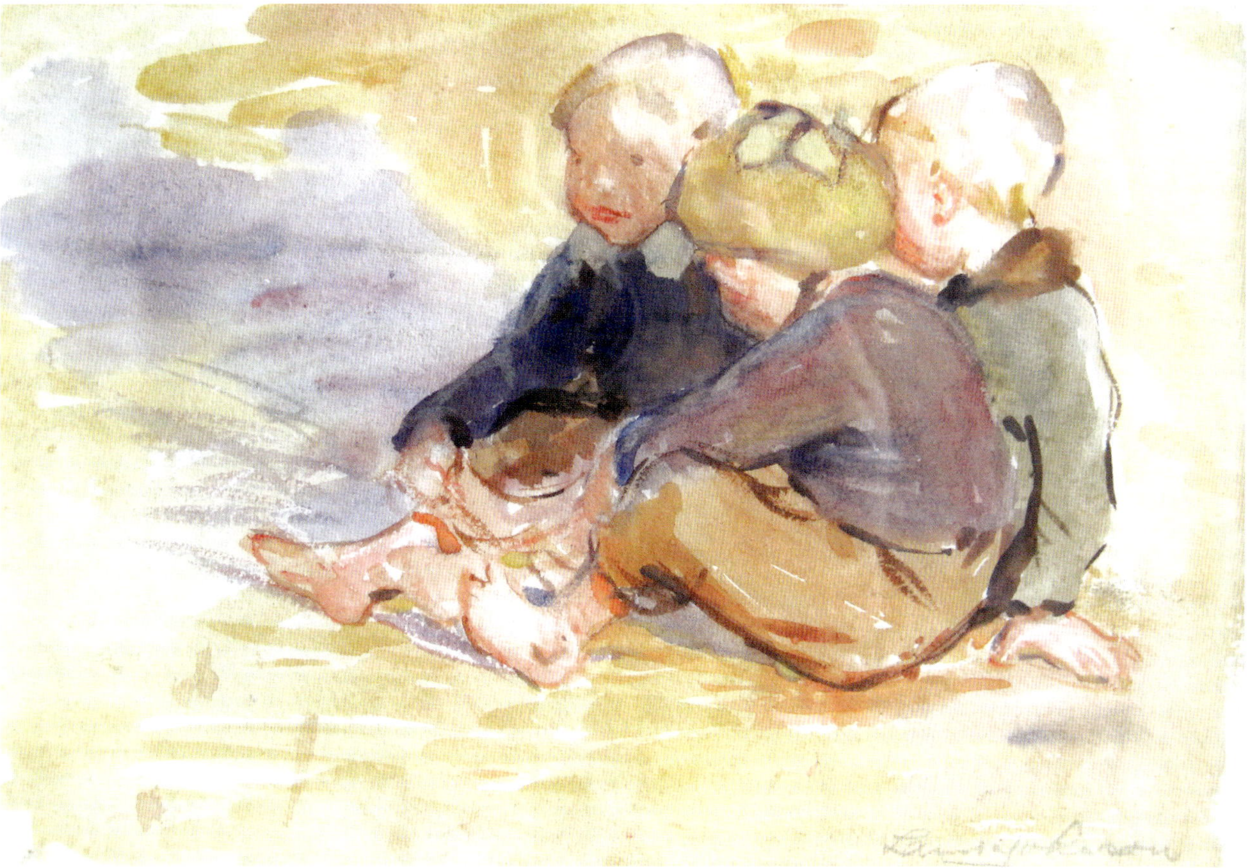

BOYS ON A BEACH
watercolour | *c.*16 x 22 cm
private collection

assurance. Perhaps because she was not in front of her chosen setting it appears more as background; the shadows on the sand and particularly the shaded foreground make more of a contribution to the whole effect. *The Beach* was a success at the Royal Academy in 1909. In his book on Lamorna Birch Austin Wormleighton describes the morning in April 1909 when Birch and the Knights were receiving news of that year's hang.[4] They were at breakfast in the cheap set of rooms in Shepherd's Market, off Piccadilly, that Laura and Harold shared with Birch from the time they went to Cornwall until they moved back to London after the First World War. Laura evidently enjoyed her success and basked in the publicity she received that Spring.

In Laura's output of this date there was, as always, a constant flow of watercolours. Those made on the beach in Cornwall in 1908-09 include *Children on the Sands* and *Beach Scene*, looking back towards Newlyn from the beach below Penzance promenade. A view of Newlyn Harbour from this period is more of a finished exhibition piece than a study. In 1908 she had submitted some work to the Old Watercolour Society with a view to showing and selling in that relatively traditional context. She was accepted as a member and that winter, in London to collect her Diploma, she stayed with Mary and Ernest Gillick at their Cheyne Row studio; the Gillicks were old friends from Nottingham Art School days. It was snowy but she promptly set up her easel in the biting cold and painted the slushy street.[5] Using watercolour in the open air in such bitterly cold weather perfectly illustrates Laura's tenacity. She was constantly at work.

It is clear that Laura was continuing with her long-established regime of sketch book drawings, followed by more studies on paper or canvas, then composition studies, all leading up to a final rendering of the complete subject on canvas. From the first two summers in Cornwall, of 1908 and 1909, it seems the whole process began to accelerate until everything merged into one sustained crescendo of work. She seems never to have stopped working, from the life around her, from posed models and from scenes she chose as settings. She seems to have had boundless energy and it was expressed in her work though bravura handling of paint. Her confidence rose and rose.

Flying a Kite was painted on a hilltop high above Newlyn harbour with Penzance in a patch of sunlight beyond; the hills on the distant horizon lead away north-eastwards to Carn Brea. 'I did a six-foot study out in the wind for that landscape. Every house, farm and field was put in… and the hills too beyond. Big studies were done out of doors of every detail…'[6] The figures are assembled from individual studies but the composition looks fresh and spontaneous. Movement and bright, breezy sunshine are painted with a subtle balance of figures and wide open space; the open path in the centre leading straight into the wide windswept view is a bold stroke. The canvas has the kind of breadth and ambition Laura had never felt able to achieve in all her years of study at Staithes or Laren. Her ability with paint seems finally to have been given free rein in her most natural response to large open-air subjects. 1909-10 saw her coming-of-age as a painter. *Flying a Kite* was shown at the Royal Academy in 1910, where it was much admired and bought by George Clausen for the National Gallery of South Africa in Cape Town.

Other works of this period include *In the Sun, Newlyn*, painted from a lower viewpoint just above the Newlyn rooftops, looking down on the long line of the quay with Mount's Bay and Penzance beyond. The girls wear the same kind of white pinafores and straw hats but the sunlight bearing down on them is still and the balance of figures with view seems much more conventional. A series of studies culminated in the more complex composition *Boys* (aka *The Boys*), of boys getting dressed after bathing in Newlyn harbour, also shown at the 1910 Royal Academy exhibition. Harold Knight's first major Cornwall paintings were *A Village Wedding* shown at the Academy in 1908 and *In the Spring*, probably painted in 1909. Both represent, although to a less dramatic degree in relation to previous work, the kind of breakthrough Laura was making. They are certainly very freshly painted and Harold's brighter

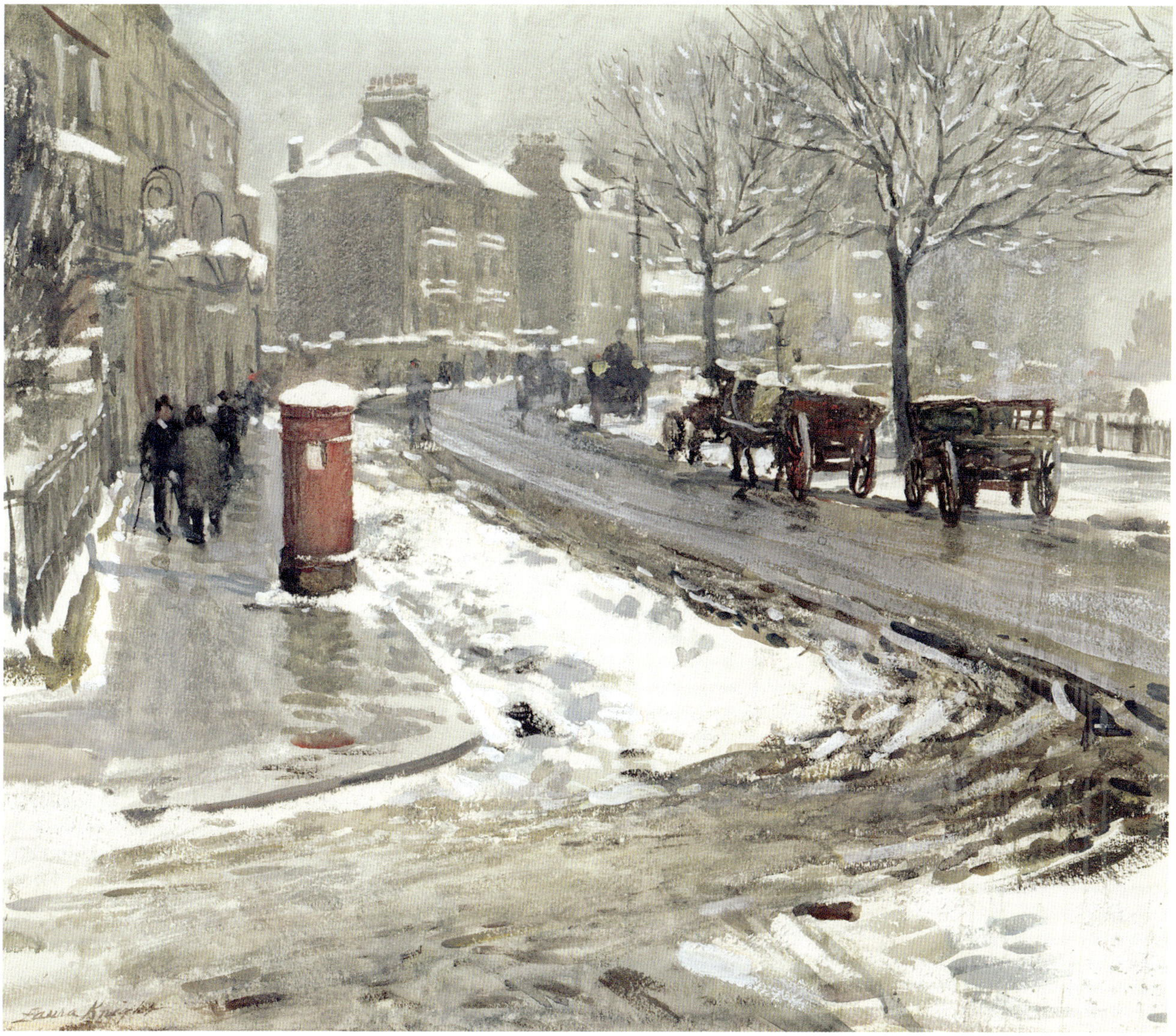

CHEYNE WALK

1908–09 | watercolour | 50 x 60.3 cm

Leeds Museums and Galleries (City Art Gallery) UK/The Bridgeman Art Library

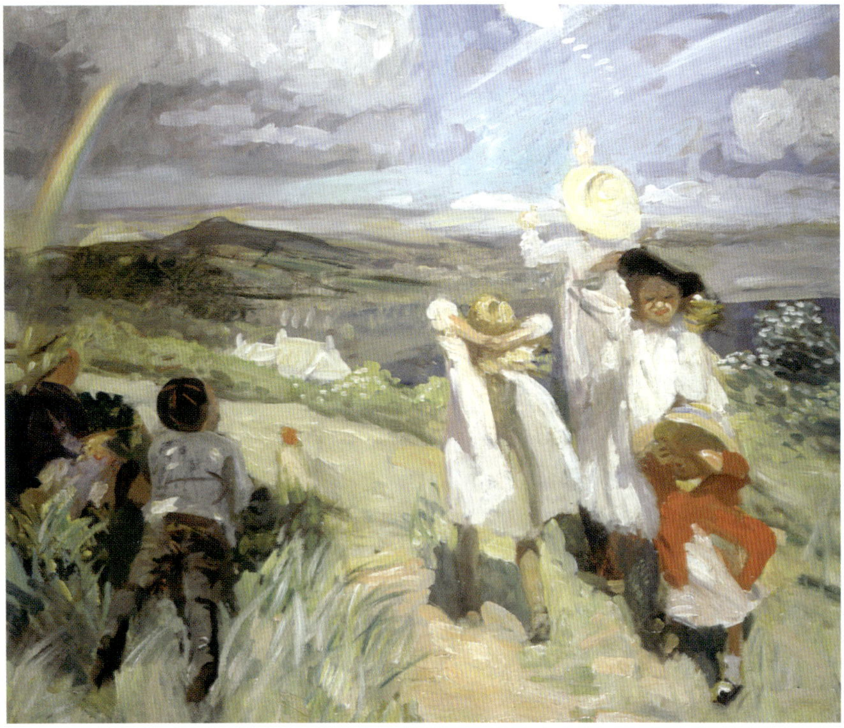

STUDY FOR 'FLYING A KITE'

*c.*1909–10 | oil on canvas

private collection

palette of colour expresses warm Cornish sunlight but the subjects seem more anecdotal, lacking the exhilarating airiness of Laura's new work. These and other paintings reflect the *plein-air* tradition, with figures set out of doors, but working directly from wide open landscape was never Harold's primary concern. He fits more closely into the successive phases of Newlyn School painting than Laura does and in any case, continuing to build a reputation as an accomplished portrait painter remained a priority for him. Though he and Laura both made good sales occasionally, at this time his portraits provided an important and comparatively reliable part of their joint income. From 1909 onwards his portrait commissions appeared regularly at the Royal Academy, while canvases like *Morning Sun* of 1910–12 show that in painting tranquil figures in interiors he was following his own inclination as much as seeking sales or commissions.

Harold also painted a number of their friends. In 1909 he began work for a large canvas with figures at a table taking tea. He included Laura as the visitor, in a wide-brimmed hat with tulle, delicately adjusting her gloves. There is a painting of Edith Florence Carter-Wood (whom Harold called Florence but whose nick-name was Blote) that is a study for the figure in profile at the left and Harold painted Florence again for the figure on the right in a painting titled *The Sonnet* of 1910-11, in which four women are grouped round a table in the open air, listening to a man reading aloud.

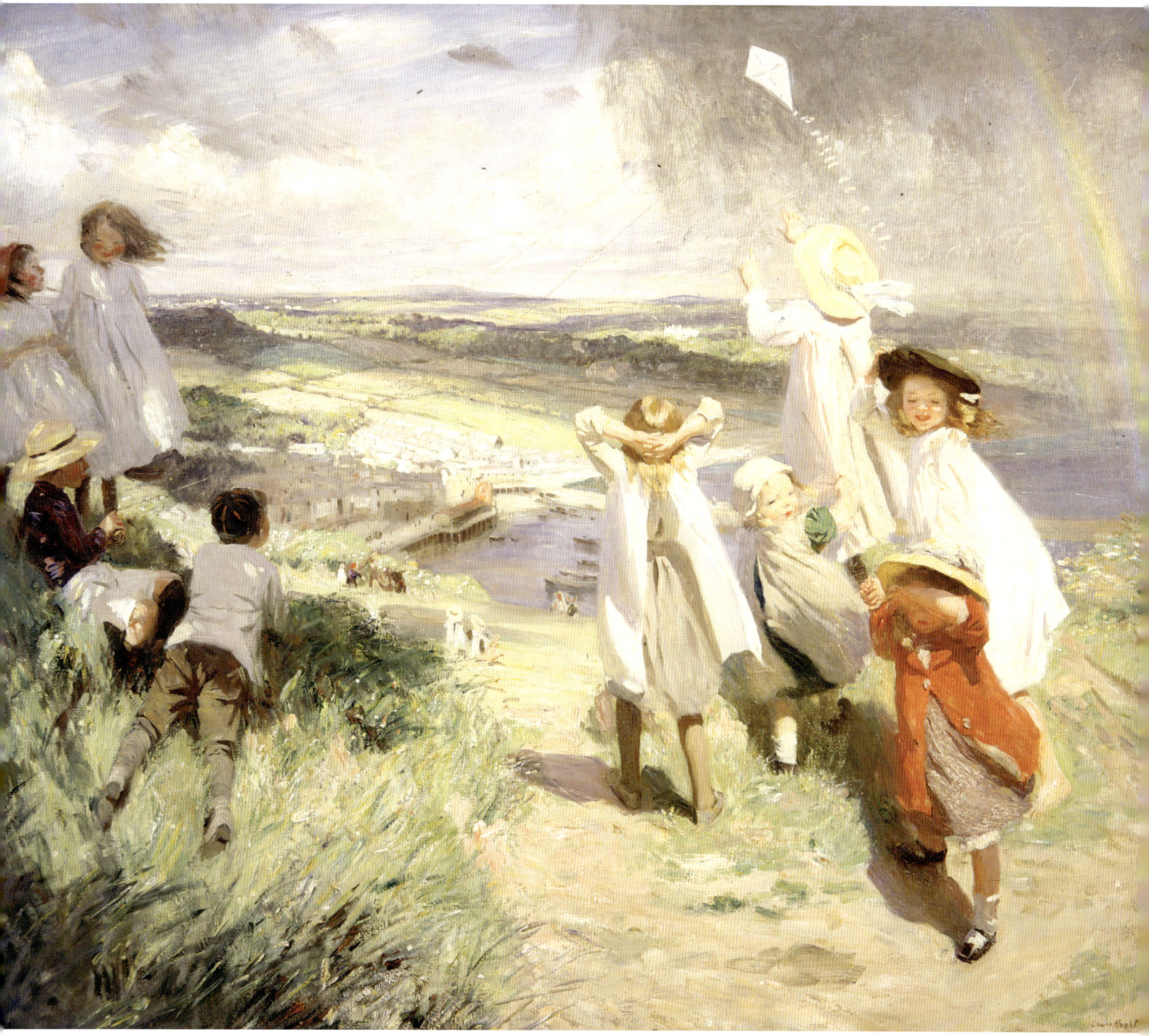

FLYING A KITE

1910 | oil on canvas | 150 x 180 cm

Iziko South African National Gallery, Cape Town

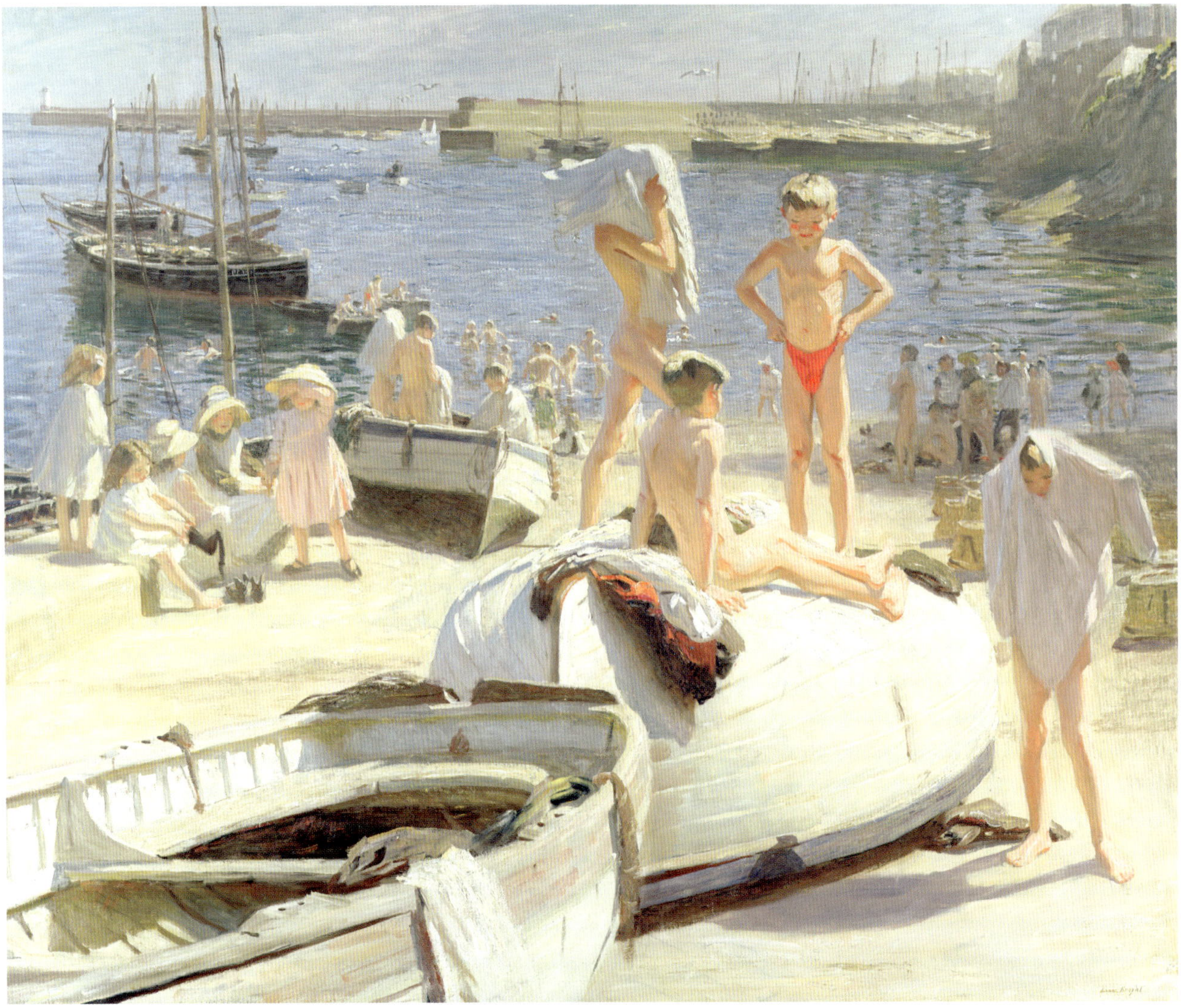

BOYS (aka **THE BOYS**)

1909 | oil on canvas | 152.2 x 183.5 cm

Johannesburg Art Gallery, South Africa/The Bridgeman Art Library

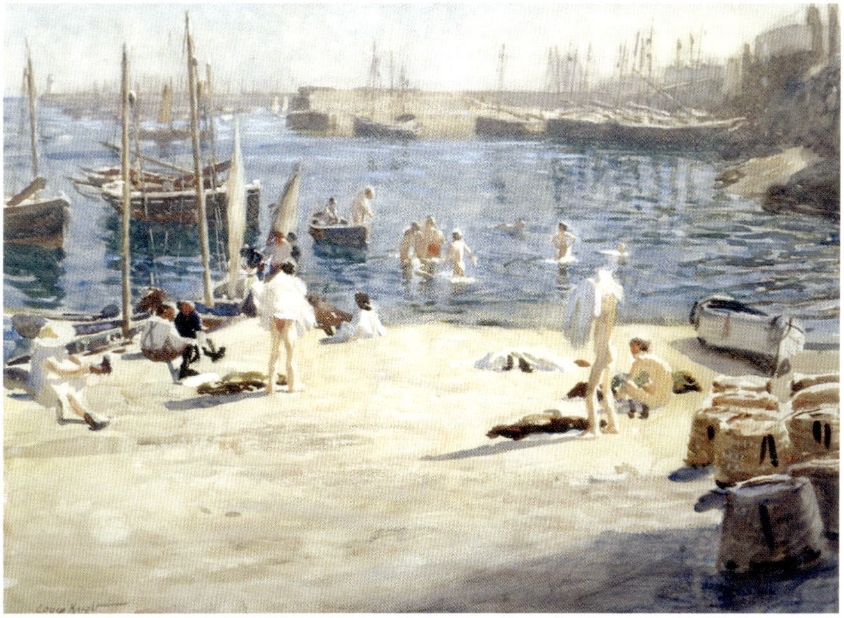

IN THE HARBOUR

*c.*1909–10 | watercolour | 45.4 x 62.9 cm

Manchester City Galleries

The figure next to Florence is Laura and the figure reading is A.J. Munnings.[7] Harold and Laura both painted their great friends Robert and Eleanor Hughes. Other friends of the pre-war years included Harold and Gertrude Harvey, and the toy-maker Phyllis Yglesias (known as Pog or sometimes Golly). Lamorna Birch was a well-established and successful painter in oils and watercolour, then and now best known for painting the beautiful wooded valley leading down to Lamorna Cove. He and his wife Houghton and their daughters Mornie and Joan were good friends of the Knights'. Mornie described Harold as '…usually an observer. He liked to sit back in a chair, wrapt in thought, drawing deeply on his pipe'.[8] Laura seemed strong and inexhaustible: 'She was so supple in her movements, dancing one minute, gesticulating the next… Even when she crossed the room with a tray of drinks she would shimmy as she went, her skirt swinging from side to side…' Mornie goes on to describe Laura continually drawing then flopping down exhausted, only to 'open her eyes and start drawing again, using anything that came to hand, old envelopes, invoices, anything. She was irrepressible.'[9]

Of the circle around the Knights in their first few years at Newlyn, Laura's particular friends included A.J. Munnings and Dod Shaw, who was to marry Ernest Procter in 1912. Munnings made extended visits to Cornwall between 1908 and 1911, when he set up a studio there. He moved in on the Knights' lodgings, persuading their landlady Mrs Beer that they would love to have him under the same roof. He was charismatic, conceited and loved to perform; he initiated parties and picnics and stirred up the genteel social world of the senior Newlyn

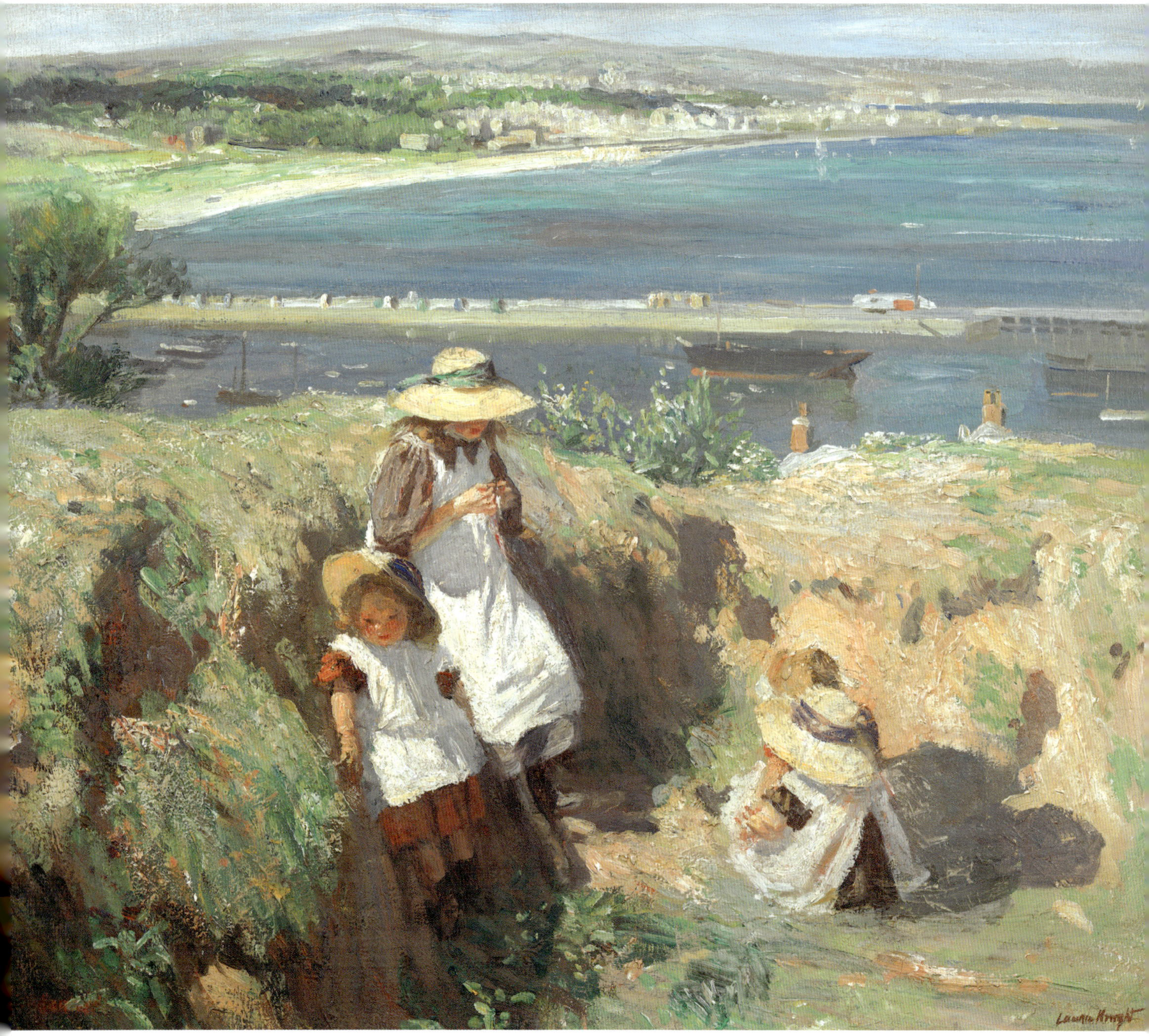

IN THE SUN, NEWLYN

*c.*1910 | oil on canvas | 63.5 x 76 cm

Richard Green Gallery, London

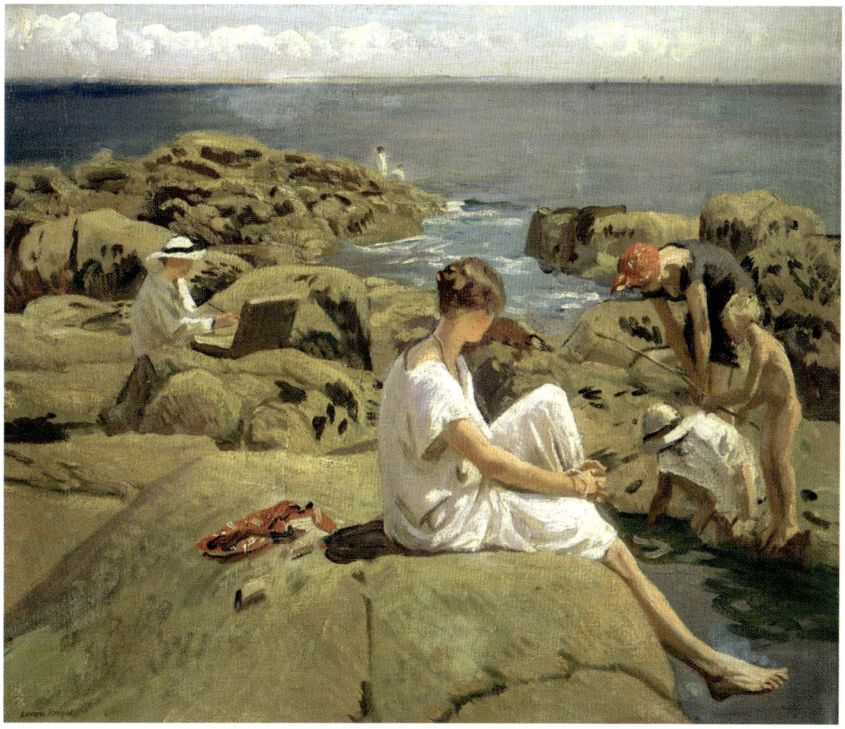

A SUMMER'S DAY AT THE ROCK POOL
oil on canvas | 51 x 61 cm
private collection

artists. He is best known as a painter of horses, from racing to hunting and gypsy ponies. He combined the life of a sociable, literary gentleman with a raucous insalubrious streak, cultivating an image of himself as at home among rough sporting types. He was completely serious about painting, however. His work was much more intuitive and freely drawn than Laura's and often painted directly out in the open air. His way of working chimed with Laura's and it is probable that its example contributed to loosening her painterly style. For his part, he admired her work from the spring of 1909, when he first saw *The Beach* at the Royal Academy. In the same exhibition, the Knights admired his painting *The White Pony*. In the first of three volumes of autobiography, Munnings describes Laura working in Newlyn: 'There, in a low whitewashed sail-loft, with a skylight, Mrs Knight – Dame Laura now – painted pictures which made the rest of us sit up… Here was a great artist who never ceased working. She possessed the energy of six; the studies for her larger canvasses were wonderful.' And he goes on 'I myself have seen her attacking these large canvasses out of doors, and when she started there was no going back. Things happened.'[10]

Dod Shaw had arrived in 1907 as a talented seventeen-year-old to attend the Forbes School of Painting. She was one of a little group of young girls living at Myrtle Cottage in Newlyn, chaperoned by Dod's mother.[11] Laura was older, of course, but was a natural friend for such 'advanced'

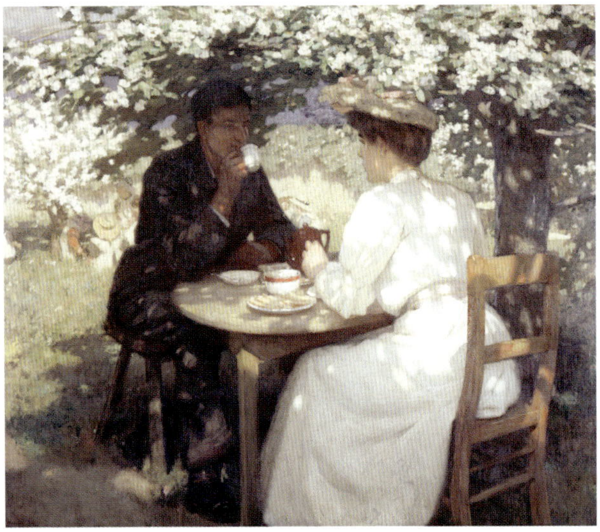

HAROLD KNIGHT
IN THE SPRING TIME (aka **IN THE SPRING**)
1908–09 | oil on canvas | 132 x 158 cm
Laing Art Gallery, Newcastle/Tyne & Wear Archives & Museums

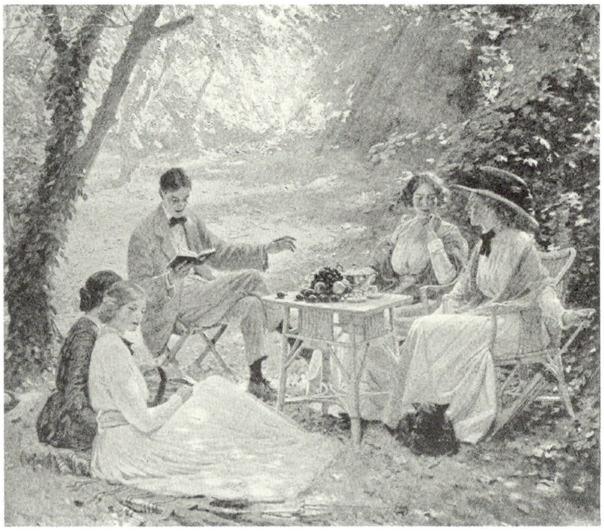

HAROLD KNIGHT
THE SONNET
1910–11 | oil on canvas
A.J. Munnings reading; Florence Carter-Wood (far right) and Laura beside her
reproduced in *The Studio*, December 1912

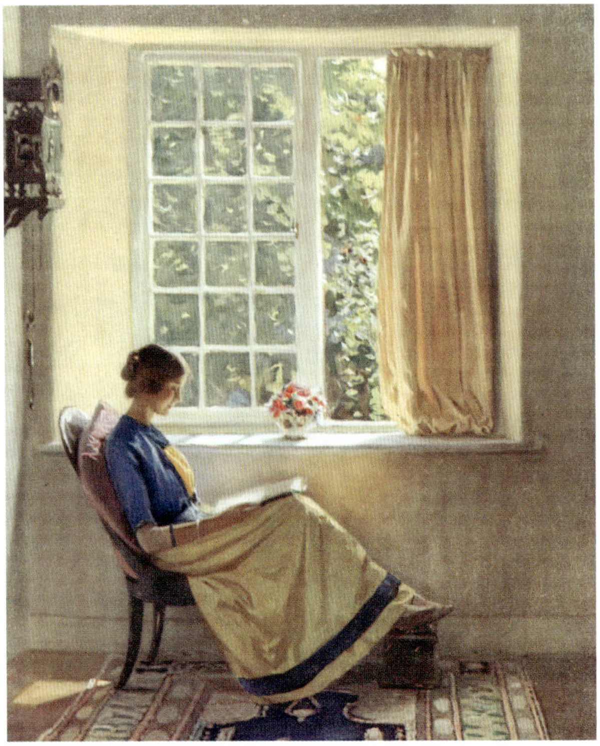

HAROLD KNIGHT
MORNING SUN
c.1911 | oil on canvas
private collection; image courtesy Richard Green Gallery, London

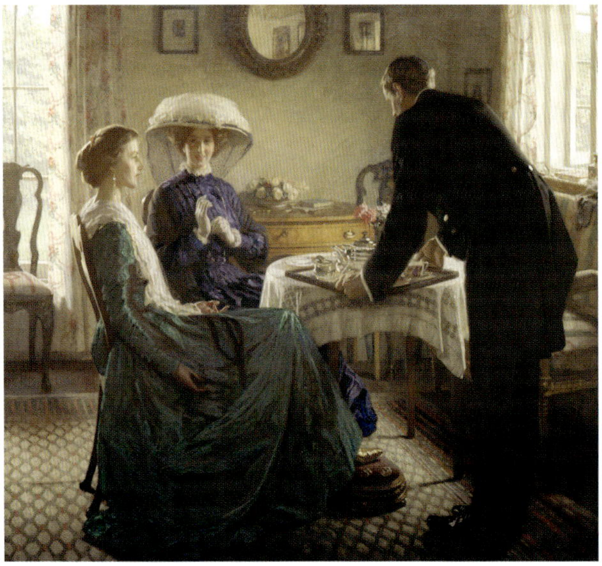

HAROLD KNIGHT
AFTERNOON TEA
1910 | oil on canvas | 188 x 198 cm
private collection; courtesy David Messum

young women. Their intellectual but ebullient company contributed to Newlyn's effect upon Laura, while the beginning of the warm and lasting friendship between the Knights and Lamorna Birch and his family was perhaps more of a steadying and supportive influence.

From the way Laura wrote of her first few years in Newlyn it is evident that she was shedding the strain from her early life. The hardship, continual shortage of money, the loss of her mother, her two grandmothers and her sister Nellie had been hard to bear. For many years she and Harold had had to struggle to make a living at painting. Through it all, Laura's strength of character and her belief that hard work would pay off in the end sustained her. Significantly, she believed in the essential quality of Harold's work and trusted that he would succeed. However irrepressibly she behaved in the new-found freedom of Cornwall, she was anchored in the strength of their relationship and in the working routine than came naturally to them both.

The development of Laura's work was paralleled by widening social horizons, and by perceptions across a broader range of contemporary art and ideas generated by lively enthusiasms and arguments among the artists she mixed with in Cornwall. In the winter of 1910–11 Roger Fry famously brought a large exhibition of Post-Impressionist paintings to London. Some of the work had been painted as much as thirty years before but recent work included shockingly radical paintings by Henri Matisse; it was a landmark exhibition. Its effects on a number of British artists have been well documented and Laura Knight was one on whom it made a deep impression.

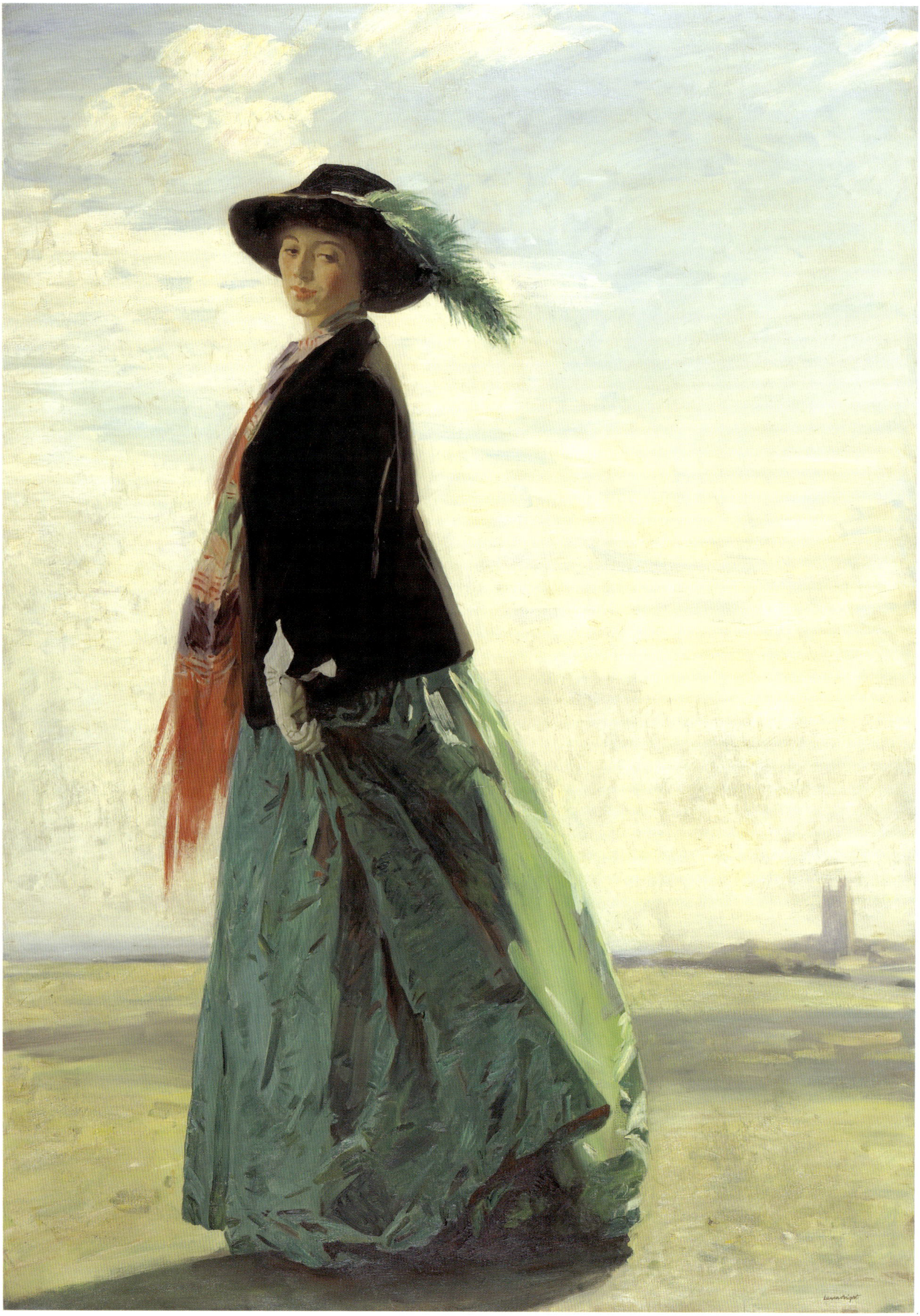

Cornwall and the early years of World War I 1910–1916

Following her success in 1910, Laura Knight was ready to take more radical steps to arrange for herself the subjects she knew she wanted to paint. In Cornwall that summer she started a series of paintings of models in the open air. Though she still drew endlessly from what she saw around her, for her major exhibition canvasses she began to concentrate on a few, mostly adult, models. She needed to rely on them to sit for the more sustained and intense sessions she required. She wanted to work from nudes in the open air – always a tricky problem in Cornwall, where disapproving locals and wandering holiday-makers could cause trouble. She made watercolour studies such as *Children Swimming* using Mornie and Joan Birch as her models but however 'progressive' her more adult friends might be, young women needed to guard their reputations carefully; though nude bathing certainly went on in the privacy of certain special secret places, for a young woman to be known to pose nude for a painting could have been a step too far. Laura's answer was first of all to hire professional models from London, and then to find locations where she could expect not to be interrupted. She and Harold were doing better financially and she writes '…we seemed to be sitting pretty. Without thinking of cost, we regularly engaged two or three models from London. Harold used these lovely girls for smaller, intimate studies of home life.'[1] Laura describes two large canvasses of this time, one of which she was not happy with and so destroyed. The other, *Daughters of the Sun*, was shown at the Royal Academy in 1911 and afterwards in a number of provincial galleries but it was damaged and Laura later destroyed it. She describes making full-size studies for these two large paintings: 'I climbed along the cliff-edge and over slippery rocks every day carrying six-foot canvasses on my head.'[2] She also describes the difficulties of having London models under her wing. Though they had been used to artistic 'goings on' since the mid-1880s, local people thought these women were particularly outrageous. Some felt provoked beyond their usual warm-hearted tolerance. These

THE GREEN FEATHER
1911 | oil on canvas
214.7 x 153.3 cm
National Gallery of Canada, Ottawa
photograph © NGC

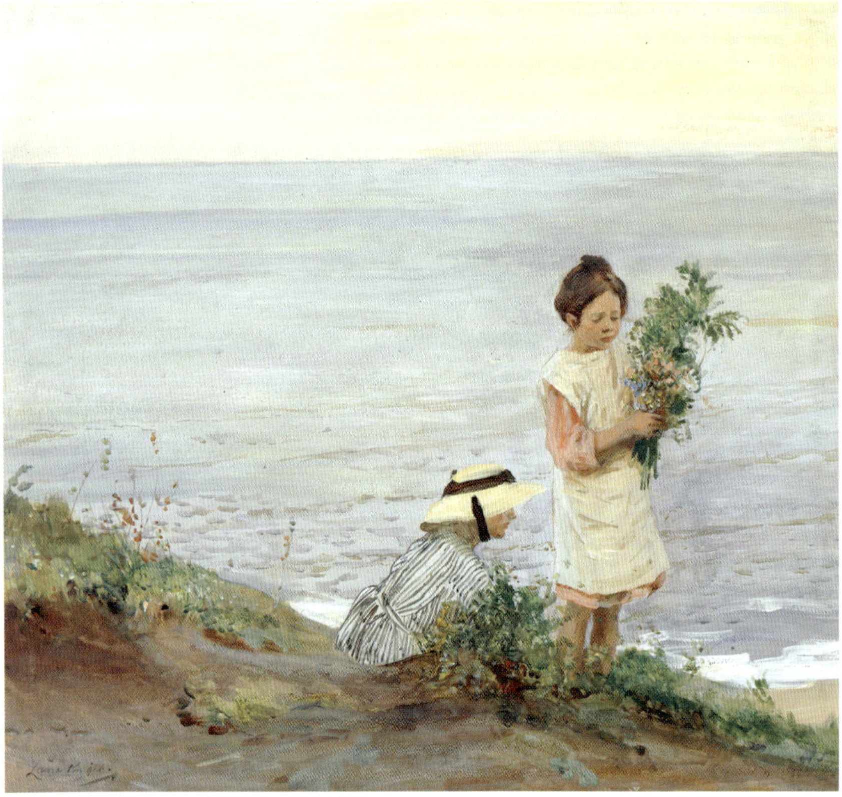

BY THE SEA

*c.*1914 | watercolour | 56.5 x 62.9 cm

private collection; image courtesy Richard Green Gallery, London

difficulties may have led Laura to turn back to painting clothed figures, as in *In Cornwall* 1912.

In October 1911 Laura set out to paint her model Dolly Snell in a green silk evening dress with a black velvet jacket, and a soft-brimmed hat trimmed with a long feather. In the great tradition of dramatic and glamorous single figures, most notably perhaps John Singer Sargent's famous *Madame X*, Laura wanted to create a *coup de theâtre* painted in the open air. She describes the whole process of the painting from prepared canvas to completion in a single day, all but a few final touches made the next morning.[3] She painted at speed, changing the light and her sky as the sunlight came and went. It was a sustained burst of energy and technical brilliance that she herself recognised as exceptional. *The Green Feather* was sent to an exhibition in America and bought for the National Gallery of Canada in 1912. It seems never to have been exhibited in Britain but remains one of Laura's most accomplished and expressive paintings.

At this time (1911–1912), Laura and Harold were lodging at Trewarveneth, at the top of Paul Hill above Newlyn village. This may have been Trewarveneth Farm House, vacated by the Gotch family in 1910, where there was studio space for Harold; he worked at Trewarveneth

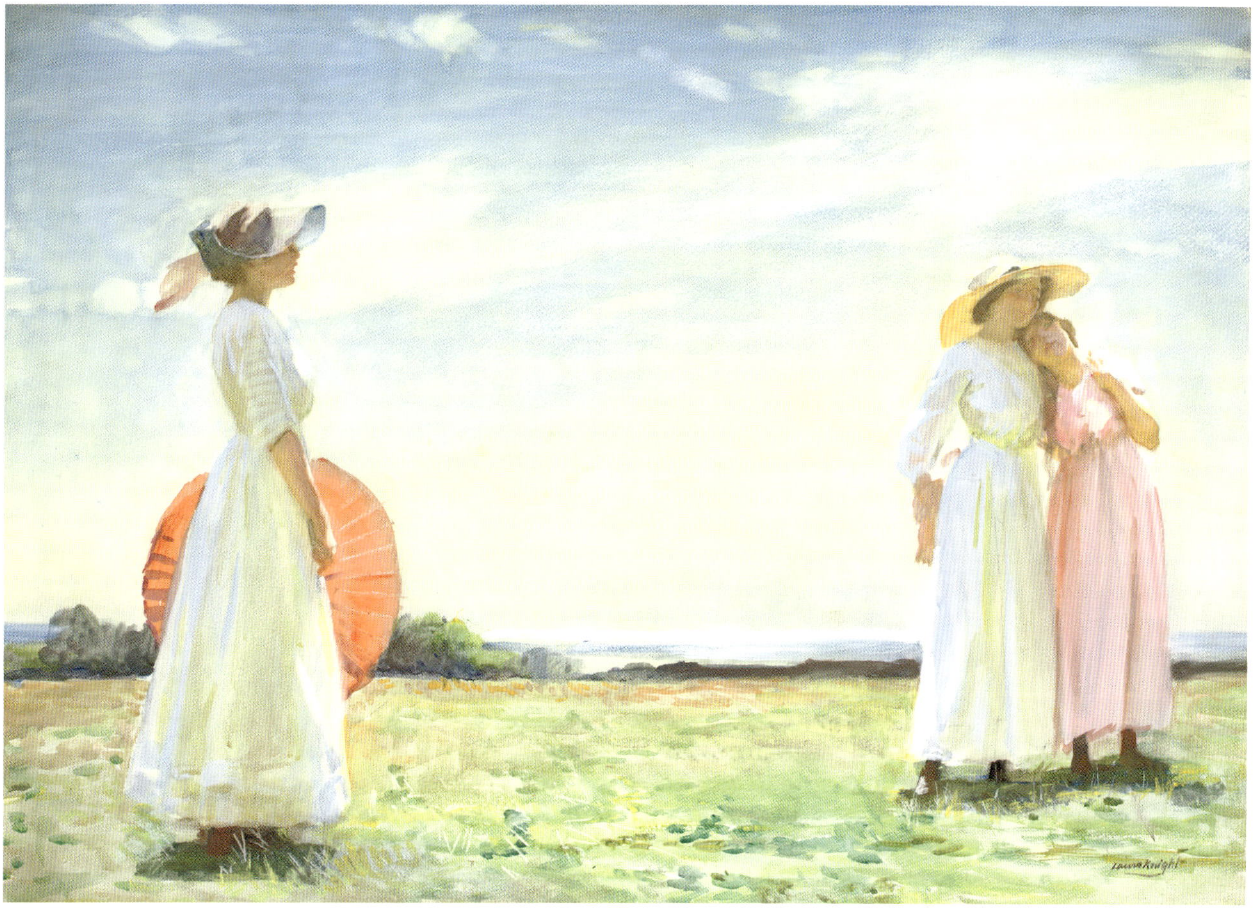

IN THE FIELDS

watercolour | 53.4 x 76 cm

private collection; courtesy Christie's Images/The Bridgeman Art Library

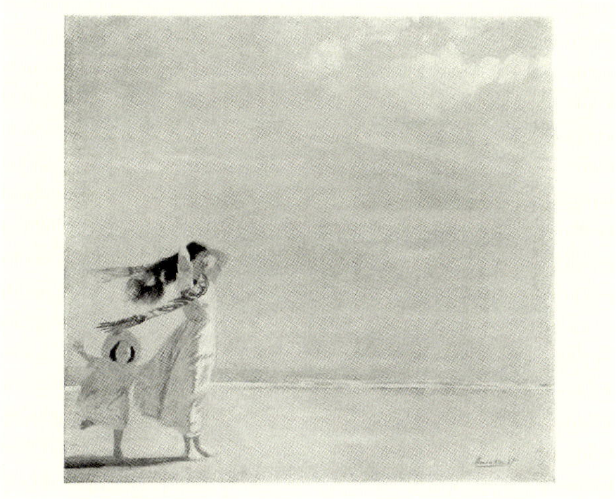

UNTRODDEN SANDS

*c.*1910–12 | watercolour

reproduced in *The Studio*, December 1912

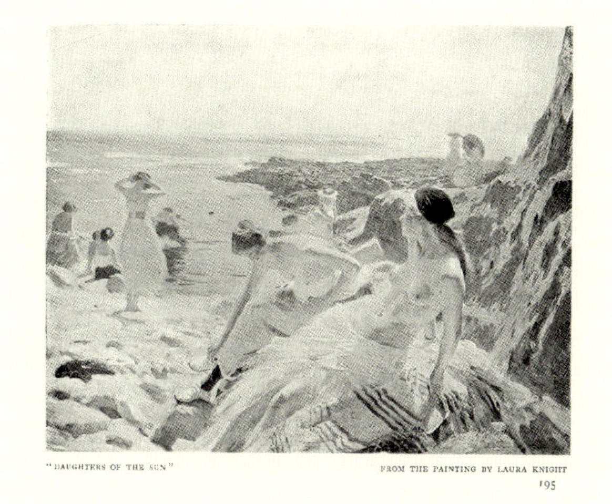

DAUGHTERS OF THE SUN

1910–11 | oil on canvas

reproduced in *The Studio*, December 1912

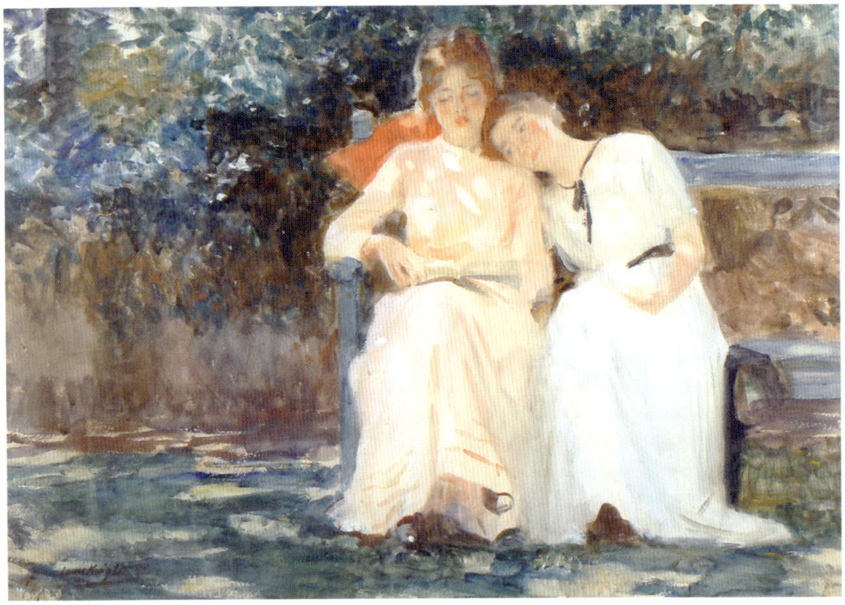

TWO GIRLS READING IN A SUNLIT GARDEN

*c.*1914 | watercolour | 52.7 x 74.2 cm

Doncaster Metropolitan Borough Council, Museum & Art Gallery

while Laura would cycle to Lamorna Cove. She worked out on the rocks or up on the cliff-tops looking down a steep perspective to the sea below. She had a studio on the cliffs near the rocky outcrop of Carn Barges, just along the coast west of the cove itself, provided by the local land-owner, Colonel Paynter of Boskenna. Through his friendship with Lamorna Birch, his tenant at Flagstaff Cottage, Paynter was generally well-disposed to artists and particularly amenable to Laura when she wanted to work at Lamorna. By 1911 Paynter, who owned the land west of the Lamorna stream, was making modest improvements in the village[4] and the following year more houses began to be built there.

At some time in 1911-1912 Harold became seriously ill and Laura ceased working to care for him. It was clearly a prolonged interruption; the Knights had to stay in Plymouth for several months while Harold received treatment and it appears that as he was recovering, Laura herself fell ill, extending even further the time in which all normal working life had to be discontinued. There was a third joint exhibition, 'Cabinet Pictures and Watercolour Drawings' at the Leicester Galleries in April–May 1912, in which Laura showed landscapes and two ballet subjects, and Harold mostly domestic subjects, called his 'modern life interiors' by Laura, who adds that Ernest Brown was delighted with their work.[5] Though no sizes are given in the Leicester Galleries catalogue, one can speculate that 'Cabinet Pictures' means relatively small work – not major exhibition canvasses. The ballet subjects were probably the first Laura showed. The Knights would spend a few weeks in London every year and besides keeping up with galleries and friends they would cram in as many theatre and ballet performances as possible.

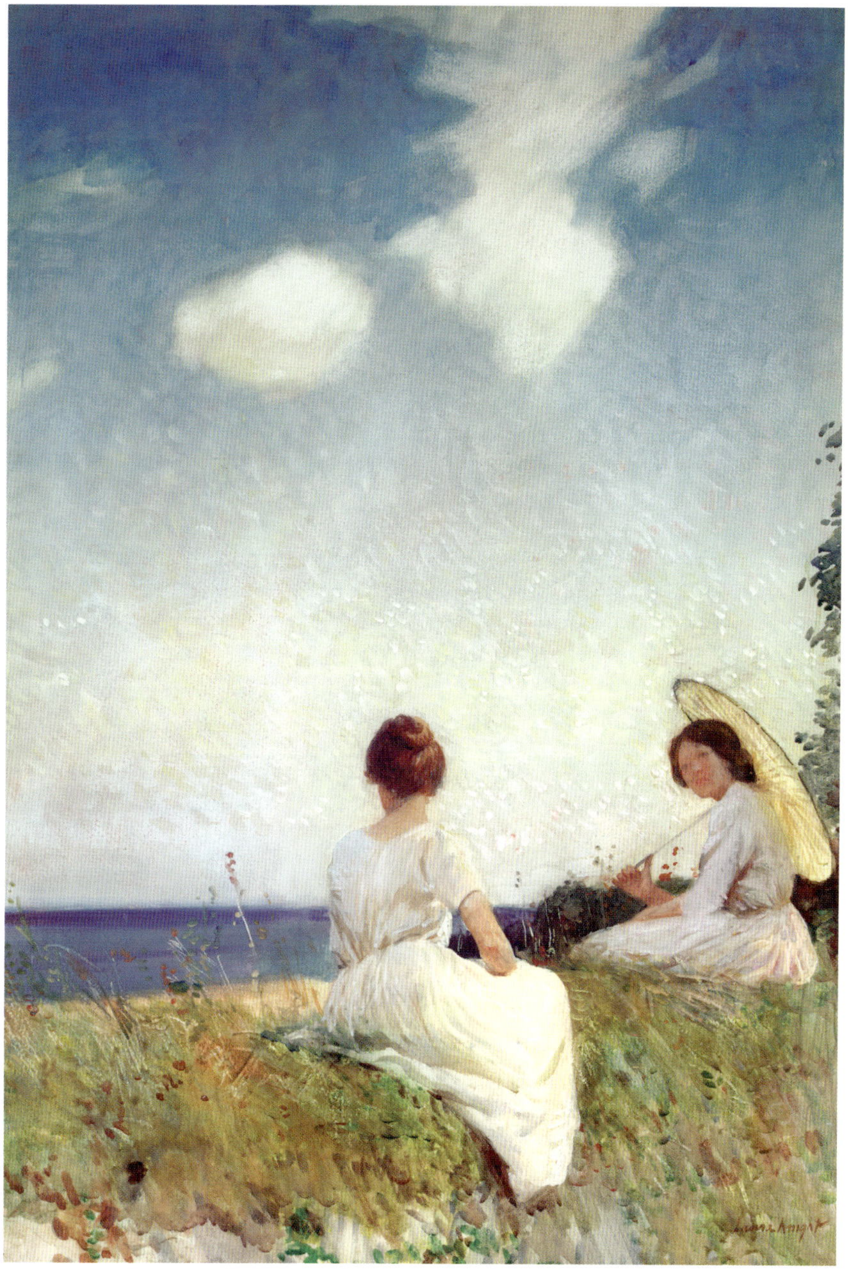

ON THE CLIFFS

watercolour | 74 x 53 cm

private collection; courtesy Sotheby's Picture Library

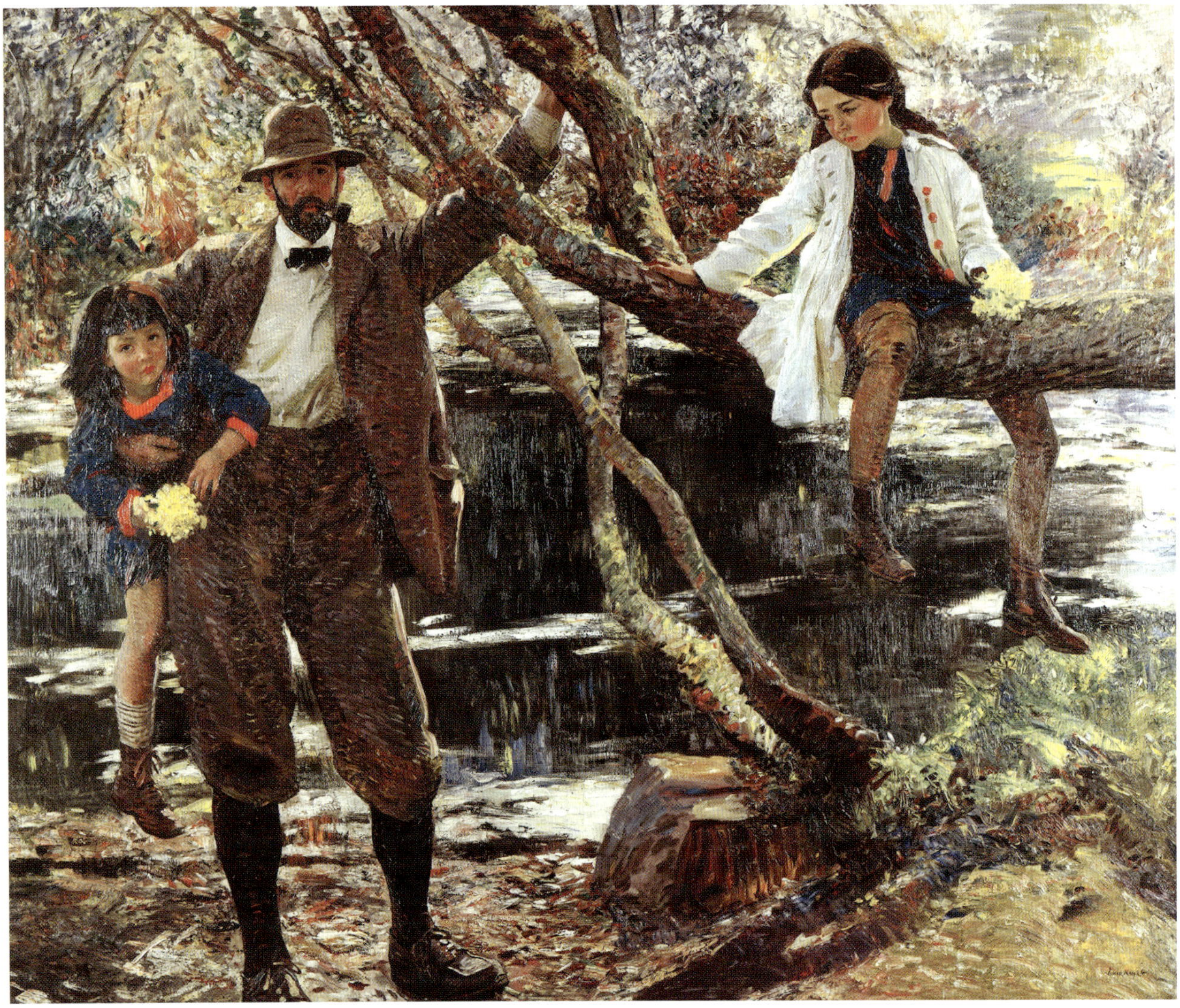

LAMORNA BIRCH AND HIS DAUGHTERS

1916 and 1933 | oil on canvas | 228.6 x 272 cm

University of Nottingham/Djanogly Art Gallery

Laura was already working behind the scenes and in practice rooms, drawing dancers and theatrical life.

While Laura was still recuperating the Knights spent a month in Lancashire where Harold had a commissioned portrait to paint. On their return to Cornwall, later in 1912 or early 1913, they moved from Trewarveneth to Oakhill, in an enclave called Trewoofe at the inland end of the Lamorna valley. Colonel Paynter had made a house out of a row of small cottages; Dod Procter's mother and Aunt Lilla had been living there, and also a friend of Lamorna Birch's, the artist Benjamin Eastlake Leader and his wife. Paynter now made further improvements in preparation for the Knights' tenure. He also provided studios: a small one at Oakhill itself and a large one built for Laura at Trethinnick, a little way down the lane to the cove. The Knights were evidently determined to stay in Cornwall and Laura enjoyed arranging a more settled and properly equipped household, and seeing their plot cleared to make a garden.[6] At Oakhill and around Laura's new studio in the long sheltered cleft of the Lamorna valley itself, there were shady streams and rocky ground and oak trees, growing low because of the wind and covered in lichen, moss and ferns. Laura set out to paint Lamorna Birch and his two daughters, in a setting reminiscent of his own best-known subjects. She used a large canvas and posed the painter with his youngest daughter Joan under his arm, while Mornie sits on a branch beside them. The ambitiously large canvas shows that Laura's new studio had increased her scope, though in the event the painting was not completed until 1933–34 when Laura reworked it and showed it at the Royal Academy.

In December 1912 the *Studio* magazine carried an article written by Norman Garstin on the work of Harold and Laura Knight. The balance of his interest and the illustrations seem to give precedence to Harold's work but Laura is well represented, including *Flying a Kite* and *The Green Feather* as well as recent work like *Daughters of the Sun* and *Untrodden Sands.* The article, and Garstin's authoritative by-line, is likely to have contributed to the reputation Harold and Laura were establishing in the context of a strong 'next generation' – after the original Newlyn School – of painters working in West Cornwall.

Laura's *A Picnic* was in the 1913 Royal Academy exhibition. It was painted at Lamorna, with Munnings lying on the grass reading poetry, and a little girl in plaits for which Lamorna Birch's daughter Mornie was the model. The scene is a simpler subject than Harold's accomplished set-piece *The Sonnet* of 1910–1911, and may in fact have been painted around the same time (though for her retrospective at the RA in 1965 Laura dates it to 1912). It should be noted that paintings are often dated to the year of their Royal Academy showing, even if painted a year or two (or occasionally many years) before. In 1913 in her Trethinnick studio, in contrast to the open-air scene of Lamorna Birch, Laura painted a studio set-piece of herself (in the red cardigan) with Ella Naper as a nude figure. Ella was an experienced model and sat for Harold Harvey and Harold Knight. This bold and confidently painted canvas looks

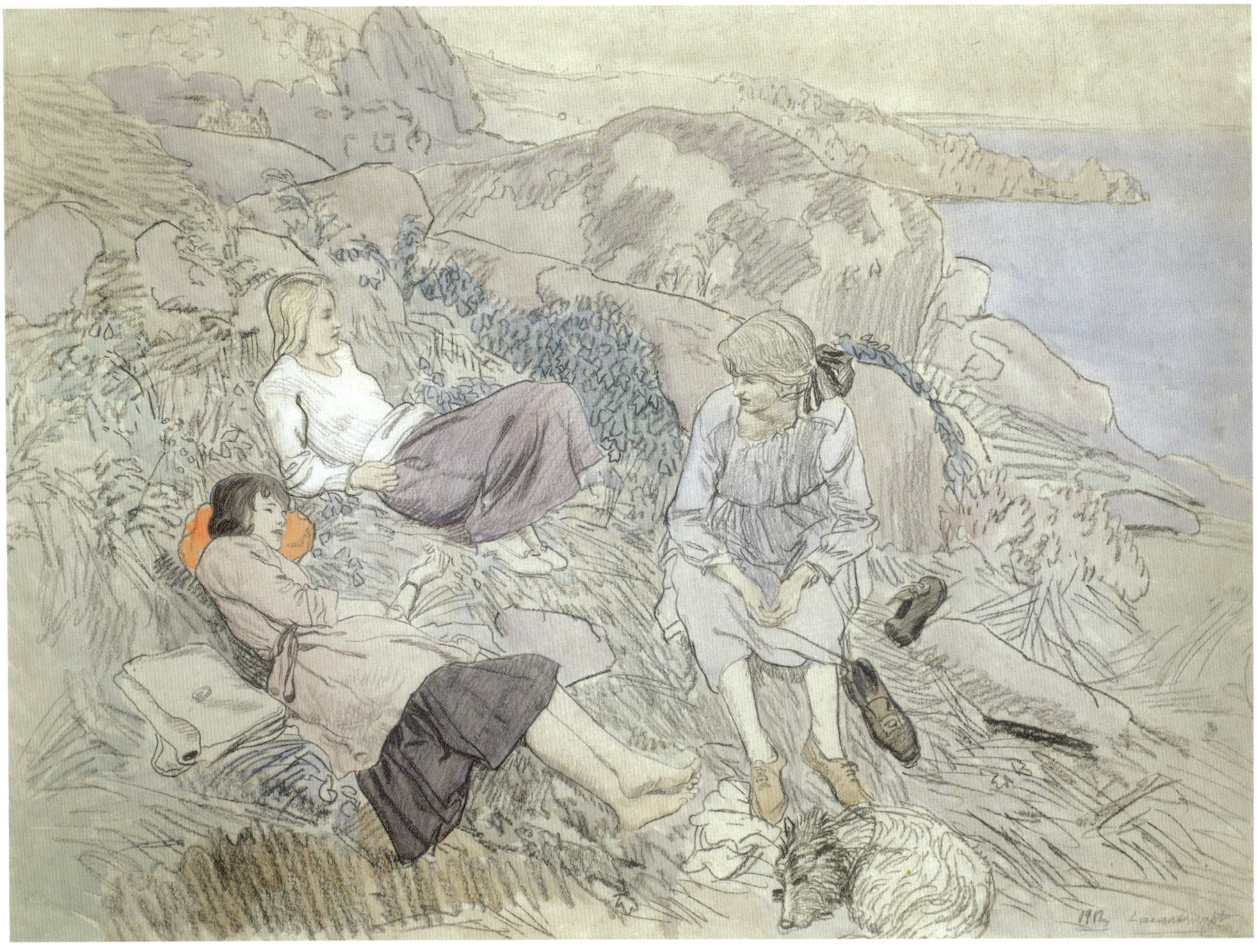

IN CORNWALL

1912 | chalk and watercolour | 54 x 76.2 cm

private collection; courtesy Editions Graphiques

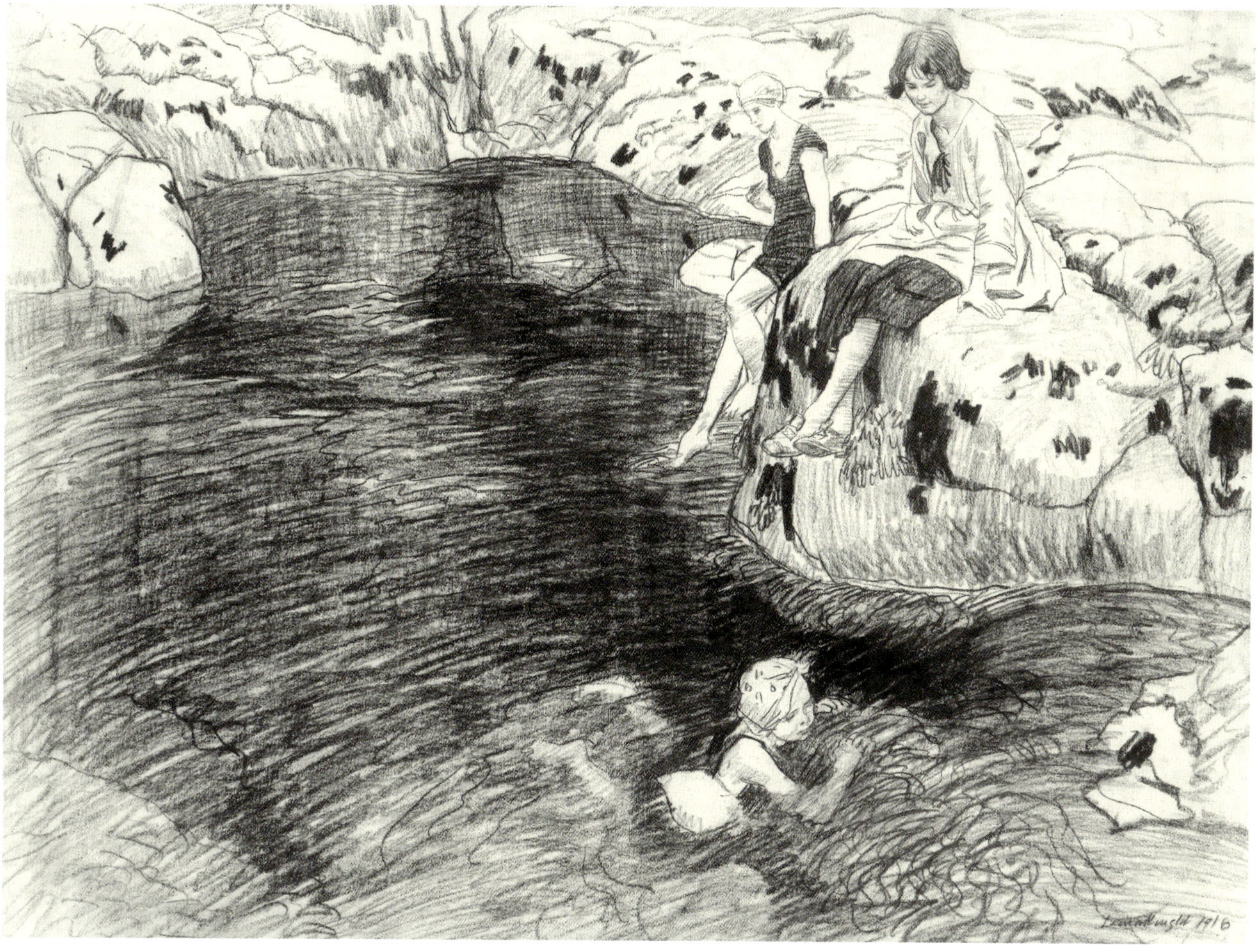

BATHERS AT LAMORNA

1916 | chalk | 56 x 76 cm

private collection; courtesy Editions Graphiques

forward to Laura's later paintings of figures in which formal painterly concerns dominate. It has become one of Laura's best known images.

There is a group of works including the watercolours *On the Cliffs*, *Wind and Sun*, *In the Fields* and *Untrodden Sands* that, rather like *Daughters of the Sun* of 1911, show Laura's most light-hearted mood. The last two were shown in the April-May 1912 Leicester Galleries exhibition. She places her models in light gauzy dresses, wearing flimsy sunhats or holding a sunshade, in open almost featureless settings. The mood is airy and the palette light, the sunny skies painted with delicate skill. Another watercolour, *Two Girls Reading in a Sunlit Garden* suggests a similar gentle atmosphere, as does the oil painting *Marsh Mallows*, for which the model was Dolly Henry (whose sad demise Laura records in *Oil Paint and Grease Paint*).[7] There is a distinct contrast between these and a drawing, visibly dated 1912, in which three models are posed on a cliff-top wearing more work-a-day clothes and in rather less elegant poses. The model on the left (and on the right in *Bathers at Lamorna*) is Phyllis Vipond-Crocker, a young girl with a characteristic forward-swinging bob of dark hair who frequently modelled for Laura (and other artists) from about 1912. This drawing certainly prefigures Laura's impressive series of cliff-top figure paintings of 1915-1917. Perhaps those works where the mood is so airy and light-hearted in fact belong to the period 1908 to 1910 (although a date of about 1913 has been suggested for one of them), or perhaps they are of a type she continued to make after 1910 for a different market – possibly one that included watercolour specialists. Only two such seem to have been shown at the Academy, *Daughters of the Sun* in 1911 and another large canvas, *The Flower* in 1912 (illustrated in *Royal Academy Pictures* that year). It may be that Laura simply moved between different ideas and treatments through this period when her work was developing so rapidly. Without concrete dating evidence, one can only speculate but it is certain that the mood of her paintings changed substantially from around 1913.

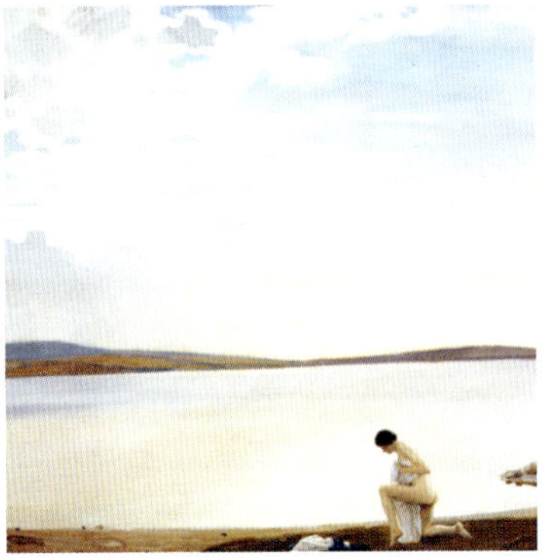

HAROLD KNIGHT
DOSMARE POOL
1915–16 | oil on canvas
76 x 76 cm
private collection
courtesy Bonhams/Phillips

In the autumn of 1913 Augustus John and his wife were staying at Lamorna and there was much socialising between the artists of the Birches' and Knights' circle. Robert and Eleanor Hughes's new house at Lamorna became the centre for many social evenings that year. In the spring of 1914 another visitor was the theatre producer Barry Jackson, who was having his portrait painted by Munnings. Jackson, the founder of Birmingham Rep, would become a life-long friend of the Knights and later introduced them to Malvern and the Herefordshire countryside. In July 1914 Munnings' wife died. She was the painter Florence Carter-Wood, but always known as Blote (short for Bloater), whom Harold had painted in 1909–10. Her death was a sad and shocking thing for Laura, who was one of the people immediately summoned when she was found, and who had tried to revive her; it was assumed she had taken poison but Laura is carefully discreet when writing of the event in both autobiographies. Years later, Laura writes feelingly to Munnings' second wife Violet, absolving him of all possible blame. She says Blote suffered from, 'a type of madness, call it what you will'.[8]

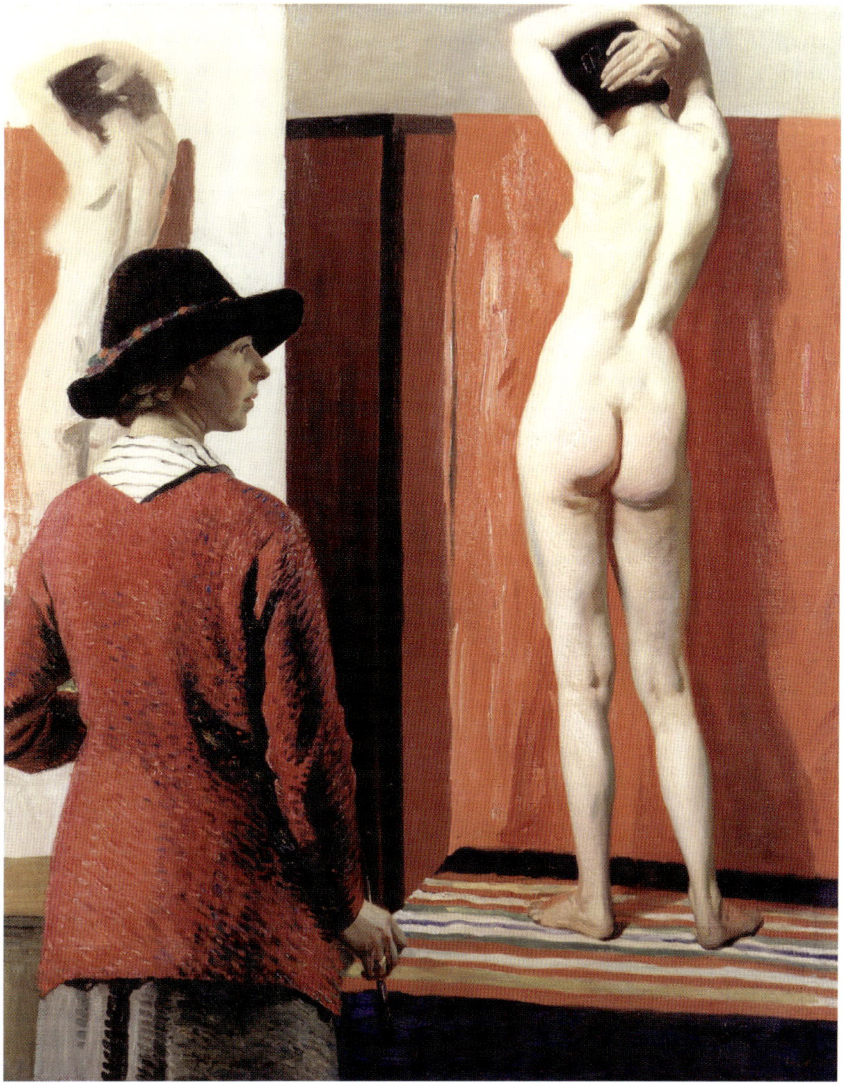

SELF PORTRAIT (aka **THE MODEL**)
1913 | oil on canvas | 152.4 x 127.6 cm

The painter Charles Naper and his wife Ella, maker of jewellery and ceramics, had arrived in 1912 and become good friends of the Knights. Their house at Trewoofe, at the head of the Lamorna valley, was completed in 1913. In 1911, while they were still living at Looe, Charles had built himself a summer cabin near Dozmary Pool on Bodmin Moor and in the summer of 1914 the two couples spent time camping out there, working in the open air.[9] The Knights made several summer visits to Dozmary with the Napers, building another cabin there in 1915; other artists also went: Harold and Gertrude Harvey, and the Birches. For Harold it became the setting for a painting of Ella Naper, taken from photographs specially posed: *Dosmare Pool* (shown at the RA in 1916). Laura's response to the bleak landscape is more direct: 'The moor was glorious up at Dozmare [sic]. The long unbroken line of Brown Gelly reflected in the pool.

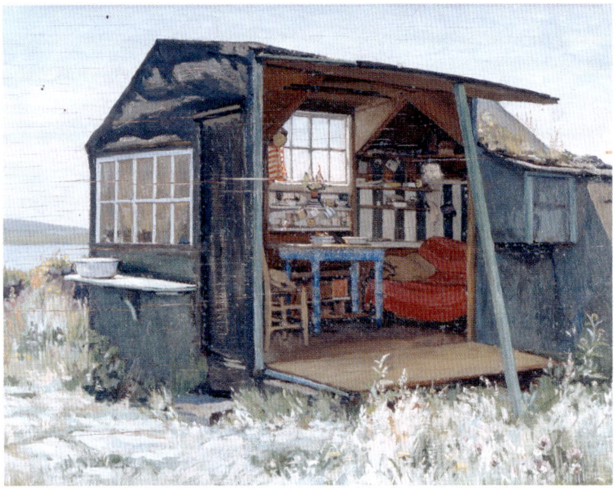

CHARLES NAPER
PAINTING HUT AT DOZMARY POOL
oil on panel
private collection/© The Artist's Estate

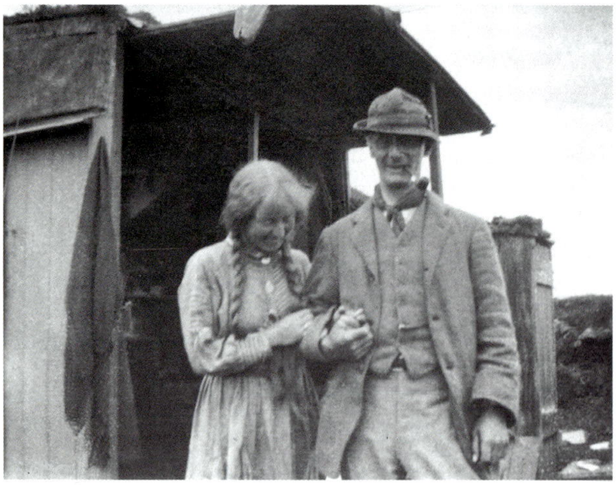

Laura and Harold, Dozmary Pool, 1914
The Naper photograph album/© The Artist's Estate

The rough grass washed and bleached, the freshness – what balm it was!'[10] And she goes on to describe a deep moorland wood with 'a thick carpet of emerald moss and bright red pine needles…' where there were '…densely packed pine trees, their trunks mast-like before overhead their branches spread and made a ceiling. Here and there a spindly beech festooned its leaves of palest green over the density of an ink-black pool, gold-spotted where the sun pierced some little hole in the fir branches overhead, turning the peat-stained clear brown water into little patches of pure gold.'[11] It seems the large canvas Laura planned was never painted but her vision of the place remains fresh on the page as she writes more than twenty years later.

Laura had paintings in the large and prestigious Carnegie International Exhibition at Pittsburgh in February 1914, including her 1913 Academy painting *The Picnic*. Her Academy painting for 1914 was *March Manyweathers*, of a man with a child on a horse with sunshine and rain in the background. She writes that it was her first attempt at painting a horse (no doubt she had been encouraged by Munnings, who painted her working on it) and that it ended up consigned to storage.[12] That year she painted watercolour views of a china clay pit, probably visiting the huge workings near St Austell while she was staying on Bodmin moor, or on the way there. It is an unusual industrial subject for Laura, pre-figuring her wartime commissions. In 1914–15 she was working on a painting of a May tree in full blossom, with a figure on the left in a black hat and a red cloak, and a girl picking wild flowers. The scene is set by a field with big granite boulders piled along its edge. Blossom, wild flowers and lush grass are painted with thick brushstrokes under brilliant sunshine. This is probably *May Blossom*, shown at the Royal Academy in 1915. There is a notable contrast with Harold's cool toned *View of Mousehole* of this period.

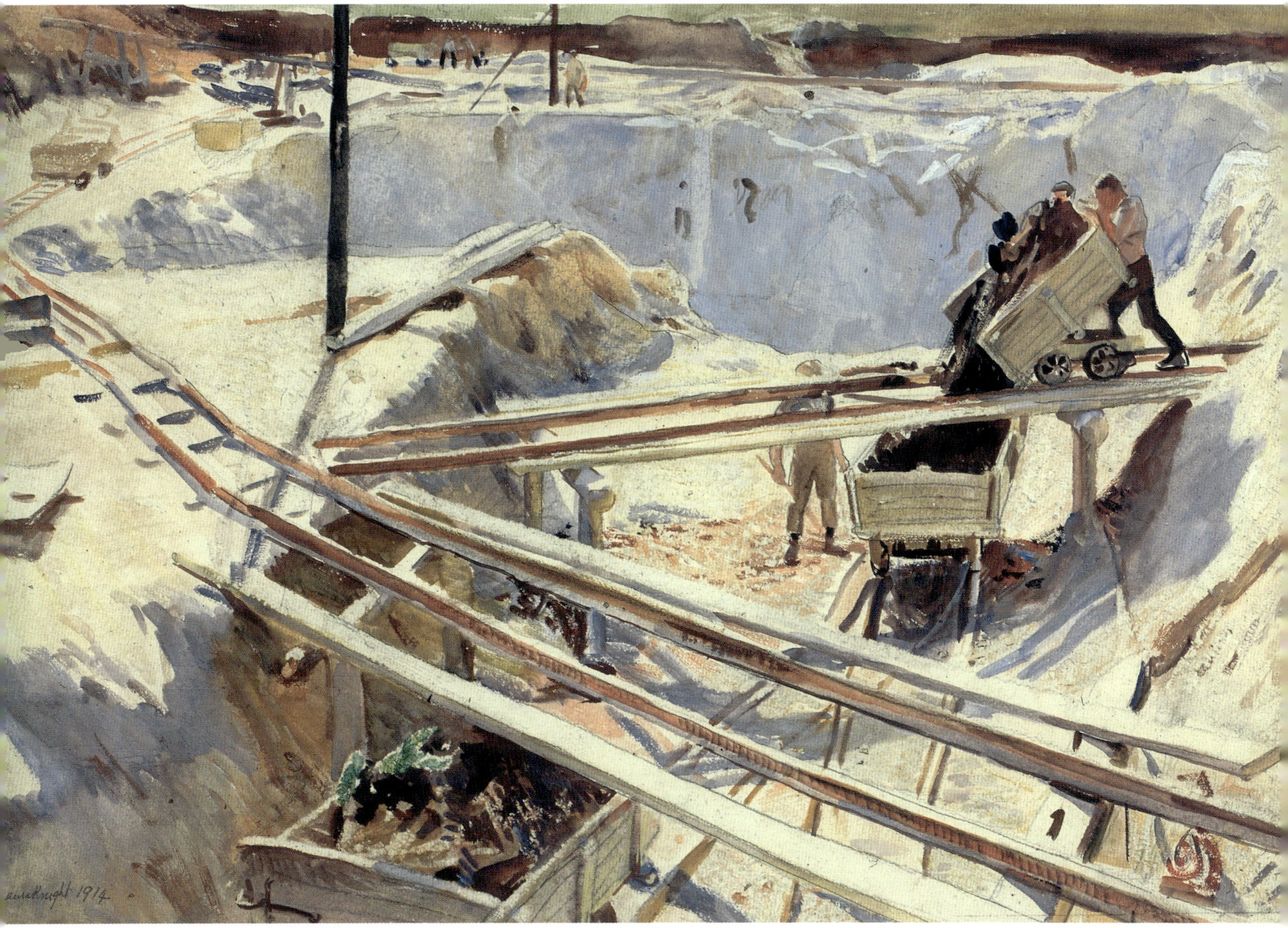

THE CHINA CLAY PIT

1914 | watercolour | 44.5 x 69 cm

Penlee House Gallery and Museum, Penzance

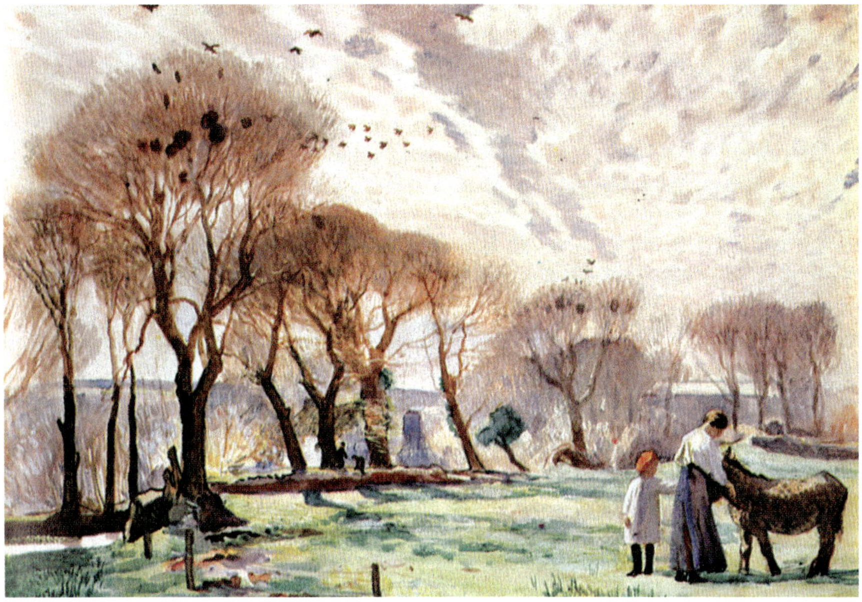

EARLY SPRING
*c.*1916–17 | watercolour | 53 x 75 cm
whereabouts unknown; image courtesy Bonhams/Phillips

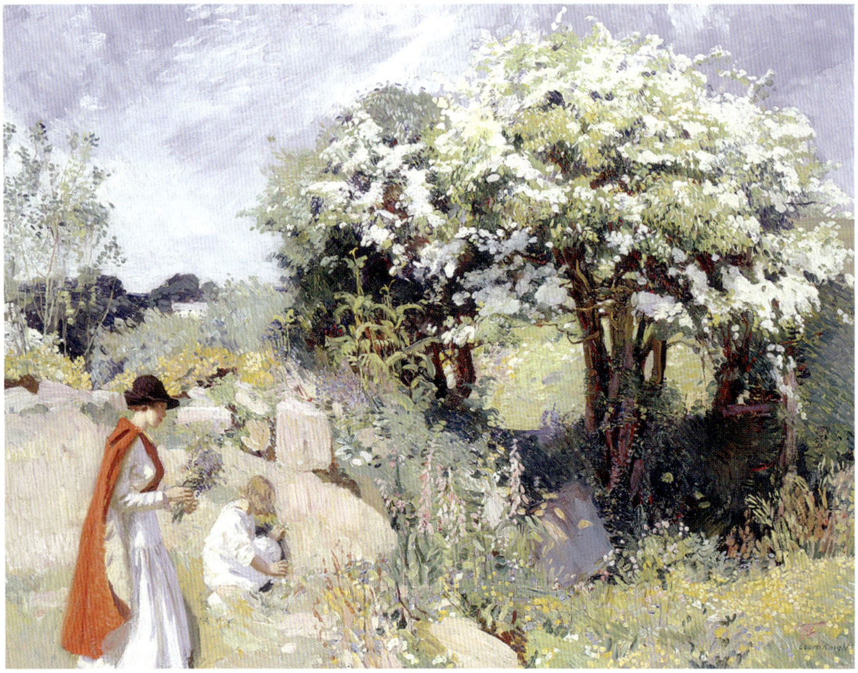

THE MAY TREE (aka **MAY BLOSSOM**)
1913 | oil on canvas | 76 x 102 cm
private collection/© Christie's Images Limited

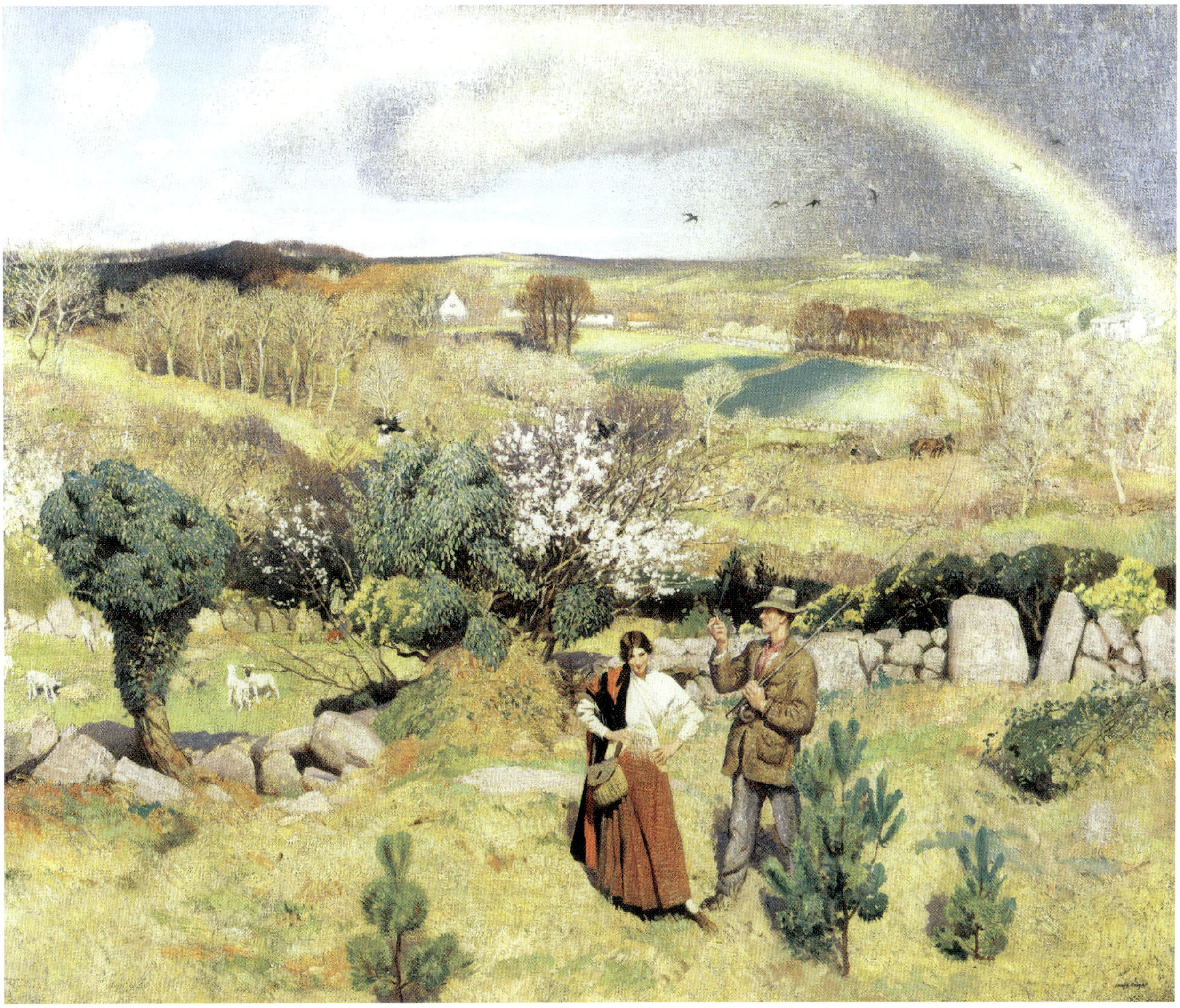

SPRING

1914 | oil on canvas | 152.4 x 182.9 cm

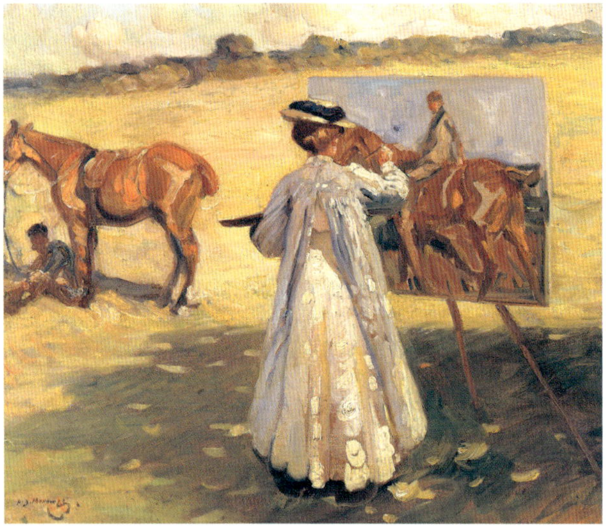

ALFRED MUNNINGS
LAURA KNIGHT PAINTING 'MARCH MANYWEATHERS'
*c.*1913–14 | oil on canvas
Norwich Castle Museum
courtesy Felix Rosenstiel's Widow & Son Ltd., London

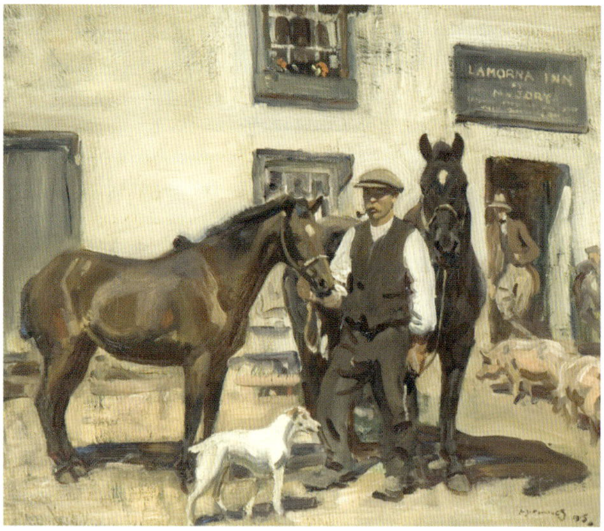

ALFRED MUNNINGS
LAMORNA INN, CORNWALL
1915 | oil on canvas | 50.8 x 61 cm
Sir Alfred Munnings Museum, Dedham
courtesy Felix Rosenstiel's Widow & Son Ltd., London

The Knights seem to have been affected only slowly by the outbreak of war in 1914. Harold, true to his own firm principles, was a pacifist and determined to refuse any action that would support war. He was eventually designated a conscientious objector and worked on the land for a while. Though Laura presumably supported his view, or certainly his right to hold to it, the situation became very difficult as people around them reacted against Harold's position. His health was in any case still poor. The Knights left Oakhill and a relatively prosperous, productive and contented way of life. They took lodgings in St Ives for a time and Harold had a studio there but Laura continued to work at Lamorna. In late 1915 to early 1916 she planned a large canvas with a wide view over the Penwith landscape in spring. In seeking to express a broad sweep of land with rain and a rainbow, she might possibly have been recalling a huge canvas by Henry Clarence Whaite that Nottingham Castle had acquired in 1893, called *The Rainbow*. Many years later, after the Second World War, she returned to painting effects of weather, notably rain and rainbows, over the Herefordshire landscape.

Setting out to make studies for *Spring* Laura describes the difficulty of working in the open because war-time regulations forbade such activity anywhere near the coast, for fear of espionage.[13] Although she had planned the wide extent of her view, the fact that direct studies for the details of the landscape had to be made piecemeal may account for the slightly theatrical atmosphere of the finished work. She did not have the freedom to work outdoors right through to the finished canvas. The figures were painted from Charles and Ella Naper, he with a

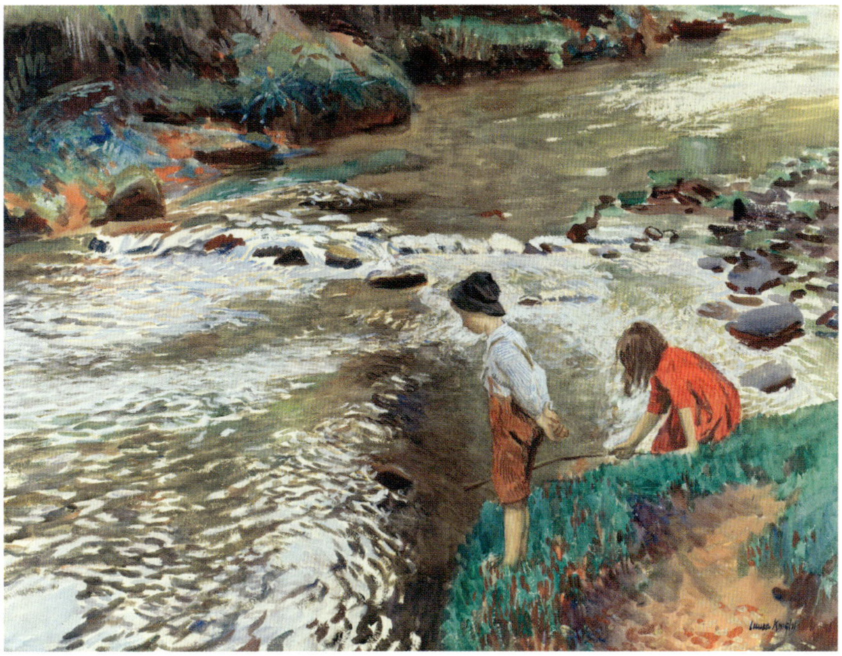

THE TWO FISHERS

pencil, watercolour and bodycolour | 56 x 75 cm

Richard Green Gallery, London

fly-fishing rod and line, and she with a fishing basket but a dancer's elegant stance. The scene is bright with sun from behind the viewpoint, a rainbow showing against a curtain of rain to the right. The landscape is typical of Penwith, fields with stone boundaries where generations of farmers have cleared their ground of granite boulders to open up small fields, and low hills on the horizon. In the foreground there are small pine trees, typical of those planted when mine-waste ground was tidied up and consequently growing stunted. *Spring* was shown at the Royal Academy in 1916 but according to a note by art historian Caroline Fox Laura worked on it again later, altering and re-altering the foreground figures[14] before it was bought by the Chantrey Bequest Trustees in 1935 and given to the Tate Collection. Indeed the figure of Charles was replaced by a boy and a dog and then painted back in again.

Laura herself notes that the painting was prefigured by her response to a valley on the moors near Staithes where she saw primroses growing: 'sheltered there, one learnt that the long winter was nearly over, in some patches of sunlight between the tracery of shadow it was almost warm. No one could take a step without crushing the virginal green and yellow that was springing from the black earth. These expeditions [up to the moors from Staithes] brought a desire to paint landscape and I went there many times, hoping to make studies for a great work.'[15] It seems that *Spring* was the fulfilment of Laura's wish to paint landscape on a large scale. It could be seen as the end of looking back to the aspirations of her earlier working life.

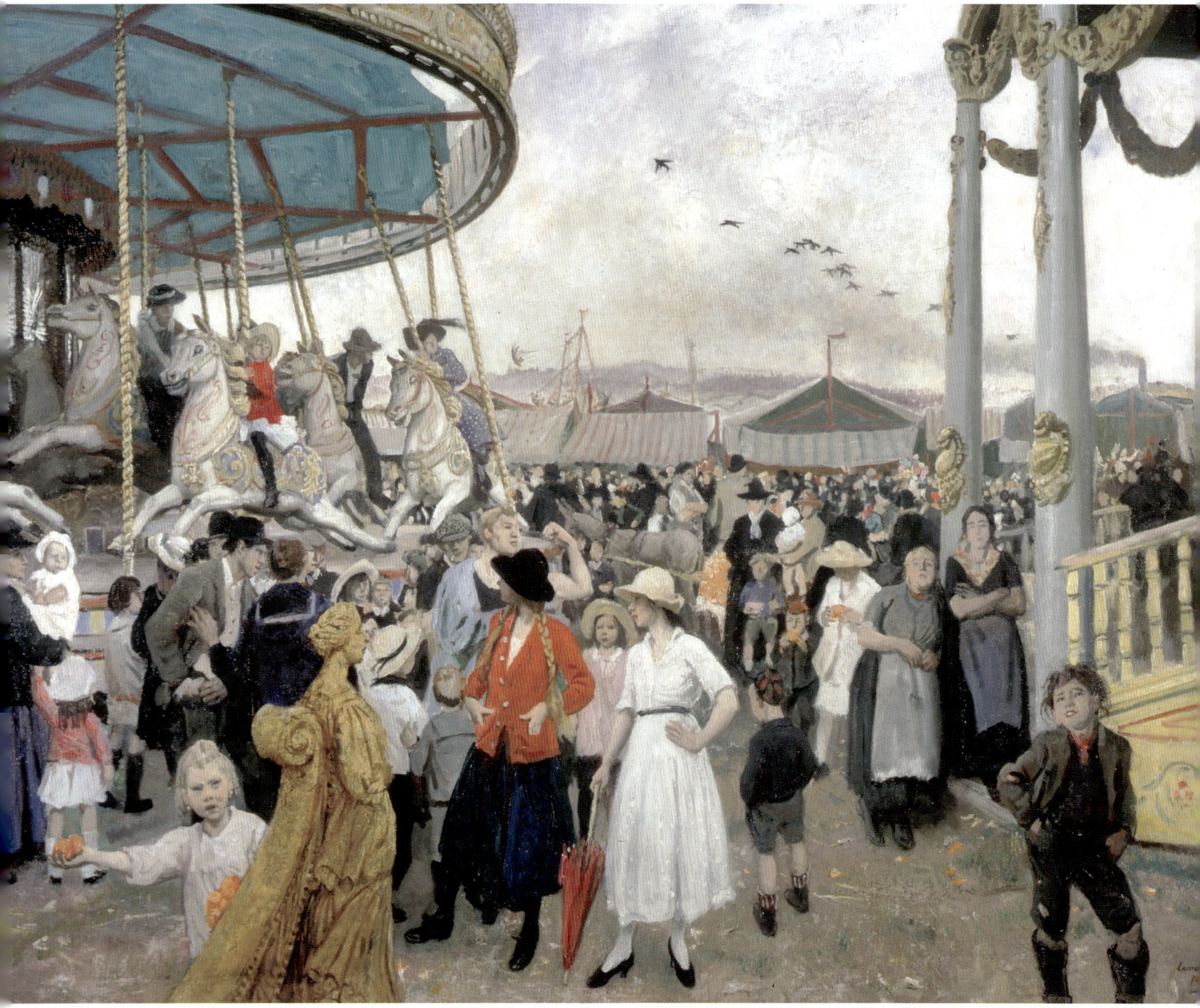

PENZANCE FAIR

1916 | oil on canvas | 116.8 x 151.1 cm

private collection, USA; image courtesy Richard Green Gallery, London

World War I and London

1915–1921

In June 1915 Laura shared an exhibition of watercolours at the Fine Art Society in Bond Street with Lamorna Birch (who had been showing there fairly regularly since 1906); there were enamels by Laura and jewelled frames by Ella Naper and an artist called Aristide Sartorio was also showing at the time. Half the artists' receipts from sales were given for the British Officers' Families Fund. Austin Wormleighton records[1] that Birch knew the gallery wanted a show suitable for war-time, with modest work modestly priced but that Laura ignored this and sent in '...a clutch of rather showy pictures including her Lamorna nudes luminously drawn against rocks and sea, some other large *plein air* studies and some impressions of the Russian Ballet.' Laura was evidently taking the best advantage of her opportunity at this gallery, whose clientele were well known to be connoisseurs of watercolours and drawings.

In 1916 while the Knights were staying in St Ives the issue of Harold's resistance to the fighting came to a head and he was sent away to work on the land.[2] They stayed in the Naper's house at Trewoofe for a time and Laura painted *Early Spring* in the meadow below the house, with figures including Ella with a donkey at the right (it was shown at the Academy in 1917). Later in 1916 Laura was confined there for a while with a broken leg.[3] In the cold winter weather of late 1916, possibly while she was staying at St Hilary with Reverend Bernard Walke and his wife Annie, and with her leg still in plaster, Laura made studies of children skating on a frozen pond. In his book *Twenty Years at St Hilary*, Walke writes of visiting Lamorna constantly that autumn and a memorable Christmas dinner there. Another artist who arrived in Newlyn during the war years was the eccentric painter Gluck (Harriet Gluckstein) and she naturally joined the Knights' circle, having a great interest in the theatre in common with Laura. Cedric Morris and Lett Haines were in Cornwall at the time (though they did not move to Newlyn until 1919) and were also friends of Laura's.

The travelling fairs that arrived annually in Penzance or Newlyn provided subjects for a number of the Newlyn and Lamorna artists and were especially attractive to Laura Knight. By this time she was confident enough to paint a fairground scene crowded with people and activity, adding piquant touches of humour here and there. There are later paintings by Ernest Procter and Lamorna Birch of a fair sited in Newlyn Harbour, while the one Laura painted in Penzance in 1916 seems to be sited on open, flat ground down below the town and close to the sea (probably where the Bolitho Gardens are now). She painted two versions of the same scene, one possibly a study for the other, which looks a rather more resolved and accomplished final version, and a number of studies. In what I suggest might be the first version of the main composition, the central figures are more static; Laura places herself in the centre with Phyllis Vipond-Crocker beside her. An old man stands at the right with what looks like a sheepskin tied like a cloak round his shoulders and behind him there is a figure that looks like A.J. Munnings, in riding boots. In my supposed second version (see p.56), there is much more flow and movement in the composition. The figure of Laura herself in the central group is posed with more verve, her hands in the pockets of the red cardigan that appears in several works of the period, notably *Self Portrait* (aka *The Model*) of 1913, while other figures in the cast have changed. Like the landscape *Spring*, *Penzance Fair* shows Laura fulfilling an ambition from her early days: as a child she always loved the Goose Fair in Nottingham – a noisy, colourful, crowded annual spectacle – and longed to be able to paint it. Laura was fascinated by the gypsies and fairground hucksters she painted in Penzance and in later years she painted travelling people in the circus, at Epsom races and in the hop-gardens of Herefordshire.

Although the years of the First World War brought difficulties and disruption to the Knights' working lives, they continued to be based in Cornwall and Laura continued to work with figures against its dramatic coastline. The regulations against working in the open air near the coast were circumvented by special permits and between 1915 and 1918 she produced a strong series of paintings that express her love of cliff-top landscapes and working in the open air. It was not only her preferred place to work but also a vital component of her subject. Painting directly from figures and place had been for many years and was still her primary concern. Furthermore, her confidence was greatly strengthened by some success and a growing reputation. During the war years Laura's work from models in the open air evidently developed from the airy lightness of *Untrodden Sands* and *Wind and Sun* towards a more contemporary aesthetic. She began to paint a clearer, more mundane reality, turning once again to close study of settings and figures. The drawings *Bathers at Lamorna* 1916 and *In Cornwall* 1912 are examples of the way Laura studied the sea shore at Lamorna cove and understood the play of changing light and colour. It was her habit to use them in paintings made in the studio as well as to paint directly on canvas in the open air. The painting *Lamorna Cove* looking down on the surface of the sea and people bathing from a boat, was probably painted in 1916-17 and may be the one shown

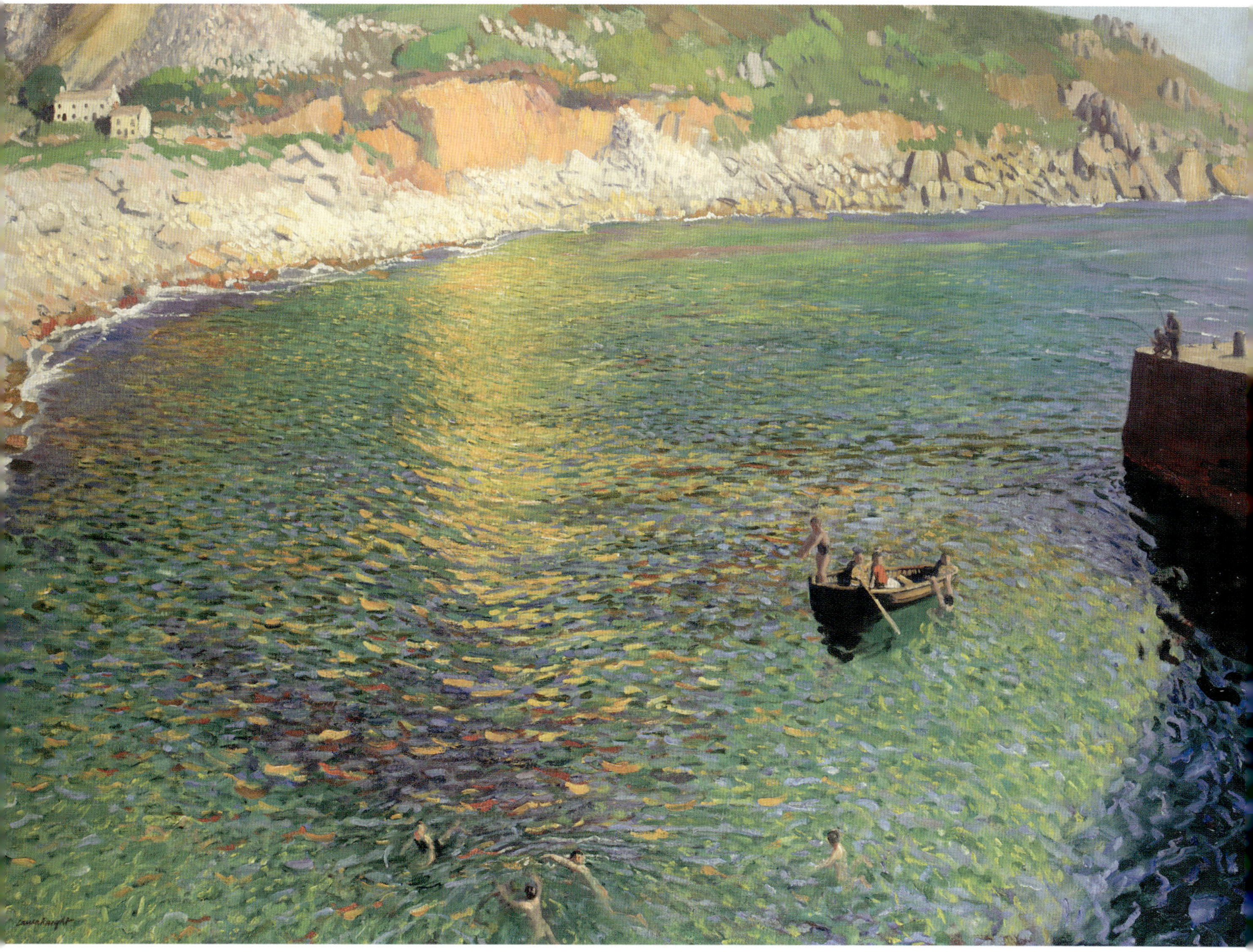

LAMORNA COVE

oil on canvas | 97.8 x 137.8 cm

private collection; courtesy Sotheby's Picture Library

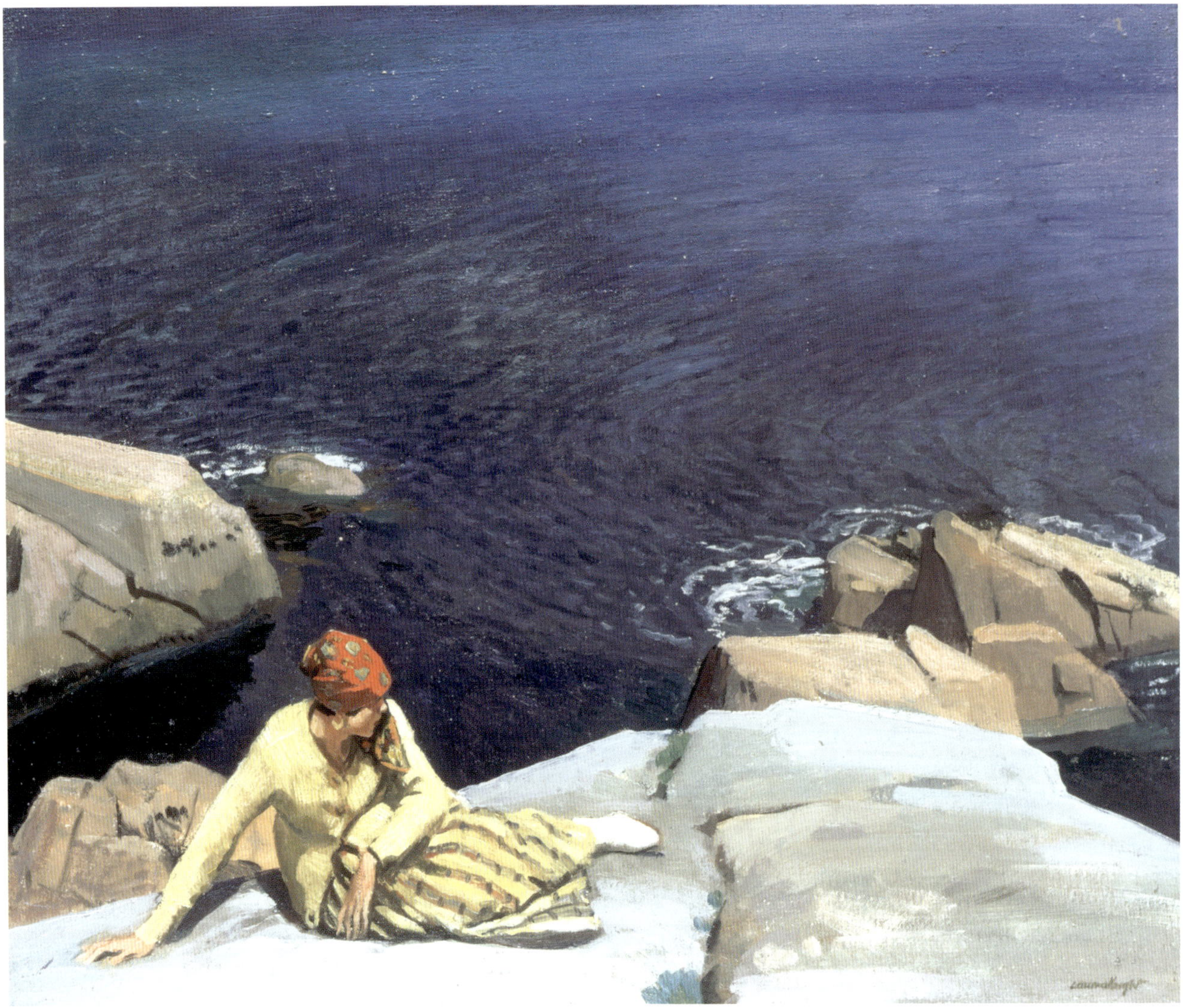

LAMORNA COVE

oil on canvas | 51 x 61 cm

private collection; courtesy Sotheby's Picture Library

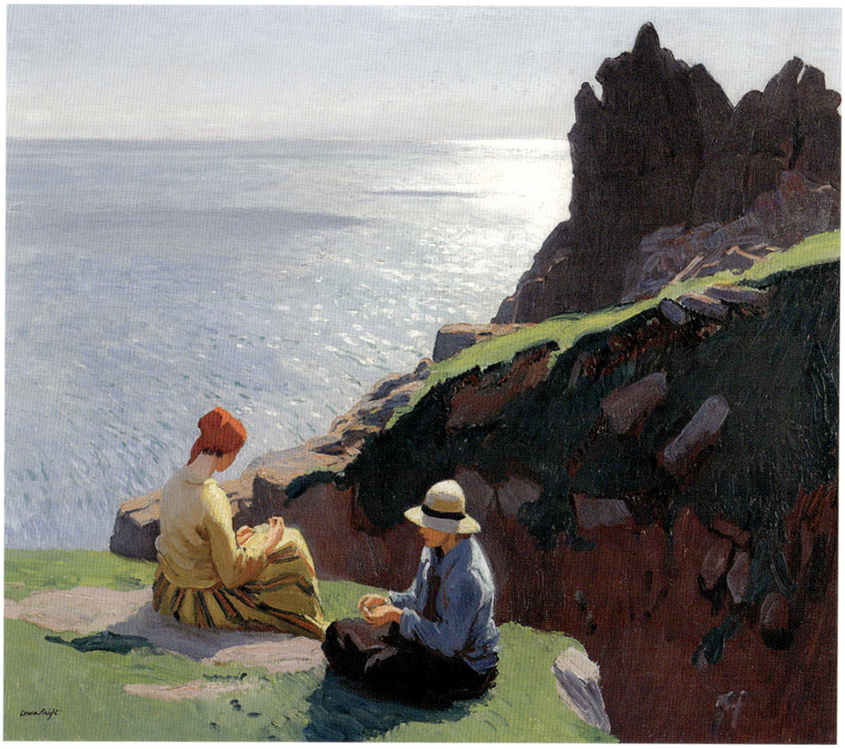

ON THE CLIFFS
oil on canvas | 63.5 x 76 cm
private collection; courtesy Sotheby's Picture Library

at the Royal Academy in 1920 (though there is a smaller painting of the same title). It is noticeable that the crane on the end of the quay appears in a watercolour study dated 1917 but not in the painting: it was probably removed during the war.

Laura Knight painted the series of canvases of clothed figures in the open air on the cliffs near Lamorna, either all in 1917, which seems unlikely even with her extra-ordinary compulsion to work, or more probably in the period 1916 to 1919 and possibly also up to late 1920. By 1919 the Knights were living in London, though they continued to spend time in West Cornwall in the summers. It seems likely that, especially on first setting up her London studio, Laura painted there from studies made in Cornwall. The paintings in this group are consistent and assured; the handling of paint recaptures some of the bravura of *The Green Feather* but the central theme is the balance of a broad sweep of rocks and ocean against sturdy feminine figures. Significantly unlike the pictorial élan of the lavishly dressed figure in the 1911 painting, these present what would then have been termed 'modern' women, self-confident and strong, and dressed in practical clothes. In fact, the figures seem to have an affinity with Laura herself, for example as she portrays herself in the famous *Self Portrait* (aka *The Model*) of 1913. The drawing *Cornwall* dated 1912 seems like a working drawing on this theme, with tones expressed by pencil

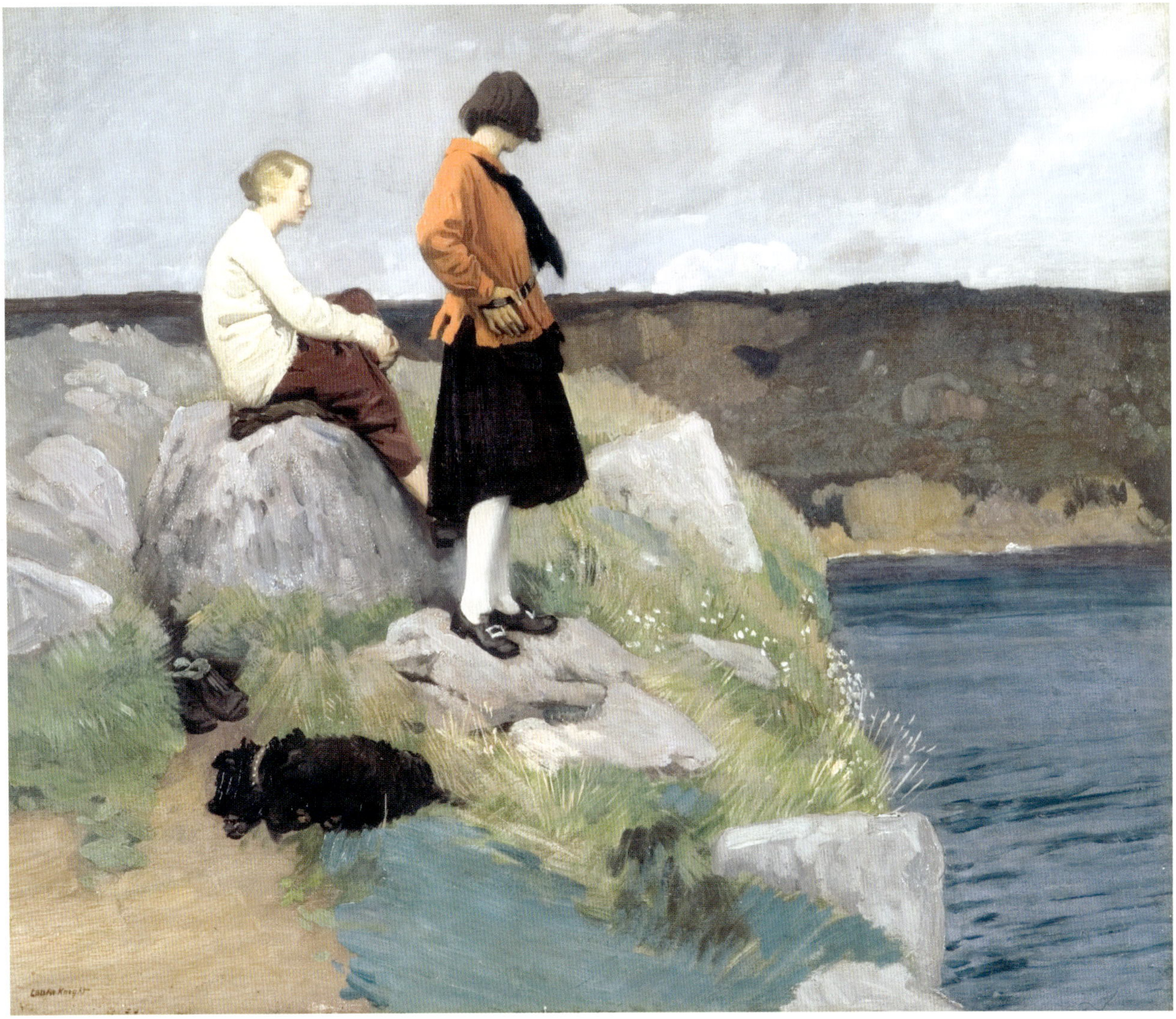

THE CORNISH COAST
oil on canvas | 64.8 x 76.3 cm
Amgueddfa Cymru (National Museum Wales)

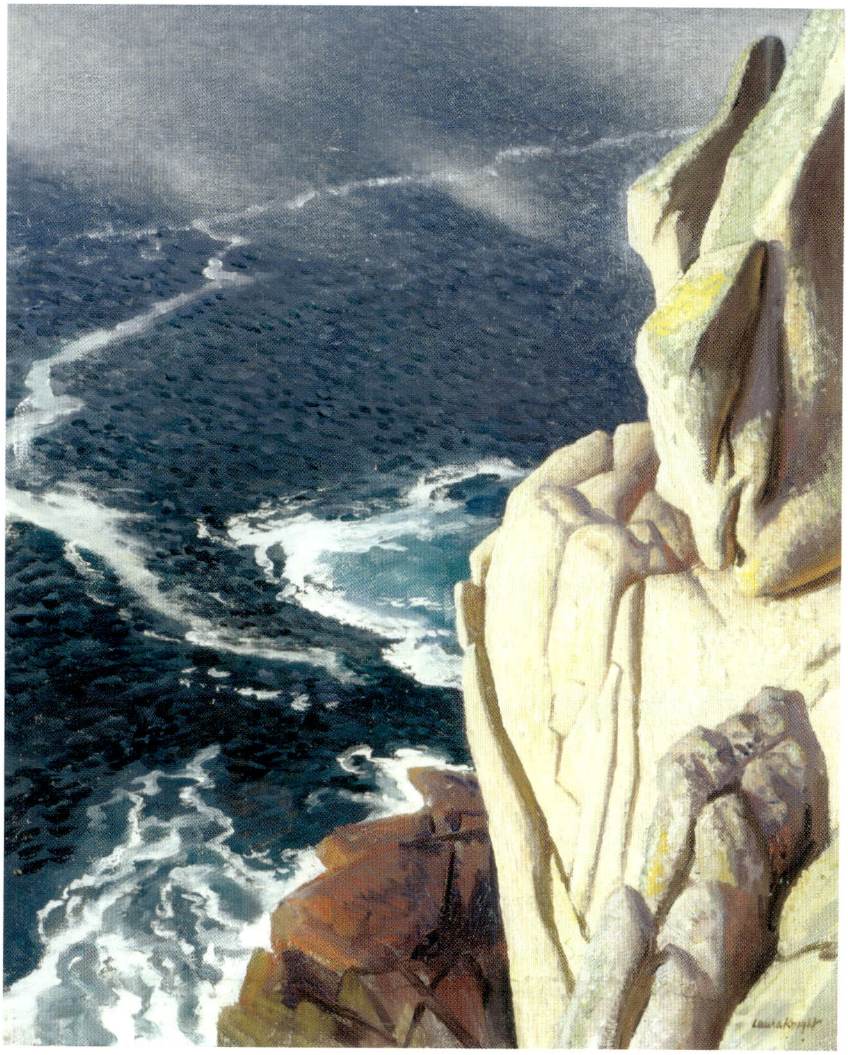

THE CRUEL SEA

oil on canvas | 76 x 64 cm

Bolton Museum and Art Gallery

shading. *The Cornish Coast* shows two women, one dark and one fair, painted from Phyllis Vipond-Crocker and Marjorie Taylor, Laura's regular models at this time. Others included Dolly Snell, whom Laura had painted for *The Green Feather* and the woman with long smooth blonde hair, often coiled into a bun at the nape of her neck, Eileen Mayo. Eileen worked for Laura for many years, right into the early nineteen thirties; she also sat for Dod Procter and for Harold Knight. Laura's black Scottish terrier Tip, who was her constant companion and appears in several works of this period, is also in *The Cornish Coast*. In *On the Cliffs* there are also two figures but they are more anonymous, seated solidly and still against the rock face; in *Lamorna Cove* a single woman looks down to rocks and a deep blue sea that fills the canvas; in both these a model wears a striped skirt and red scarf that also appear in a painting of Harold's – it seems there was a 'costume box' of clothes to be deployed.

In *The Pool* (aka *The Dark Pool*) and *The Cruel Sea* Laura seems to touch upon slightly more disturbing connotations, beyond formal painterly concerns with a figure against rocks and sea.

The first war-time commission Laura received was through the critic J.P. Konody. Laura writes in *Oil Paint and Grease Paint* that this was in 1916 (and Janet Dunbar's book gives it likewise) but it may have been 1917. The Canadian War Record authorities suggested a large painting on the theme of soldiers doing physical training as one of a series they were commissioning; 1917 was the year conscription was initiated in Canada. Laura settled on boxing as the most likely subject and made many studies, watercolours and canvases from direct observation of Canadian soldiers in their training camp at Witley, near Godalming in Surrey. In the final painting she set the figures of two men in a boxing ring against a wide expanse of cloudy sky, effectively underlining their heroic athleticism. Some of the work she made at Witley was included under the title *Camp Life* in Laura's exhibition at the Leicester Galleries in February 1918 but she also showed many Cornwall subjects including *The Green Sea* and *Phyllis by the Sea*. Tantalisingly, we cannot now be sure whether titles like *By the Sea* or *On the Rocks* are any of the other paintings from this series illustrated here.

At the end of the war the Knights decided to settle in London though they retained studios in Cornwall and planned to spend time there in the summer. When they arrived in January 1919 they first of all lived at 3 Ranulf Road on the borders of West Hampstead, where Harold had a studio. Laura describes renting Roger Fry's studio in Gower Street for a few months, though she says she never used it.[4] Although the rooms they had shared with Lamorna Birch in Shepherd's Market had been more central, it is likely that the Knights were naturally drawn to St John's Wood by friends there and by its colourful history as a place where successful artists had lived since the 1870s: it was an area full of artists, musicians and theatre people. The Knights' need was for inexpensive living and working space and by 1920 they were settled in two studios in a yard off the Finchley Road end of Queen's Grove.[5] They rented two studios side by side along a balcony over some garages. Each had 'a cupboard kitchen, a tiny living room and an attic'.[6] They contrived living and working and space to entertain. Their circle in London rapidly grew into a richly cultured and colourful milieu with dancers, musicians and popular entertainers as well as other artists. Laura was working backstage and in rehearsal rooms, leaving open-air subjects for summer time in Cornwall as she developed her work on ballet and theatre subjects.

In 1921 the *Studio* magazine published the first of what was intended to be a series of special large-format publications under the title *Modern Painting* with the work of Laura and Harold Knight, accompanied by an introduction by Ernest Halton. He describes their work to date and points out that there was an affinity between Laura and Harold's exhibited work in their early years but that by 1921 it had diverged. The plates

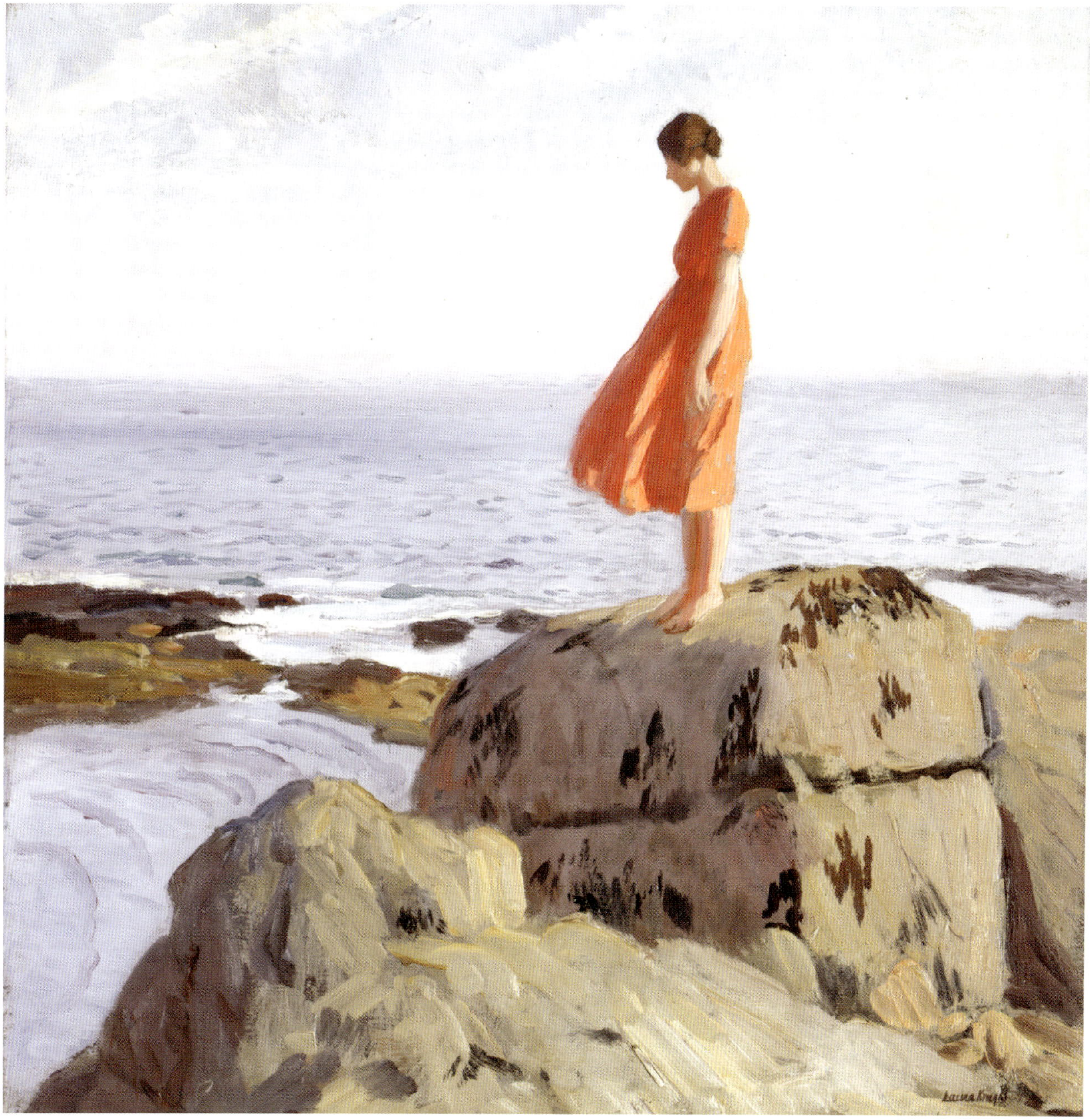

THE POOL (aka **THE DARK POOL**)
*c.*1917 | oil on canvas | 45.8 x 46 cm
Laing Art Gallery, Newcastle/Tyne & Wear Archives & Museums

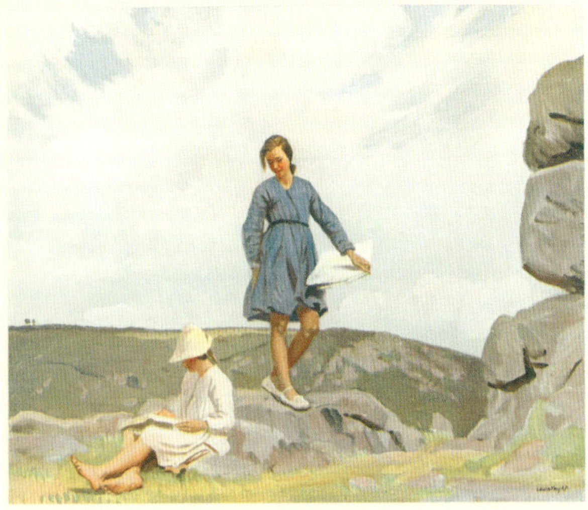

THE YOUNG ARTIST

oil on canvas

reproduced from *The Studio* magazine special edition 'The Work of Laura and Harold Knight' 1921, plate IV

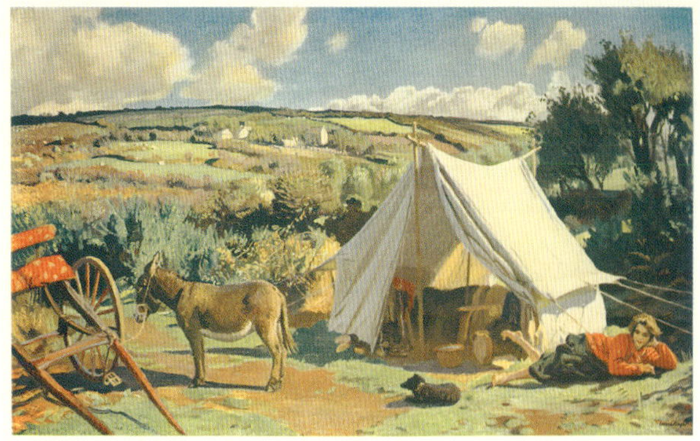

THE CAMP

oil on canvas

reproduced from *The Studio* magazine special edition 'The Work of Laura and Harold Knight' 1921, plate III

of Harold's work include three figure paintings – like Ernest Procter and Harold Harvey, he was painting a certain kind of elegant domestic interior with connotations of feminine beauty and connoisseurship – but there was also *Dozmare Pool*, for which Ella Naper was the nude model. Laura's paintings appear to follow seamlessly on from the series of figures against seascapes. They include *By the Sea* and *The Young Artist*, in which a central figure stands against the sky, asserting an almost heroic character for the role of a contemporary woman painter. There is also *The Camp* with a tent, a donkey, Laura's little black dog Tip, and a figure in red, with low Penwith hills on the horizon. This composition, by depicting the kind of working camp Laura so loved to set up, seems to contain a great deal of her feeling about painting in the open in Cornwall. It was probably painted from studies made while camping at Lamorna in the summer of 1919. The idyllic charm of the scene is significant in that it was painted at a time when Laura was beginning work in London. She was looking back on a phase of her work when her greatest strengths were developed, and on places where she had found the most productive subjects with which to take her work forward.

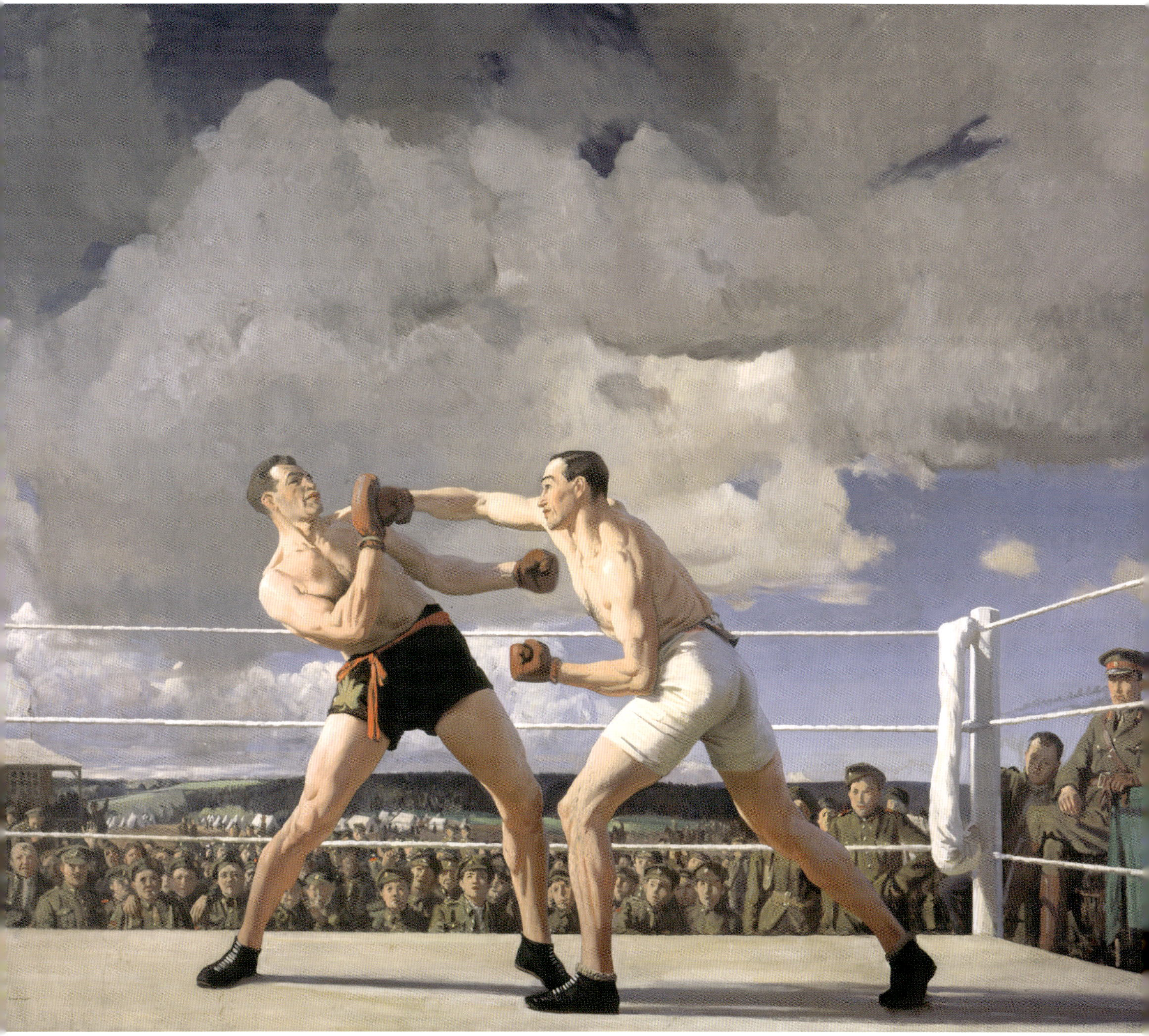

PHYSICAL TRAINING IN WITLEY CAMP

*c.*1917 | oil on canvas | 304.8 x 365.7 cm

Commissioned for the Canadian War Memorial

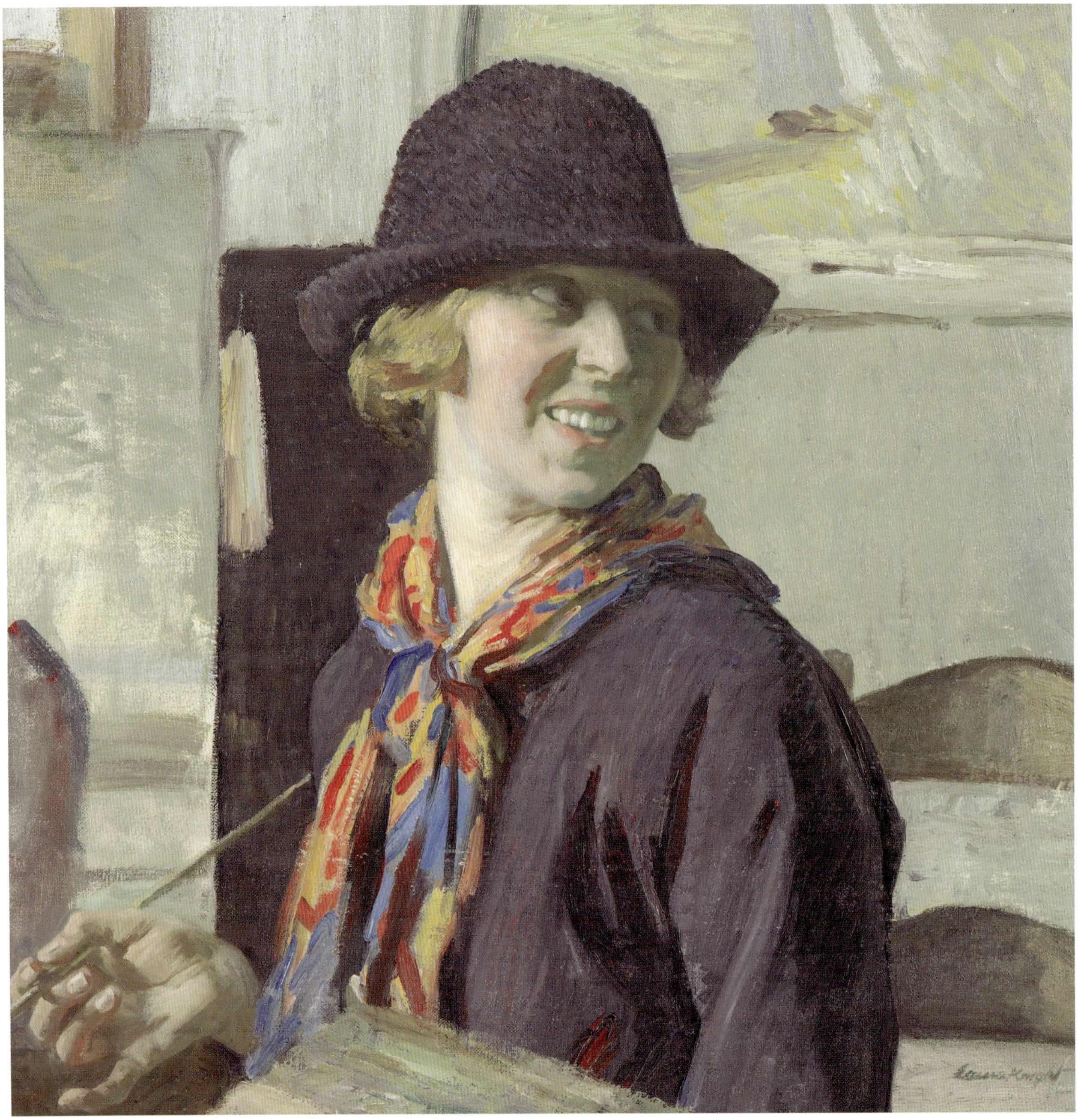

SELF PORTRAIT

*c.*1921 | oil on canvas | 59.5 x 59.5 cm

Museum of New Zealand Te Papa Tongarewa; gift of Mr and Mrs D.A. Ewen 1936

London and Cornwall 1921–1935

In London in the early 1920s Laura and Harold Knight attracted a widening circle of people from the worlds of ballet, the theatre and music. Their parties at Queen's Grove Studios were evidently casual and convivial, often with impromptu performances; the cultural élite of London replaced and greatly extended the bohemian élite of artistic circles in west Cornwall, though they kept many of their friends from Cornwall too. Munnings reports that they might be found at the Chelsea Arts Club or the Café Royal, immersed in the liveliest of artistic circles.[1] Harold was receiving good portrait commissions and Laura was working on ballet subjects. She was also still working with professional models, including the blonde-haired and smoothly beautiful Eileen Mayo.

In April 1922 the Alpine Club presented a substantial one-person exhibition of Laura's recent paintings and drawings. The Club's large galleries off Conduit Street could be hired by artists or dealers and a diversity of artists showed there, including Roger Fry, Alfred Munnings and Augustus John. Laura's exhibition included a *Self Portrait* that shows a smiling, confident, energetic woman – clearly at the height of her powers as a painter. In his catalogue introduction, E.V. Lucas writes: 'All artists are enviable in that their occupation is with beauty, but Laura Knight is peculiarly so, in being free to divide her time in such an ideal way: in summer among the rocks and pools and moorlands of the Delectable Duchy, and in winter in the dressing room of Lydia Lopokova.' The exhibition included land- and seascape subjects from Cornwall but there was also the important painting *Carnaval* (bought from the exhibition for the collection of Manchester City Art Gallery), in which the cast of dancers for this ballet are posed across the canvas in a formal composition quite unlike her directly observed drawings and paintings of dancers.

While she was still preparing for the Alpine Club exhibition, Laura Knight was invited to be selector of British artists for the big International Art

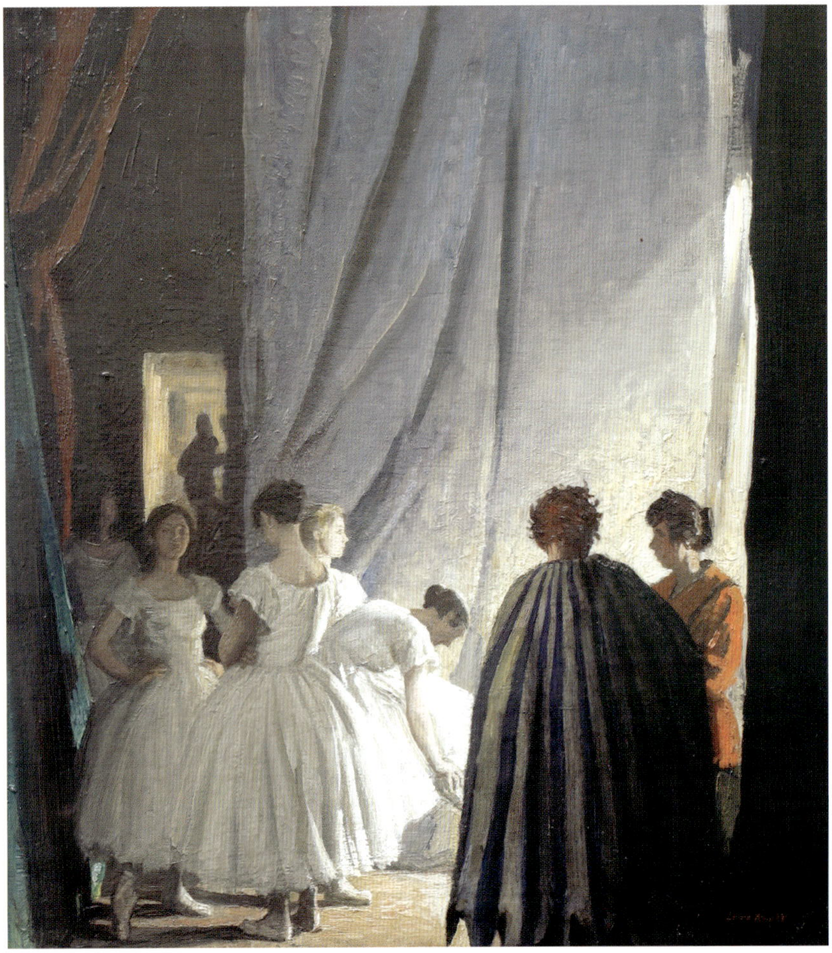

BEHIND THE SCENES (aka **DANS LES COULISSES**)
*c.*1921 | oil on canvas | 63 x 57 cm
Falmouth Art Gallery

Exhibition at the Carnegie Institute in Pittsburgh. She went to America for the final selection procedure and the opening, travelling by liner (and, as always, making studies as she went). She knew it was all a great honour and she very much enjoyed the whole process, even if it removed her from her working routine and from Harold for many weeks. There was a considerable amount of publicity about her in England: in effect this was the beginning of her being known beyond the world of art. In America Laura enjoyed lavish hospitality and was taken from city to city to see great museums and private collections, notably that of Mrs Havemeyer, one of whose rooms '...packed with canvasses from ceiling to floor, held nothing but Degas studies and pictures.'[2] An article in the short-lived *International Studio* magazine, April 1922, introduced Laura to an American audience, noting that she was the first woman to be asked to serve on the Carnegie Jury. The article illustrates *Summer*, a painting of children and a greyhound on a harbour wall that is probably the painting of this title shown at the Royal Academy in 1921.

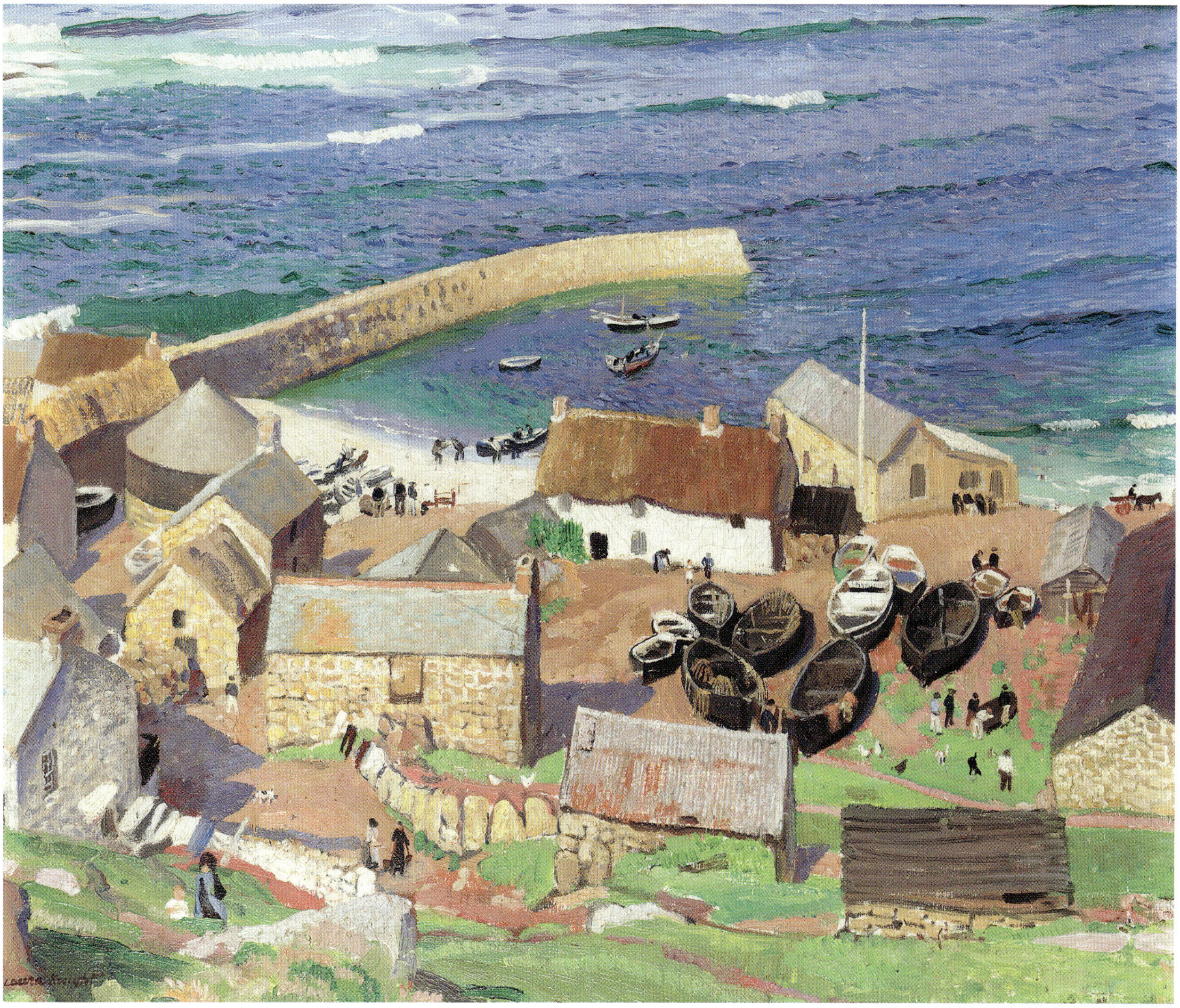

SENNEN COVE

oil on canvas | 51 x 61 cm

private collection; courtesy Sotheby's Picture Library

The Knights had retained studios in Cornwall and Laura's painting hut on the cliffs at Lamorna so that they could continue to spend time there in the summer months. At this period, they were particularly close friends with Pog Yglesias, who 'camped out' with them at Lamorna, and W.H. Davies, the tramp turned writer who stayed with them for a time in Cornwall. Laura, as always, was attracted by eccentricity, intrigued and ready to engage with it. In the summer of 1922 the Knights stayed at Sennen Cove, taking Pog with them. 'Harold and I slept in what had been a coastguard's lookout with windows nearly all round, right at the edge of a cliff, where the spray often came right over and splashed on the roof – I adored the sound of it when in bed at night.' She goes on: 'we stayed right into the winter, glorying in our wild perch, doing immense quantities of work.'[3] Laura writes of looking at the rocks of the Cornish coast with El Greco's *Toledo*, seen in America, before her eyes: 'I concentrated on the study of rocks and cliffs. I have a love of the granite blocks that border that coast, their poise is a study that never palls. Their dramatic possibilities in combination with the sea and sky fitted well with my mood, which was attuned to the "trenchant" work I had seen.'[4]

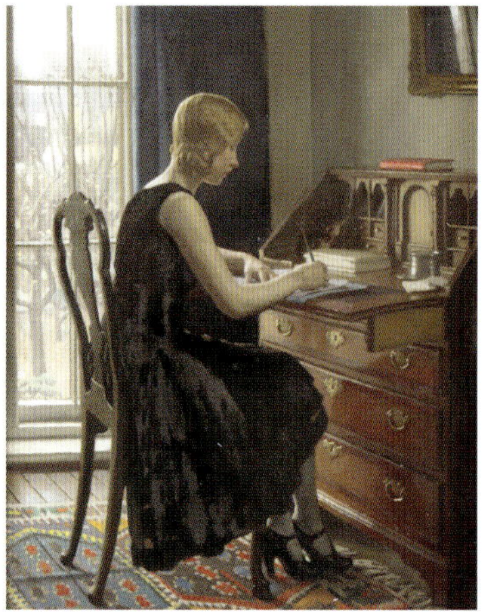

HAROLD KNIGHT
GIRL WRITING
1930 | oil on canvas
28 x 24 cm
Grundy Art Gallery, Blackpool

Later in 1922 the Knights moved into a house with a studio in Langford Place near St John's Wood tube station.[5] It was only a couple of streets further in towards the centre but certainly a more salubrious St John's Wood address and a good substantial house. Harold set up his studio there while Laura retained one of the Queen's Grove studios. There is a painting of Harold's titled *Girl Writing* that Caroline Fox notes as a portrait of Laura.[6] He paints her as elegant and calm in the Langford Place interior, where the living accommodation was rather more conventional than it had been at the Queen's Grove studios. Between Harold's painting and Laura's 1921 *Self Portrait* there is a marked contrast, while looking at them both alongside the professional press photograph of her from the Hulton Archive taken in 1923 (see p.7) gives an intriguing three-faceted view of Laura at this time.

Laura had had a watercolour in the Venice Biennale of 1910 and in 1924 she was one of three Artist Commissioners for the event. She and Harold, and Harold Harvey and Munnings were all included in the British section of the exhibition that year. In 1925 the Knights were in Cornwall again in the summer, staying part of the time at Mousehole and seeing all their friends. By this time and into the late 1920s it was becoming more obvious that Laura and Harold's work was further apart. Harold was continuing to paint elegant interiors with figures such as *The Seamstress* and *Bric-a-Brac* while executing portrait commissions, while Laura was ever more engrossed in the theatre and then also the circus and circus people's lives.

In the early 1920s Laura Knight began to make etchings and by the end of the decade she had achieved a considerable output.[7] Her subjects were often dancers, drawn freely on the plate with drypoint or shadowed with deep tones of aquatint. There were some Bank Holiday revellers on

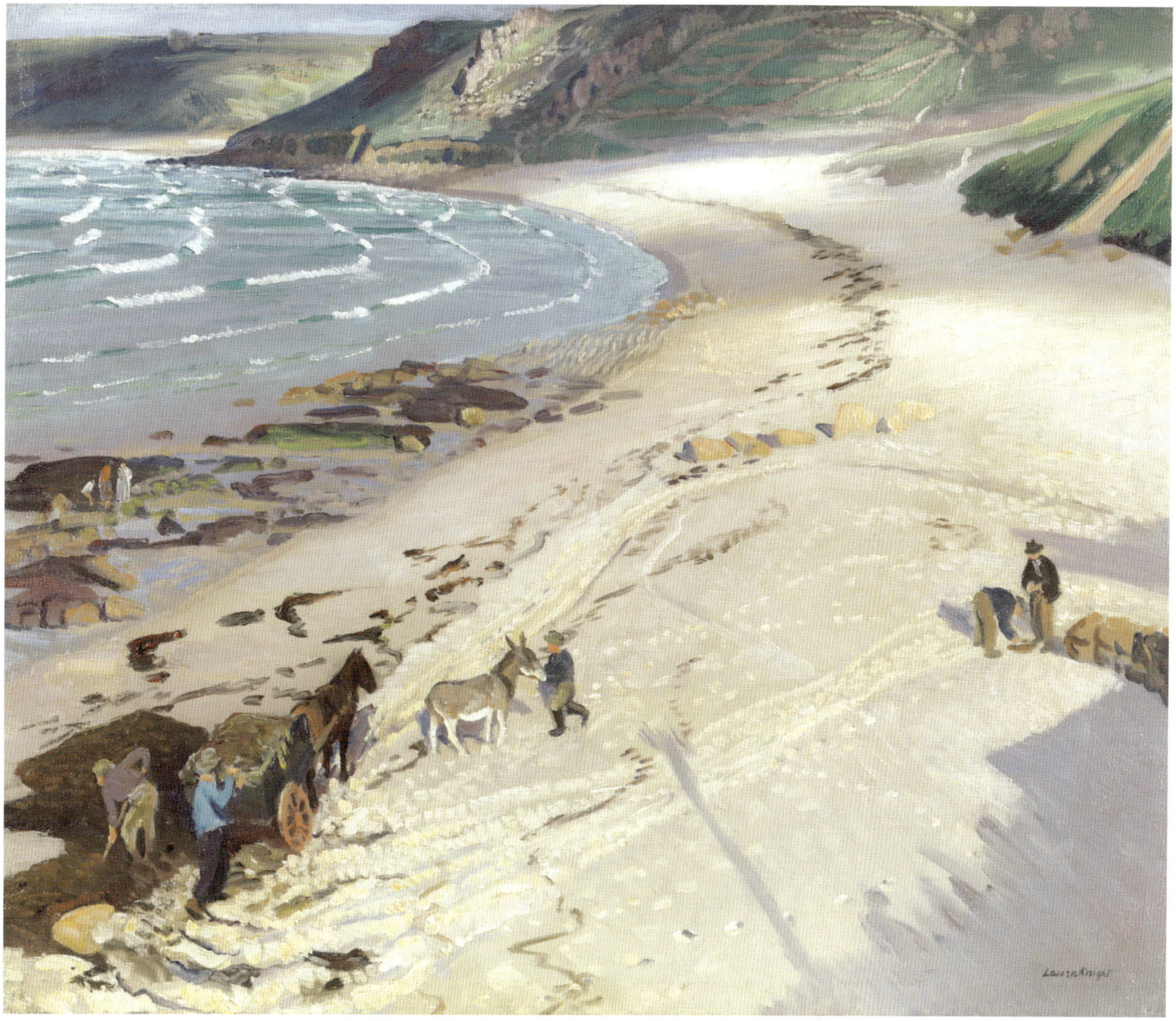

GATHERING SEAWEED, SENNEN COVE

oil on canvas | 63.5 x 76 cm

private collection; image courtesy Messum's

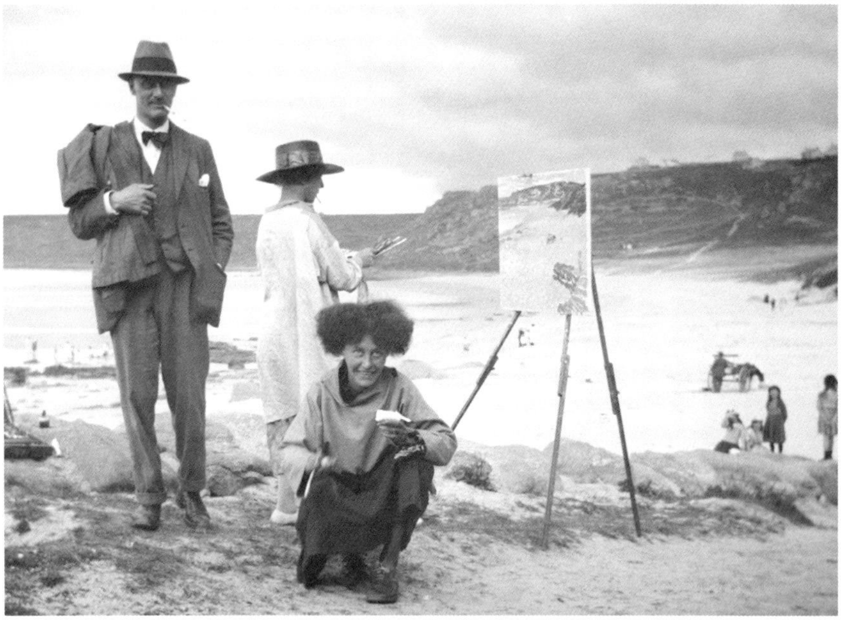

Harold and Laura (painting *Sennen Beach*) with Pog Yglesias

Hampstead Heath and a delicately observed drypoint of *Country Girls* but circus and ballet subjects predominate. There were relatively few land- or seascapes. Two exceptions are *Cornish Harbour* and *Drying the Nets, Mousehole Harbour.* There is also a pencil drawing of Mousehole of this date, possibly made with an etching in mind; the Knights stayed in the village several times through the 1920s and were living in a cottage in Love Lane in the summer of 1929.[8] Between 1924 and 1930 she also made plates of circus and fairground people, several of which are illustrated in *Oil Paint and Grease Paint* (as they were easier to reproduce than paintings). By 1925 she was an Associate of the Royal Society of Painter-Etchers. In 1932 she was featured by *Studio* magazine as no.29 in the series *Modern Masters of Etching*; in his introduction Malcolm Salaman says she was taught by the printmaker John Everett and inspired to try aquatint by Goya's *Caprichos.* Laura herself writes of the excitement of a new medium and describes the making of plates and printing[9] but evidently soon tired of the chore of editioning and fulfilling customers' orders.

This book looks at Laura Knight's work in the open air and therefore does not set out to cover the complete range of her subjects, nor her very extensive work in the theatre or the circus. Some examples are included, however, to show how she operated in a close, highly charged artificial world, and in the case of the circus the artificial 'open air' of a Big Top. In *Oil Paint and Grease Paint* she writes of fresh subjects being essential: '...Inside is a burning passion to solve new mysteries – a horse – a land-scape, sky or sea – a lion – a figure in movement or in stillness– a street, a crowd or a portrait of a man, woman or child – a dog, a cat. It is

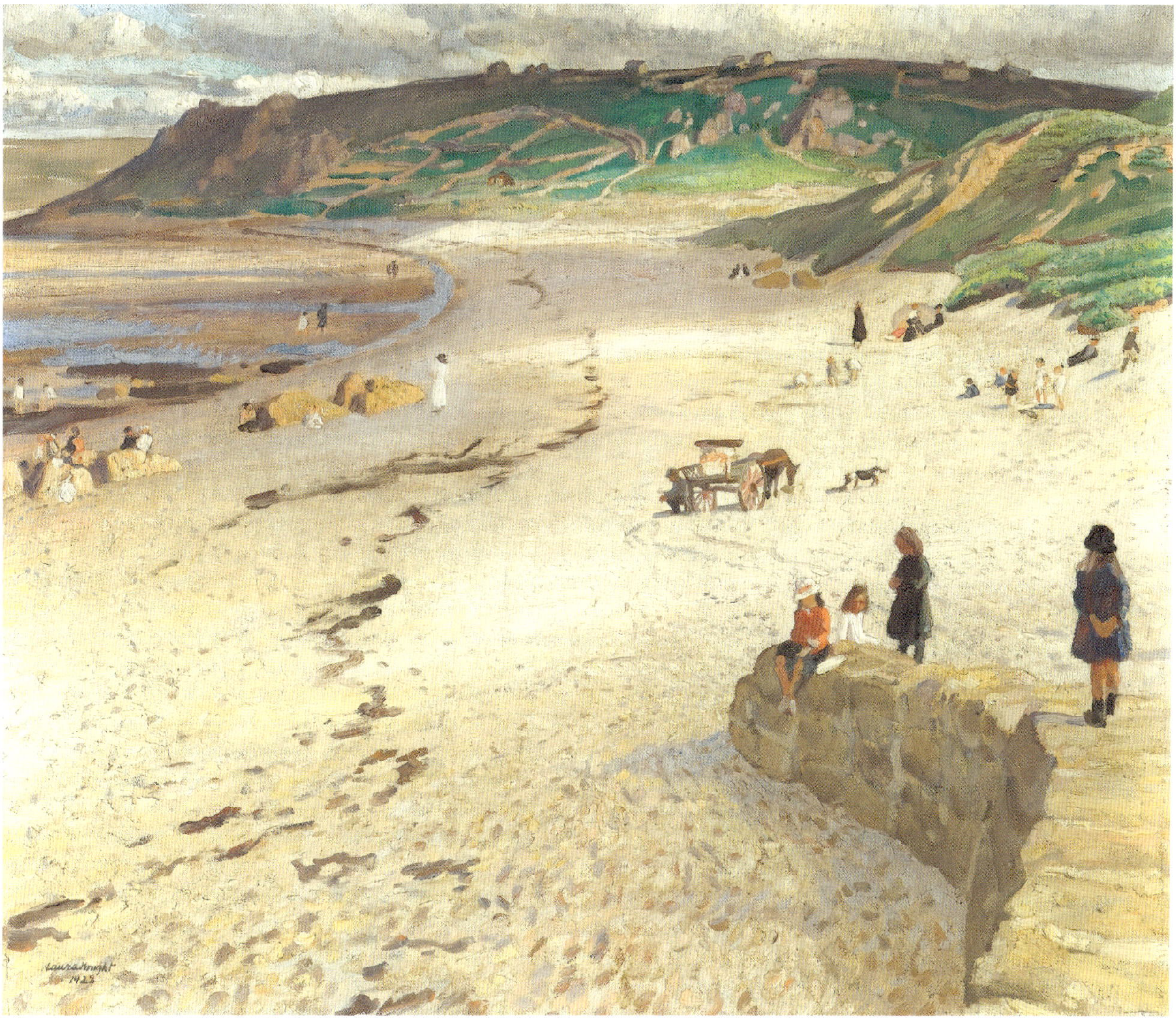

SENNEN BEACH

1923 | oil on canvas | 64 x 76 cm

private collection; courtesy Sotheby's Picture Library

ridiculous, one person cannot paint everything and work in all mediums.'[10] Touching upon Laura's immersion in the world of her subject, Harold cautioned her to concentrate on the work she is making and less on the lives of her models but she writes '...with fisher-people, the theatre, the circus... I cannot withhold the vital interest that burns inside me for the work they themselves do and what it means to them... Painting, music, ballet, theatre, circus, art and physical skill, what joy to project oneself in each, to feel the daring of the acrobat, the control of the artist, in understanding and sympathy to live many lives in one.'[11]

During the late 1920s and early 30s Laura Knight painted figure subjects, some of them essays in the depiction of a single nude female figure, often with a powerful erotic charge, painted from models in her London studio. In a letter to Eileen Mayo, who was working in Cornwall at the time, Laura writes that she is busy working on a figure painting but needs Eileen to return to London in order to finish the head.[12] This underlines the fact that Laura's practice was to assemble her subjects and her compositions from parts observed and usually individually studied. Besides the kind of intense formal paintings of flesh Laura made at this period, there are paintings of a single clothed figure set in the kind of plain country interior she knew so well in Cornwall, such as the well-known *Susie and the Washbasin* of 1929. In paintings of this date of a single female figure, Laura's work comes closest to that of Dod Procter. Dod's monumental paintings of women in simple work-a-day clothes were painted in the mid-1920s and culminated in the painting with which she achieved the greatest public success: *Morning*, shown at the Royal Academy in 1927. The model for Dod's sleeping figure was Cissie Barnes, a local Newlyn girl. Billie Waters, another Newlyn girl, sat for Laura in 1927.[13] Dod also used the fair-haired model Eileen Mayo for more mannered figure paintings, and between 1925 and 27 she made a number of paintings of babies. In 1927, Laura made studies and paintings of the black American babies and children she saw on her second trip across the Atlantic. Harold had portrait commissions in America, including one to paint an eminent surgeon at the Johns Hopkins Memorial Hospital in Baltimore and Laura went out to join him there. She was moved and enthralled by the faces of the children she saw in the wards and obtained permission to draw and paint them.[14]

Laura Knight was elected an Associate of the Royal Academy in 1927; the fact that she showed only one work in that year's Summer Exhibition is probably due to her extended trip to America. Harold Knight was elected ARA in 1928 and when he wrote to the Napers to thank them for their congratulations he describes a celebratory dinner with Robert and Eleanor Hughes, Munnings, John (Lamorna) and Mornie Birch, Ethel Bartlett, Reid Dick and his wife, and Dod and Ernest Procter '...we had a most uproarious evening'.[15] In the summer that year Manchester City Art Gallery presented 'Pictures with a Subject' including Harold and Laura with a few other artists working in Cornwall. In March 1928 Laura had a substantial exhibition with Messrs Ernest Brown and Phillips at the Leicester Galleries. It included paintings and drawings of Cornwall,

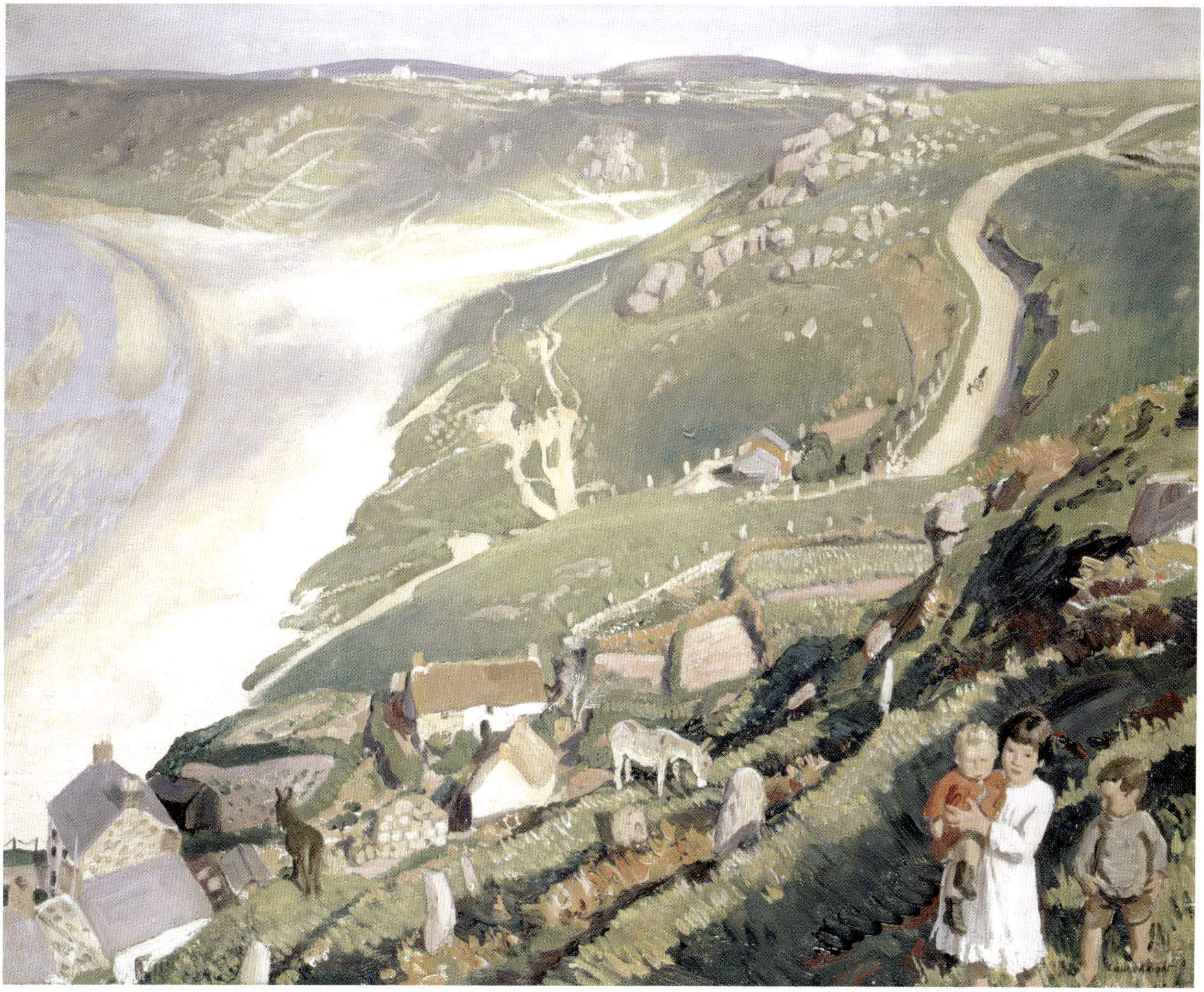

AUTUMN SUNLIGHT, SENNEN COVE

*c.*1922 | oil on canvas | 61 x 73.7 cm

Birmingham Museums and Art Gallery/The Bridgeman Art Library

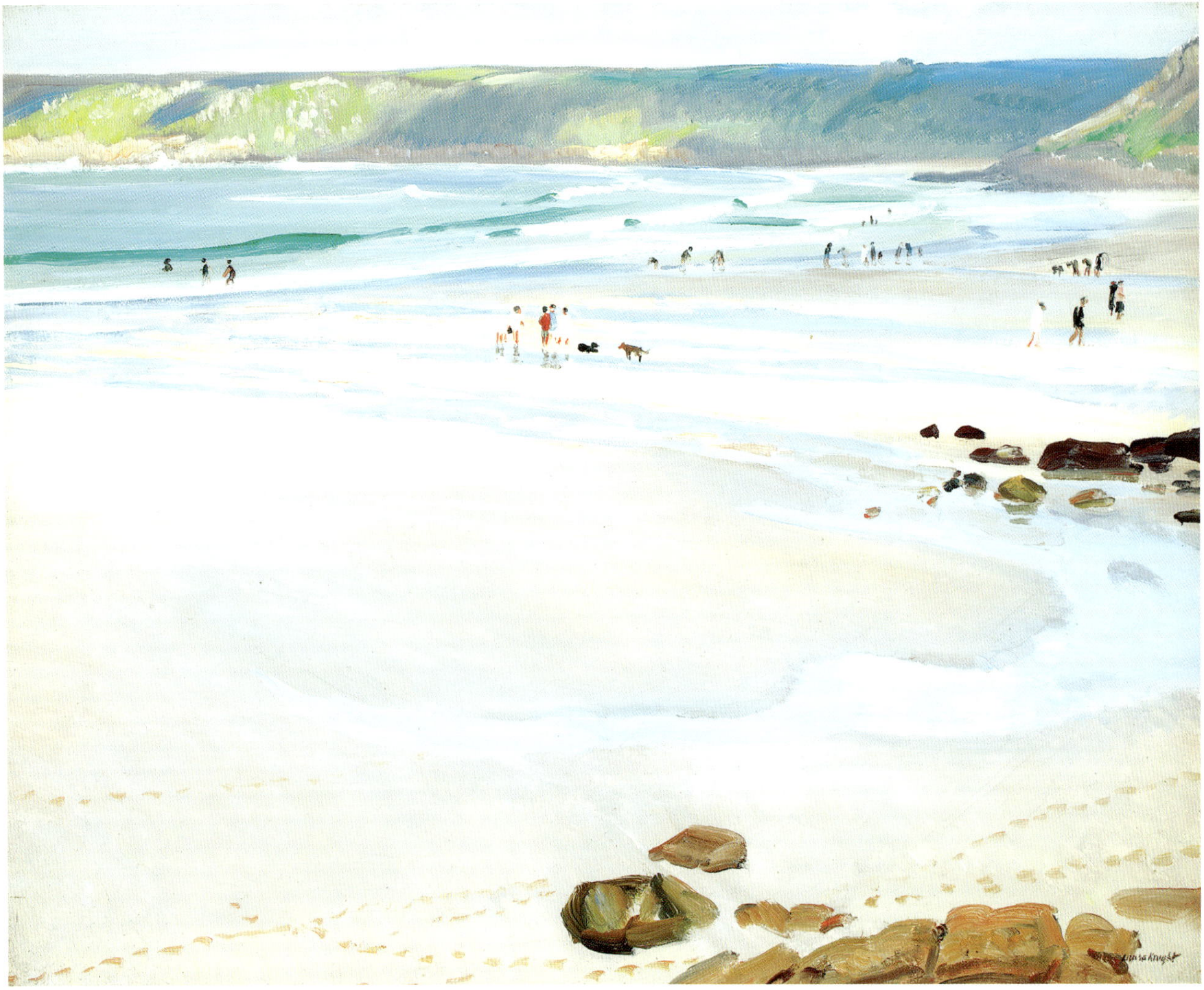

SENNEN COVE

oil on canvas | 61 x 76 cm

private collection; courtesy Sotheby's Picture Library

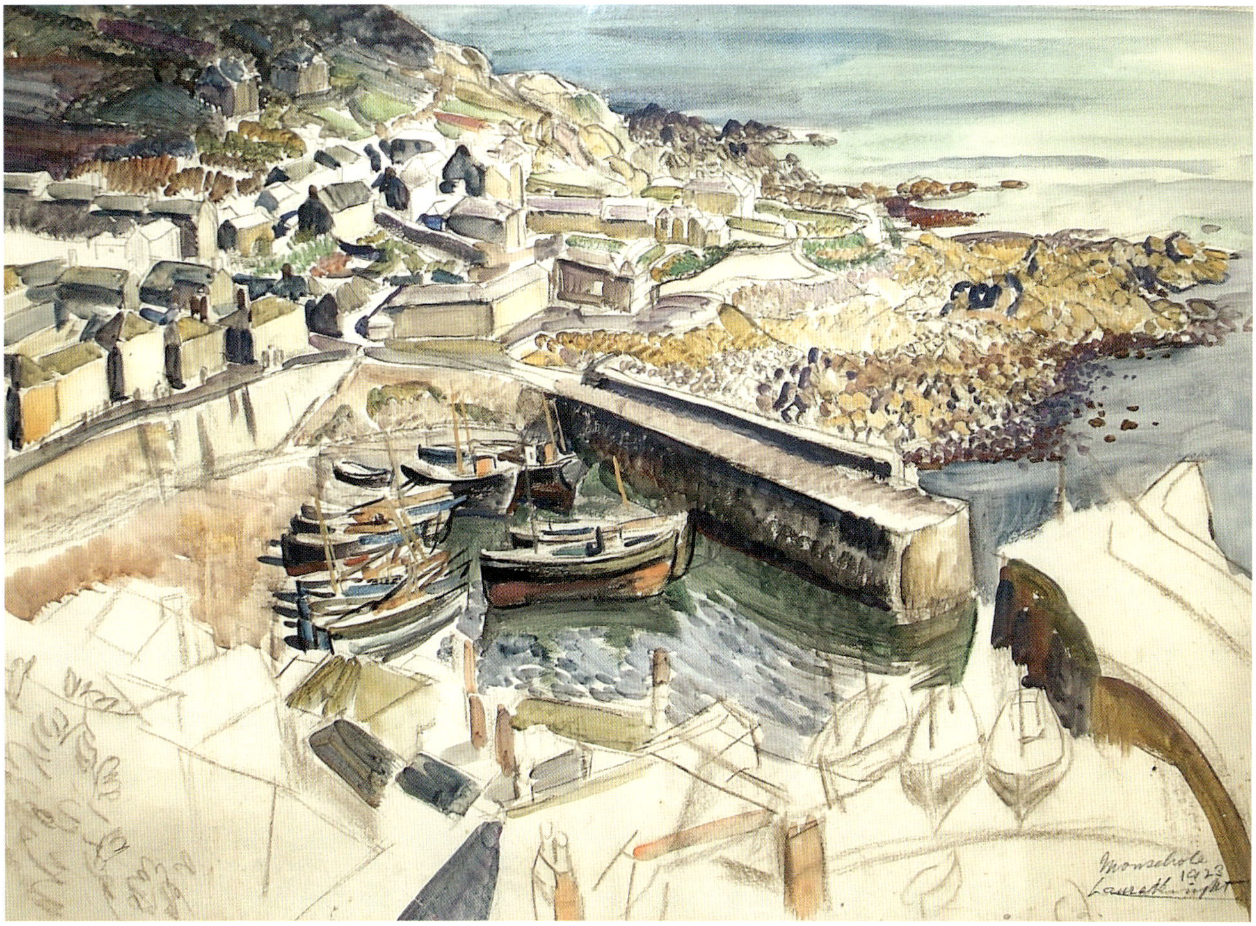

MOUSEHOLE

1923 | chalk and watercolour | 54 x 76 cm

private collection; courtesy Rosebery's Auction House

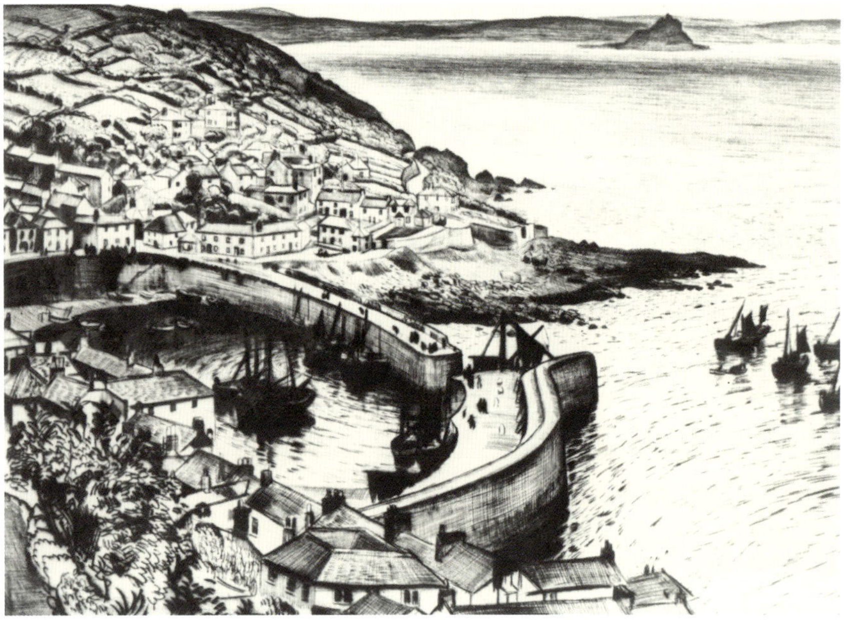

A CORNISH HARBOUR

1926 | drypoint | 25 x 35.2 cm

private collection; image courtesy Belgrave Gallery, London

circus subjects and black American children from her work in the Baltimore hospital. In the catalogue, the long list of public collections owning her work was impressive; it included Cape Town, Johannesburg, Melbourne, Toronto and Ottawa as well as Manchester, Oldham, Leeds, the British Museum and the V&A. The exhibition marks a point in her career when Laura was well established though apparently as far as ever from being settled. At some point in the late nineteen twenties as time spent in Cornwall grew less and less, she gave up her studio in the Lamorna valley (and it was later bought by Gluck).

At the end of the decade and through the thirties she continued to work at a tremendous pace, spending long periods away from home with the circus or at a Romany camp. Laura had achieved great public recognition and was held in high esteem – marked most notably in 1929 when she was created a Dame Commander of the British Empire. She answered a deluge of congratulatory letters and enjoyed plenty of publicity on the occasion. At this time she undertook some portrait commissions for friends and friends-of-friends, including the pianist Ethel Bartlett, wife of Rae Robertson, also a pianist; the couple were close friends of the Knights': Harold had painted Rae in the 1920s and his portrait of Ethel was exhibited at the Royal Academy in 1930. At Malvern in 1932, Laura drew and painted George Bernard Shaw. Her circle of friends continued to expand. It included such people as the wealthy property developer George Cross, whose country house at Compton Chamberlayne in Wiltshire the Knights visited with Lamorna Birch in the 1930s. Laura was invited back, as a distinguished guest, to Haddon Hall in Derbyshire,

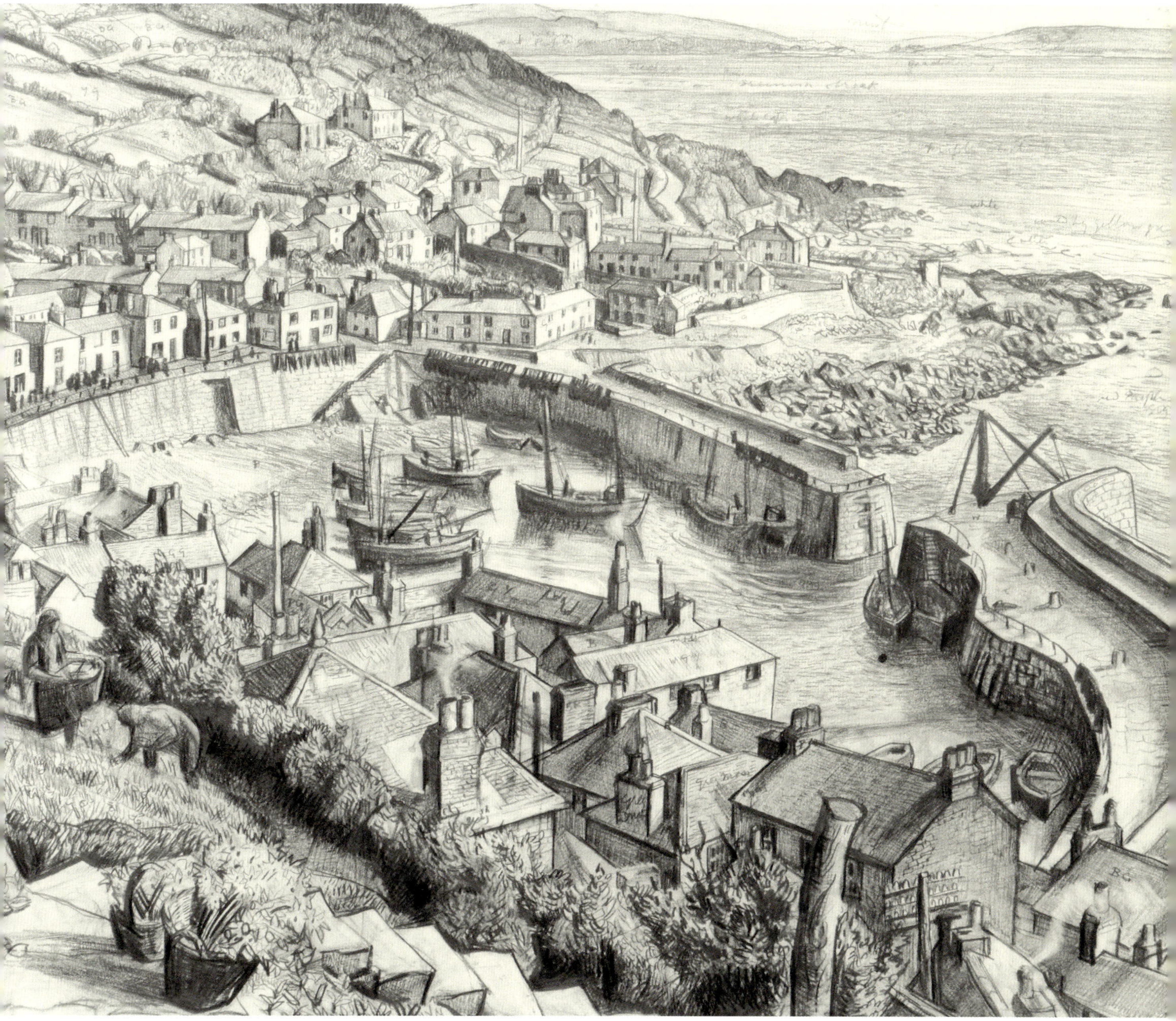

MOUSEHOLE

1923 | pencil | 47.6 x 55.9 cm

private collection; courtesy David Lay

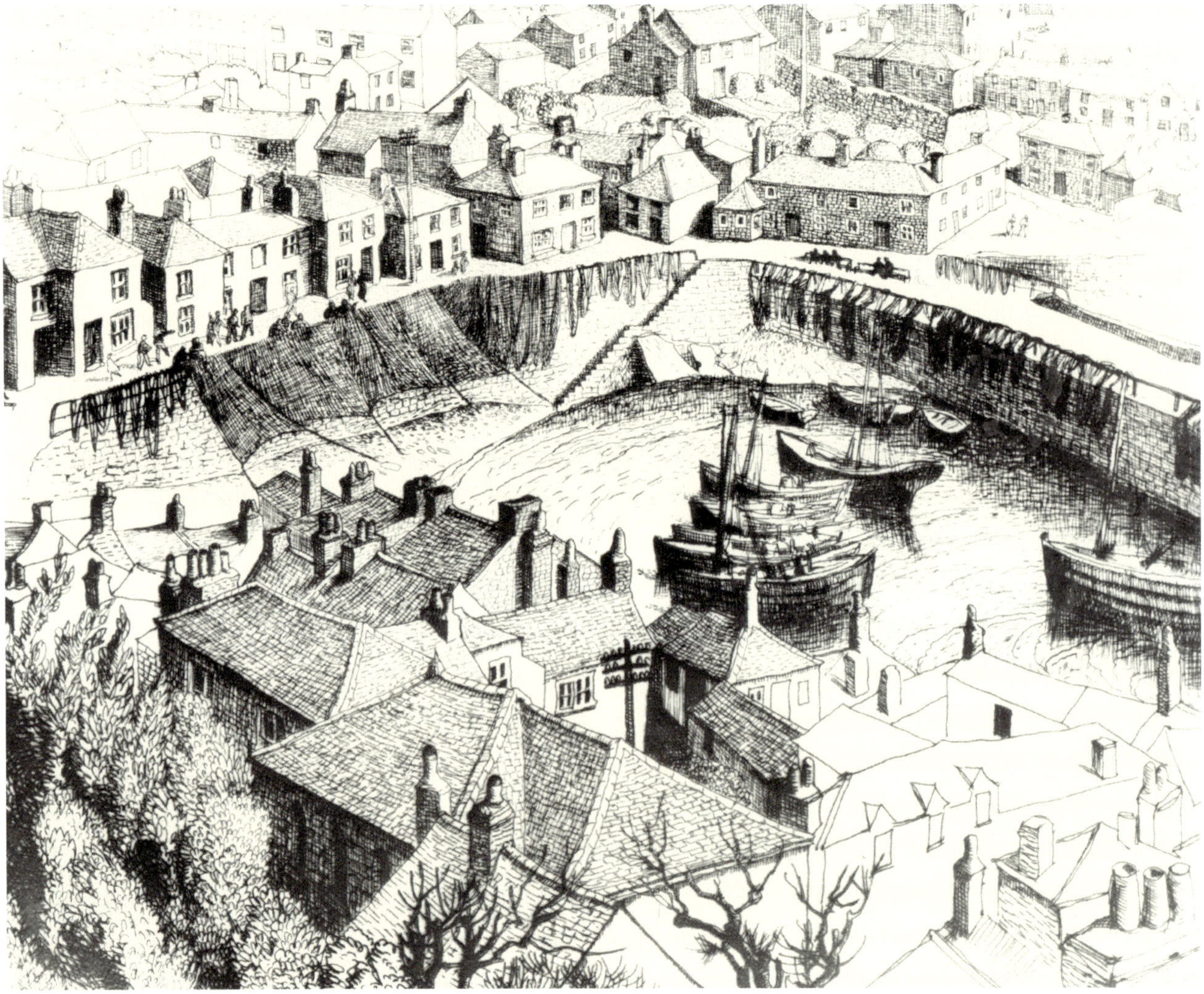

DRYING THE NETS, MOUSEHOLE HARBOUR

etching | 20.5 x 25 cm

private collection; image courtesy Belgrave Gallery, London

the beautiful house and park where she used to go sketching with her mother more than fifty years before; 'the dawn was just breaking ... when I awoke, and getting out of bed I saw before me one of my pet subjects to try to paint: the gracious lift of dark by the light.'[16] In about 1936-38 Laura was commissioned by Eileen Unwin, a friend and an important patron to her, to paint her prized Suffolk Punch mare on her farm at Billingshurst in Sussex.[17]

In 1924 Laura made costume designs for *Les Roses* for Diaghilev's Ballets Russes,[18] and in 1933-34 she was among the artists invited to make designs for the decoration of English bone china for E. Brain & Co's Foley pottery, including a distinctive design based on Noah's flood with torrential rain and a dove with olive branch. She also designed earthenware for the range produced by Clarice Cliff for A.J. Wilkinson, including circus motifs and a leaf pattern. In 1921 Laura produced a poster design of rugby at Twickenham for the London Passenger Transport Board and about 1929, more designs including *The Yorkshire Coast* for the London and North Eastern Railway. In the second half of the 1930s she was again one of the artists commissioned to make illustrations for posters for London Transport. She also made designs for glassware for Stuart & Sons and in 1937 Wedgwood commissioned a design for a loving cup, for their range of commemorative designs for the Coronation (and which, because of the Abdication, they had to amend so hastily).

Laura Knight's large exhibition at the Alpine Club in October-November 1930 was titled 'Circus Folk' but it included a number of landscape subjects. Ernest Brown and Phillips presented Laura's work in the galleries there when, as in her large exhibition in 1922, she needed more wall space than their gallery could accommodate. Her exhibition of watercolours and drawings at their own Leicester Galleries in May–June 1934 was also mainly circus works with some landscapes studies painted in Malvern. In September 1931 the Usher Gallery in Lincoln presented a substantial exhibition of Laura's work including loans of earlier paintings from public collections: *The Beach* from the Laing Art Gallery in Newcastle and Oldham's *Newlyn Old Harbour*, for example. The Laing presented an exhibition of work by Laura and Harold Knight in 1933, including some of Laura's best known earlier paintings and a similar selection was shown at Nottingham Castle Museum in 1934.

Laura Knight went to the Derby meeting on Epsom Downs for the first time in 1931, probably at A.J. Munnings' suggestion, and returned to draw and paint there every year through the 1930s. As she had been used to doing in Cornwall before the First World War, she improvised ways and means for working directly from what was happening all around her. She wanted especially to paint the gypsies, for whom the Epsom races were a traditional gala occasion. She also worked at the races at Ascot, drawing the crowds under umbrellas on a rainy race day. For her paintings of gypsies through the 1930s, Laura began to develop a looser, sketchier way of painting, though she also sometimes condensed her studies into more resolved and intense formal portraits.

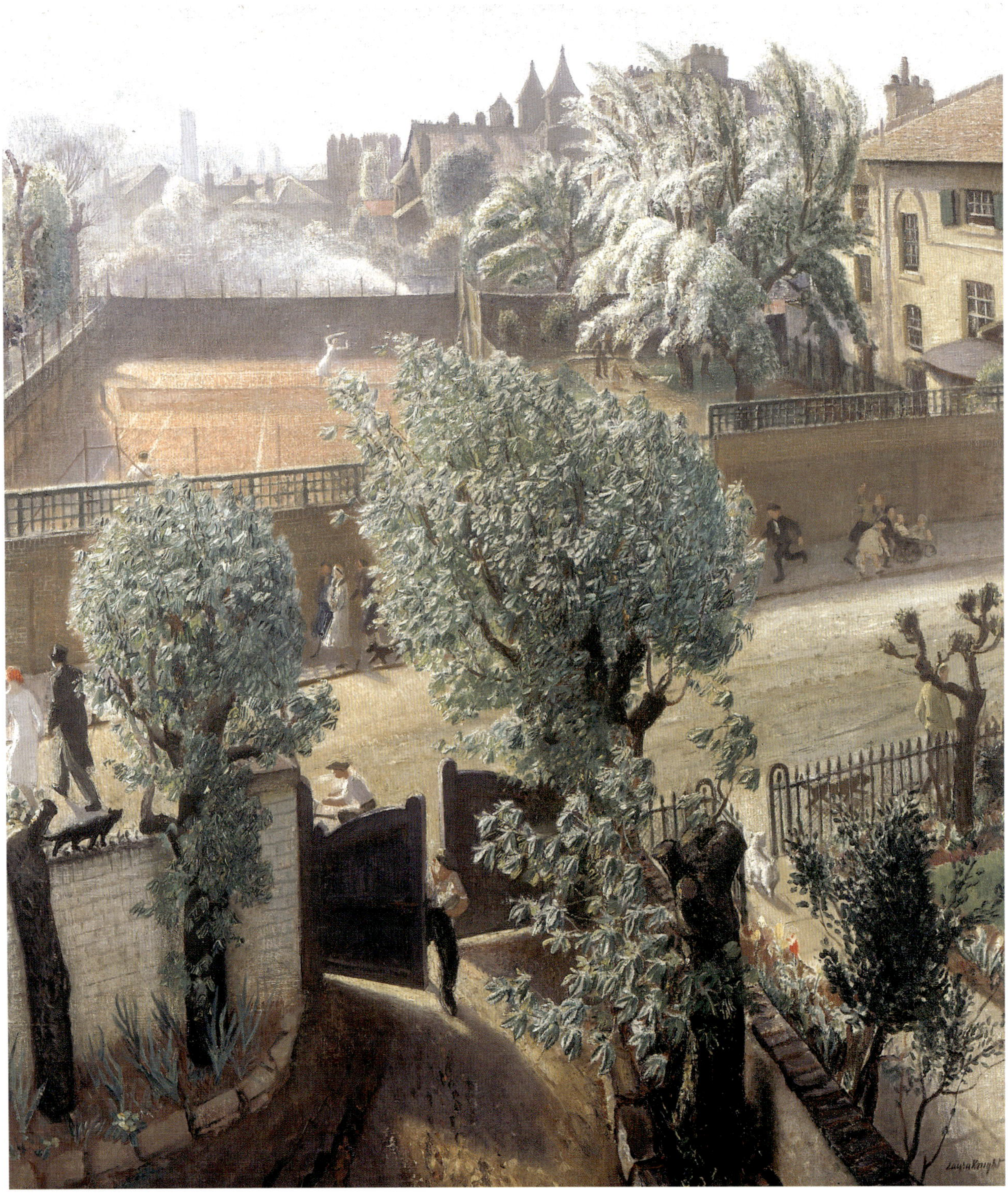

SPRING IN ST JOHN'S WOOD

1933 | oil on canvas | 130.2 x 115.6 cm

National Museums Liverpool (Walker Art Gallery)

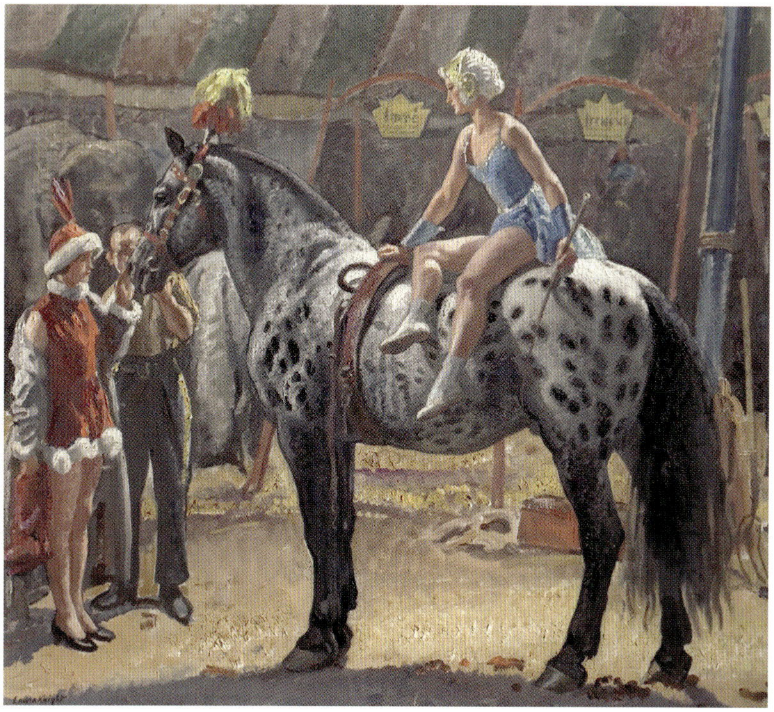

ELSIE ON HASSAN (aka **ELSIE AND HASSAN**)
*c.*1929–30 | oil on canvas | 68.6 x 76.2 cm
Nottingham City Museums and Galleries

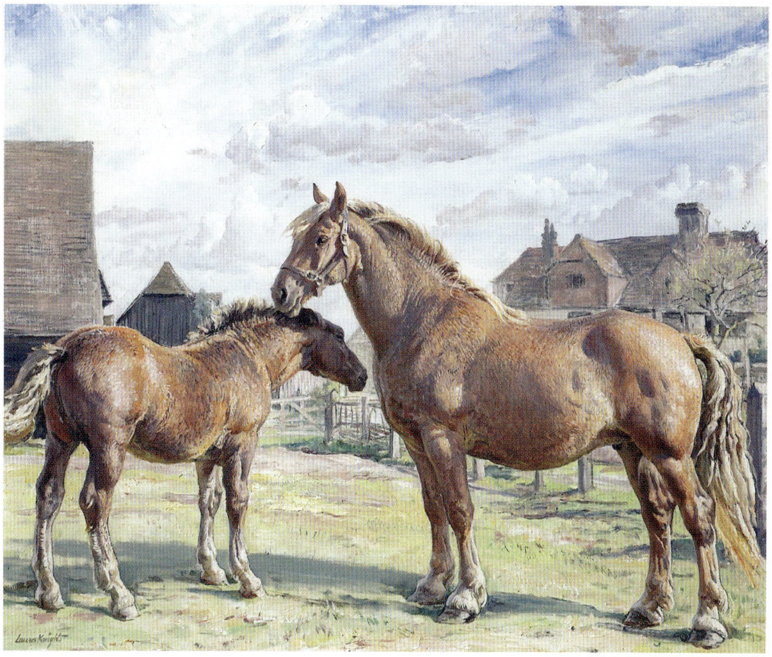

SUFFOLK MARE AND FOAL
(aka **SUFFOLK MARE PARHAM PRUNELLA AND HER FOAL**)
*c.*1939 | oil on canvas
The Suffolk Horse Society, Woodbridge

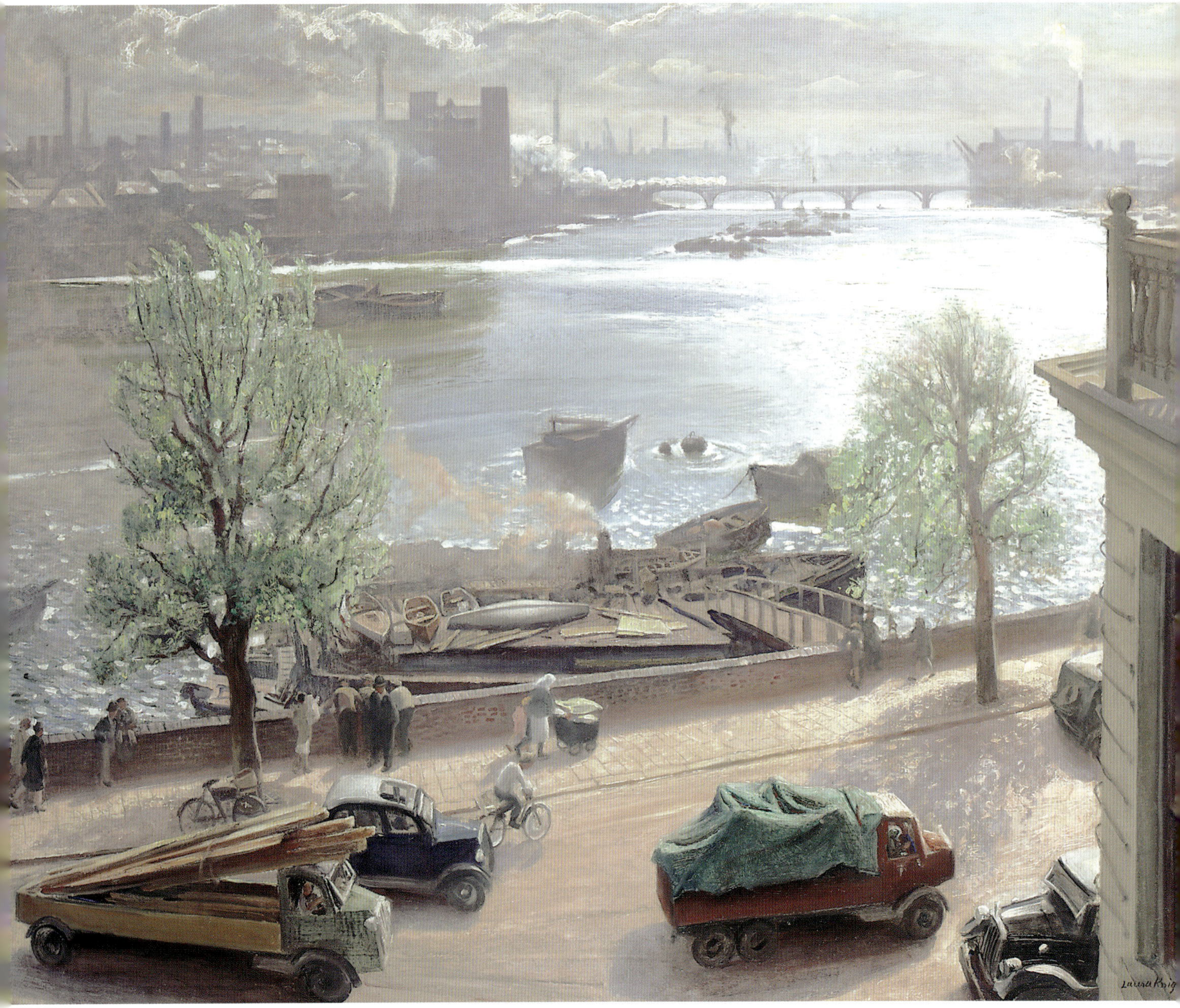

STUDIO WINDOW

*c.*1934 | oil on canvas | 101.5 x 127 cm

private collection; Christie's Images/The Bridgeman Art Library

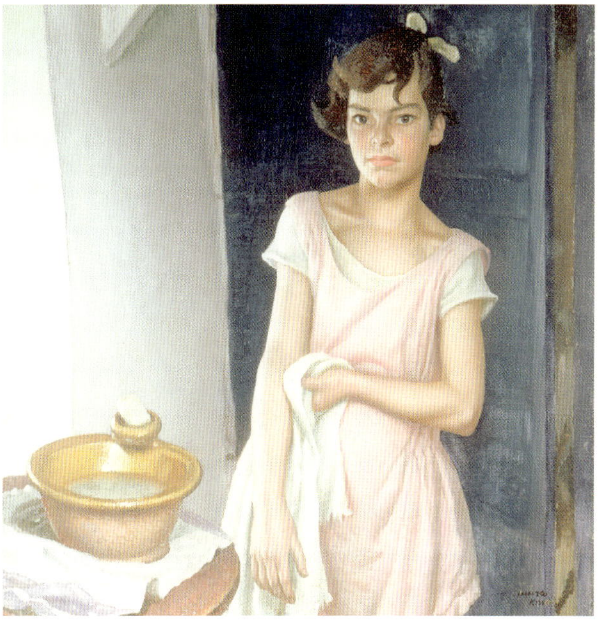

SUSIE AND THE WASHBASIN

1929 | oil on canvas | 61 x 61 cm

Harris Museum and Art Gallery, Preston/The Bridgeman Art Library

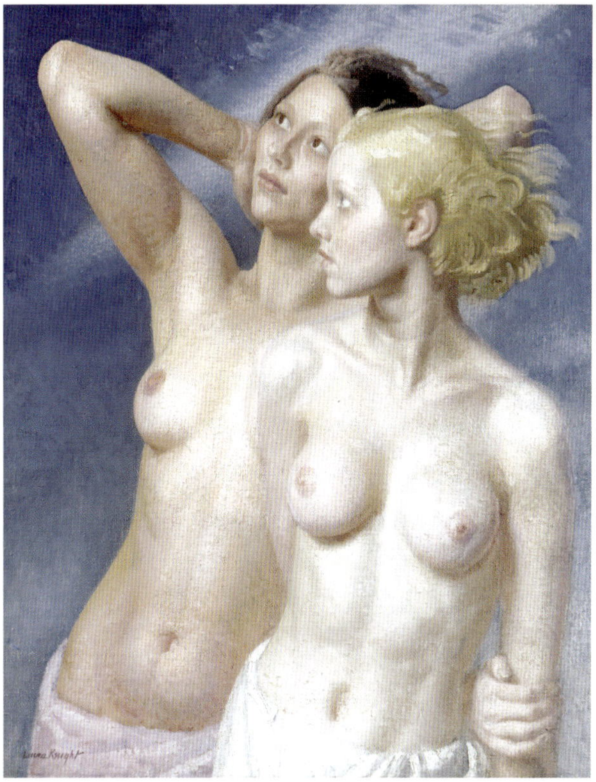

DAWN

*c.*1936 | oil on canvas | 75 x 59 cm

© Royal Academy of Arts, London; photograph John Hammond

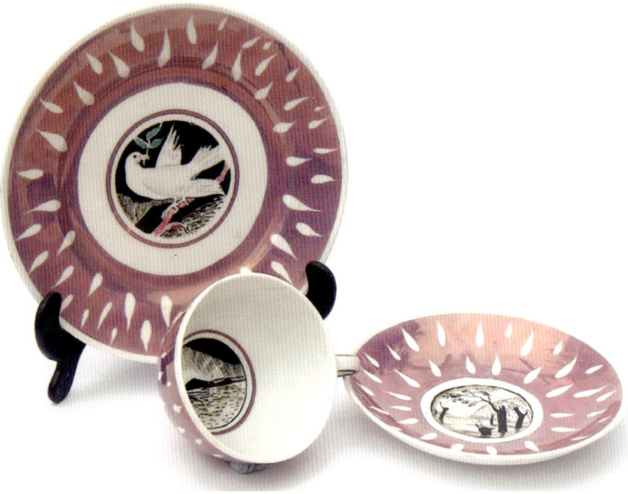

English bone china (1933–34) with biblical flood decoration designed by Laura Knight, and made by Brain & Co at their Foley Pottery Works
private collection

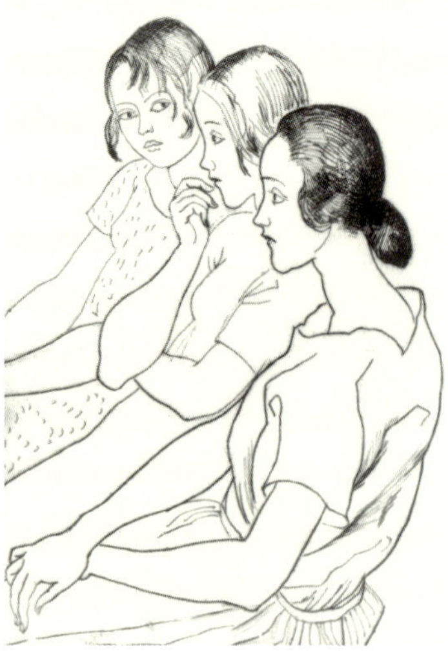

COUNTRY GIRLS
etching and drypoint
23 x 16.8 cm
private collection; image courtesy Belgrave Gallery, London

In 1933 Laura painted the view from her house in Langford Place, *Spring in St John's Wood* and at around the same time she painted the view from a friend's studio in Cheyne Walk, looking down on the Thames and away south-westwards to Chelsea Harbour and the railway bridge with a steam train crossing. In 1934, her usual activity curtailed by an injury to her knee, Laura Knight set out to write the first of her two autobiographies, *Oil Paint and Grease Paint*, published by Ivor Nicholson and Watson in 1936. She worked on the manuscript at home: 'On the scrubbed table of the balcony at 16 Langford Place lies a pile of papers covered with scribbled notes… my hands and arms are covered with pencil sharpenings – I might have been drawing for months. The creepers hanging in festoon from above and the chestnut trees in summer leaf almost hide the flats that block our view of old St John's Wood, which I painted two years ago, *Spring in St John's Wood.* The pear trees have gone, the tennis court has gone.'[19] Laura's book concludes with a wistful reminiscence of Cornwall and thoughts on the nature of being an artist. Laura's warmth and her urge to understand the lives of other people shines through: 'I am thankful to have known the tasks and struggles of common life, joy and despair like any other mortal. I am just a hard-working woman who longs to pierce the mystery of form and colour…'[20]

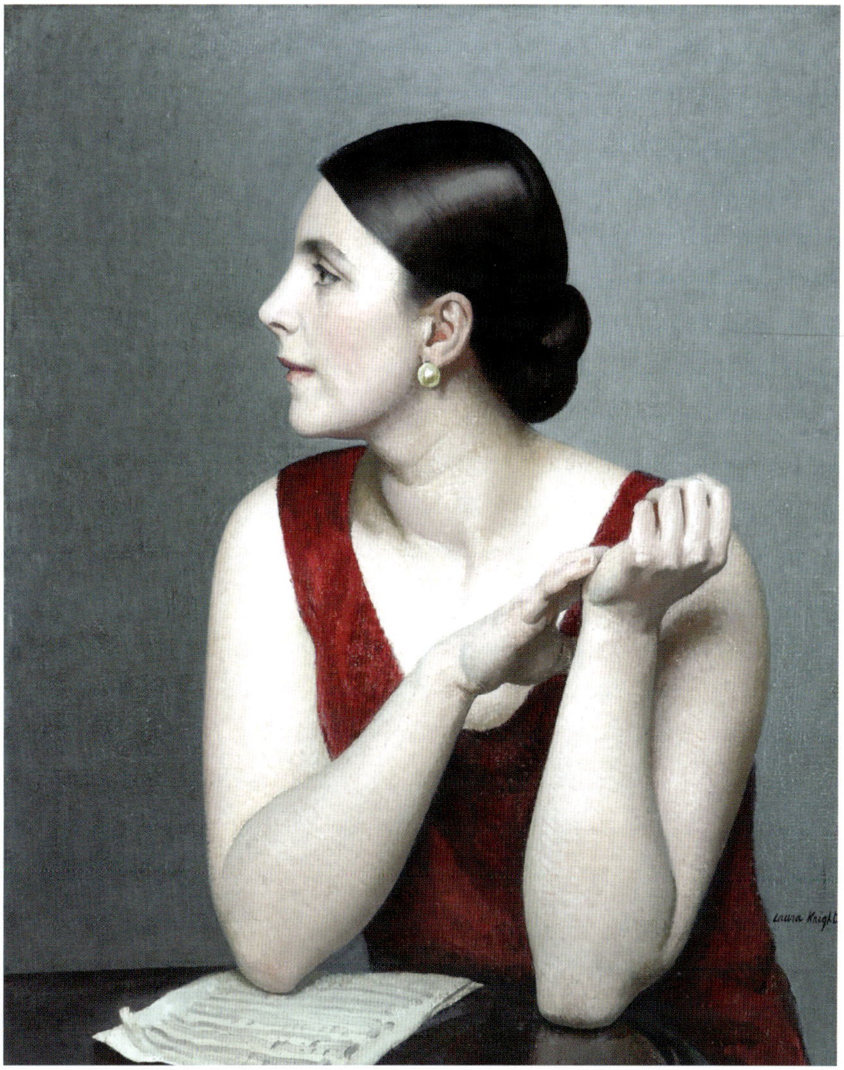

ETHEL BARTLETT

*c.*1926 | oil on canvas | 76 x 63.5 cm

Atkinson Art Gallery/reproduced by kind permission of
Sefton MBC Leisure Services Department, Arts and Cultural Services

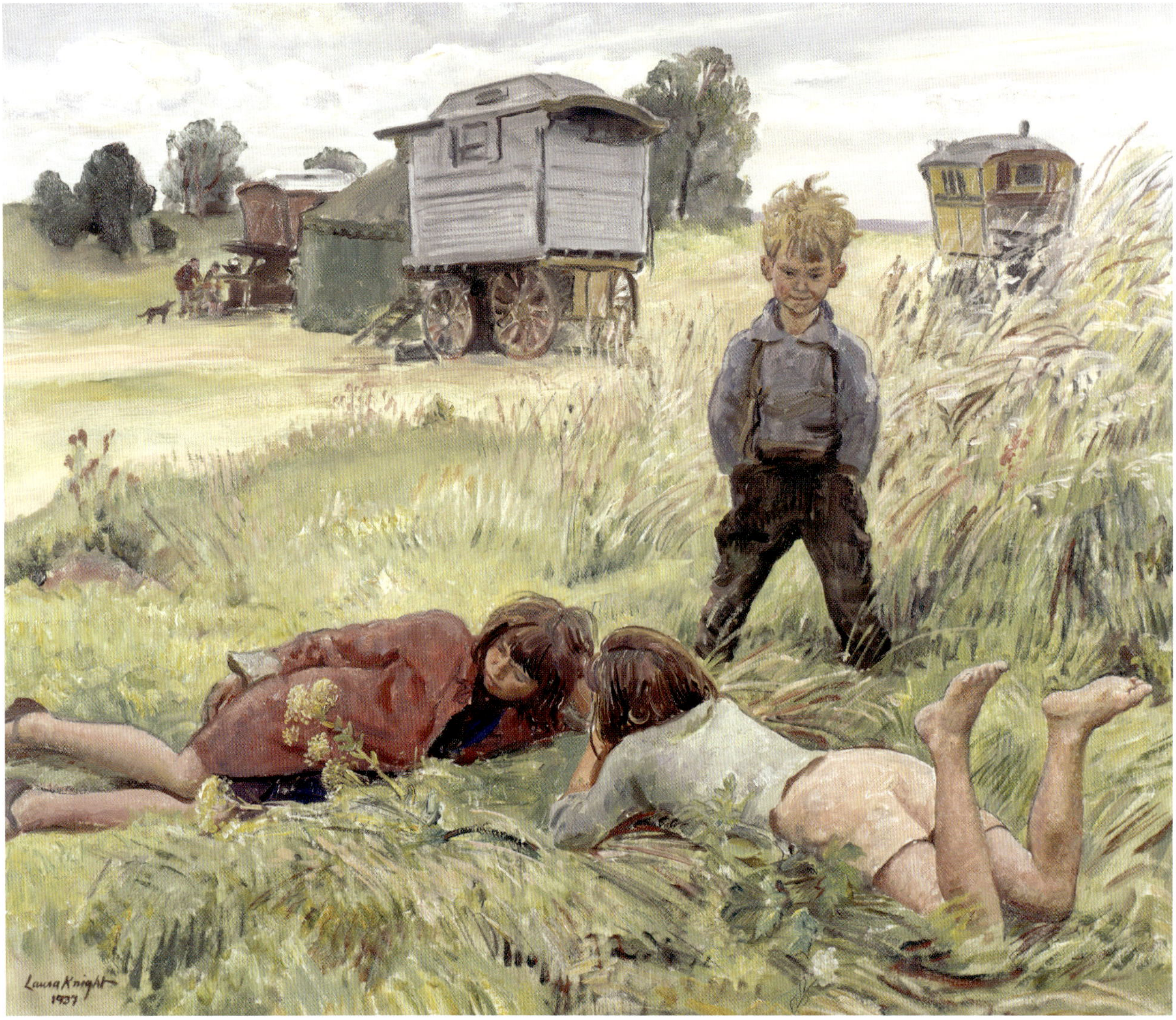

YOUNG GYPSIES

1937 | oil on canvas | 63.4 x 76.2 cm

Worthing Museum and Art Gallery, Sussex/The Bridgeman Art Library

Malvern and the early years of World War II 1932–1942

Romany people Laura met at Epsom races suggested she should visit their large camp on the common at Iver in Buckinghamshire. She went out from London many times through the late 1930s to make studies, watercolours and paintings. At that time, real Romany families were still living the travelling life in the traditional ornate painted wagons. Laura was fascinated by their looks and the way they lived, bound by tradition and a tight-knit family hierarchy. Their disconnection from the normal run of contemporary life attracted her and she appreciated their ways and means of survival as well as the dignity of their matriarchs. *Young Gypsies* was probably painted in the camp at Iver, as was the portrait *A Gypsy*. Of working at Iver Laura writes, 'It was one of the most inspiring times of my working life. An immense wild rose-bush, gaudy with bloom, that flourished on the common, typified the gypsy in its freedom of bloom and thorn. I was at home with these people – found them kindly and willing to pose…'[1] Many of Laura's paintings of Romany people are sketchier, lighter in handling than some earlier paintings. It seems that her urge to depict their lives, rather than to seek a painterly expression for her own life and ideas, led to a more illustrative way of working. It is possible to speculate that while she was in Cornwall, surrounded by serious painters, she naturally engaged in the same kind of endeavour whereas when she followed her desire for particular subjects to its furthest extent she became isolated from formal painterly concerns, or at least kept them subsidiary to her need to depict her subject. Her lifelong habit of drawing, making studies and painting direct from her subjects contributed to the consistent direction of her mature work.

In November 1935, under the auspices of the British section of the Artists International Association Laura joined with Eric Gill, Duncan Grant, Augustus John, Henry Moore and Paul Nash to gather an exhibition 'in protest against fascism and War', held at 28 Soho Square. In 1936 Laura's work appeared in Frank Rutter's ambitious fortnightly publication *Modern*

Masterpieces with five large colour plates in each issue. *Ballet Girl and Dressmaker* and *The Bedroom* were featured, and also Harold's *The Letter.* In Part 20 Rutter discusses Laura's success at the Royal Academy – '…the first woman Academician for more than a century'. From about 1935 Laura took a studio at 28 Finchley Road; the building bore a plaque to the poet Thomas Hood[2] and so became known as her 'Hood' studio. While working there she injured her leg and to aid her recovery Harold took her to Malvern that year.

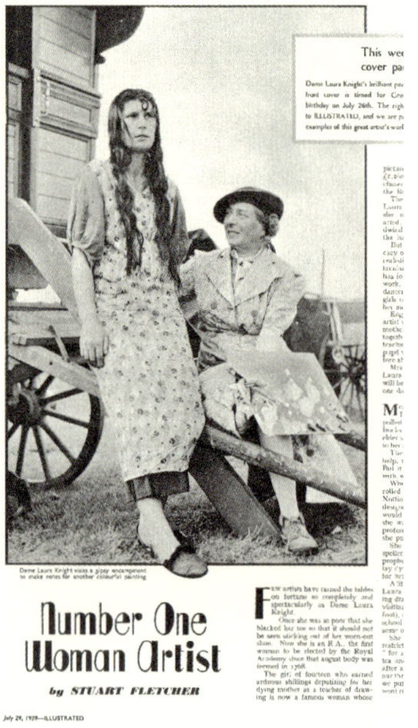
Dame Laura Knight visits a gipsy encampment to make notes for another colourful painting

Number One Woman Artist

by STUART FLETCHER

Few artists have turned the tables on fortune so completely and spectacularly as Dame Laura Knight.

Once she was so poor that she blacked her toe so that it should not be seen sticking out of her worn-out shoe. Now she is an R.A., the first woman to be elected by the Royal Academy since that august body was formed in 1768.

The girl of fourteen who earned arduous shillings deputising for her dying mother as a teacher of drawing is now a famous woman whose

July 29, 1939—ILLUSTRATED

Laura featured in *Illustrated* magazine, 29 July 1939

private collection

The Knights' friend Barry Jackson had a small house near Malvern, Blackhill East, high on the slopes of the Herefordshire Beacon (also known as British Camp), the high point towards the southern end of the range of Malvern hills. Jackson gathered parties of theatre people, artists and musicians there and from about 1931 through the 1930s, the Knights were part of a large circle of frequent visitors: 'Among [the guests of] Sir Barry Jackson have been Lord Sandwich, Lady Rhondda, Sir Granville Bantock, Miss Irene Vanburgh, Dean Inge, Dame Laura Knight and Mr Harold Knight.'[3] Jackson had been the creative force behind what had become an annual Festival in Malvern since 1929 and by the early 1930s he was particularly engaged in presenting plays by George Bernard Shaw at the theatre in the town. Among other friends of Laura and Harold's in and around Malvern were J.R. Allardyce Nicoll, the distinguished theatre historian and his wife Josephine, who was a puppeteer; both were friends of Barry Jackson's and also involved in the Malvern Festival. Marjorie and Morris Averill of Severnbank, Shrawley were friends and important patrons of Laura's in the 1930s. From 1935, when she met its Principal Victor Moody, until its demise later in the 1950s, Laura was involved with the art school in Malvern. She championed opportunities for 'artisan' students and the teaching of the basic skills of drawing and painting from nature. Another particular Malvern friend was Dr John Richardson, a GP and sculptor. From 1933 the Knights stayed in the Mount Pleasant Hotel in the centre of Malvern, and Laura painted a view looking down on its terrace and the street below. From the town they walked up to the high paths and got to know the dramatic landscape, with its steep vistas and winding lanes. Laura made a painting titled *Love Lane* of the view looking down the steep Green Valley on the eastward side of the hills (apparently known to locals as 'Happy Valley'), and a drypoint of the same subject (reversed). She began to find subjects in the broad expanse of farmland spread out far below: the Severn Valley through Worcestershire and Gloucestershire to the east, and Herefordshire to the west. She looked for rooms with windows looking out to the east: 'I got a rage for painting dawns… September month is the best time – in contrast to the suns and clouds "doing their stuff"; strands of grey mist wreathe the landscape, the trees appear to have no roots, and church spires no naves to prop them up.'[4] In a characteristic little burst of lyrical description, Laura writes of a Malvern view: 'On this late August day, the air is keen on the hills' smooth switchback; under a stunted hawthorn six newly clipped grey-white sheep find haven. The cries of children tobogganing down a grassy mound, a terrier's sharp barking, voices of trippers climbing round from

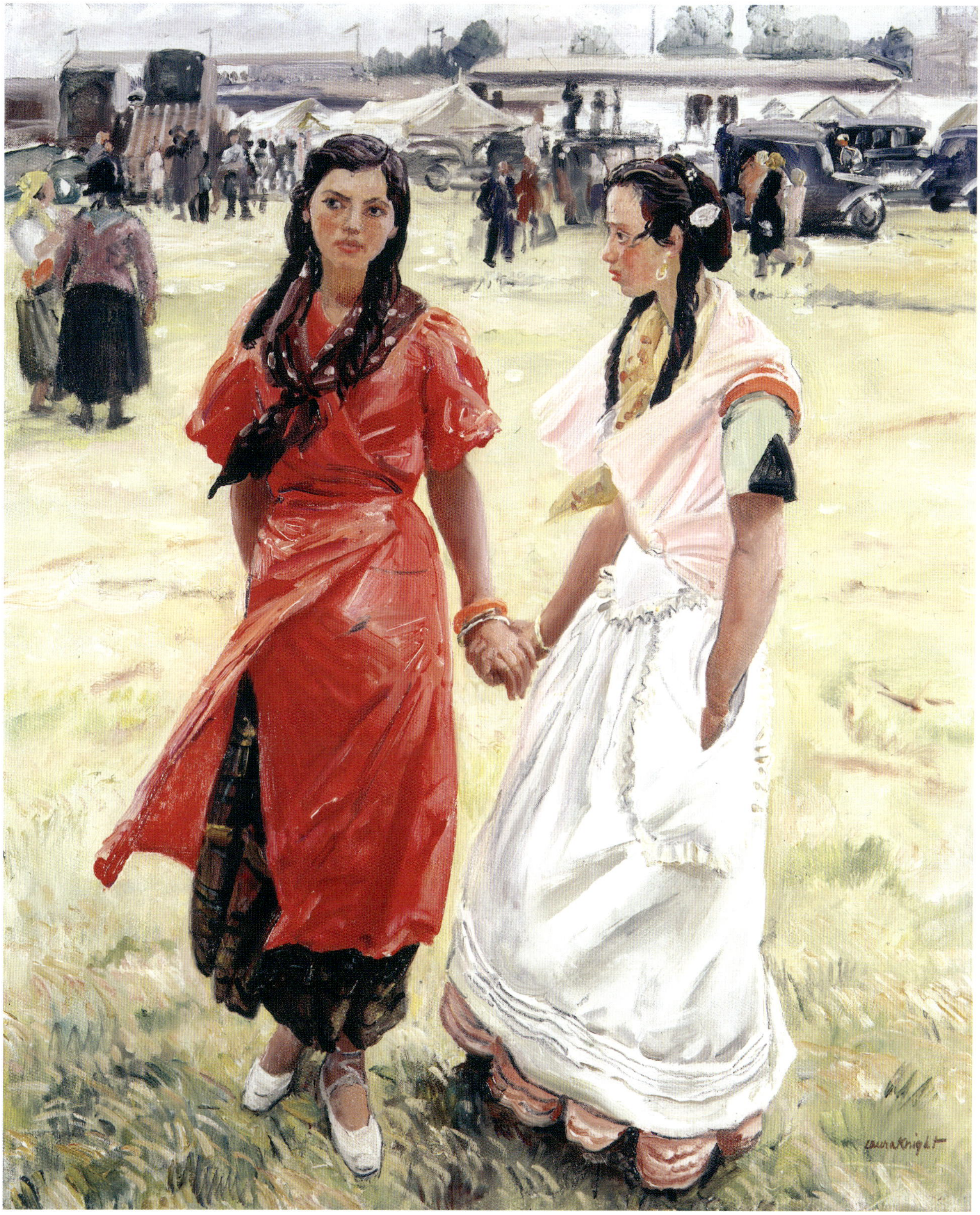

ASCOT FINERY

*c.*1937 | oil on canvas | 76.2 x 63.5 cm

Dundee Art Galleries and Museums

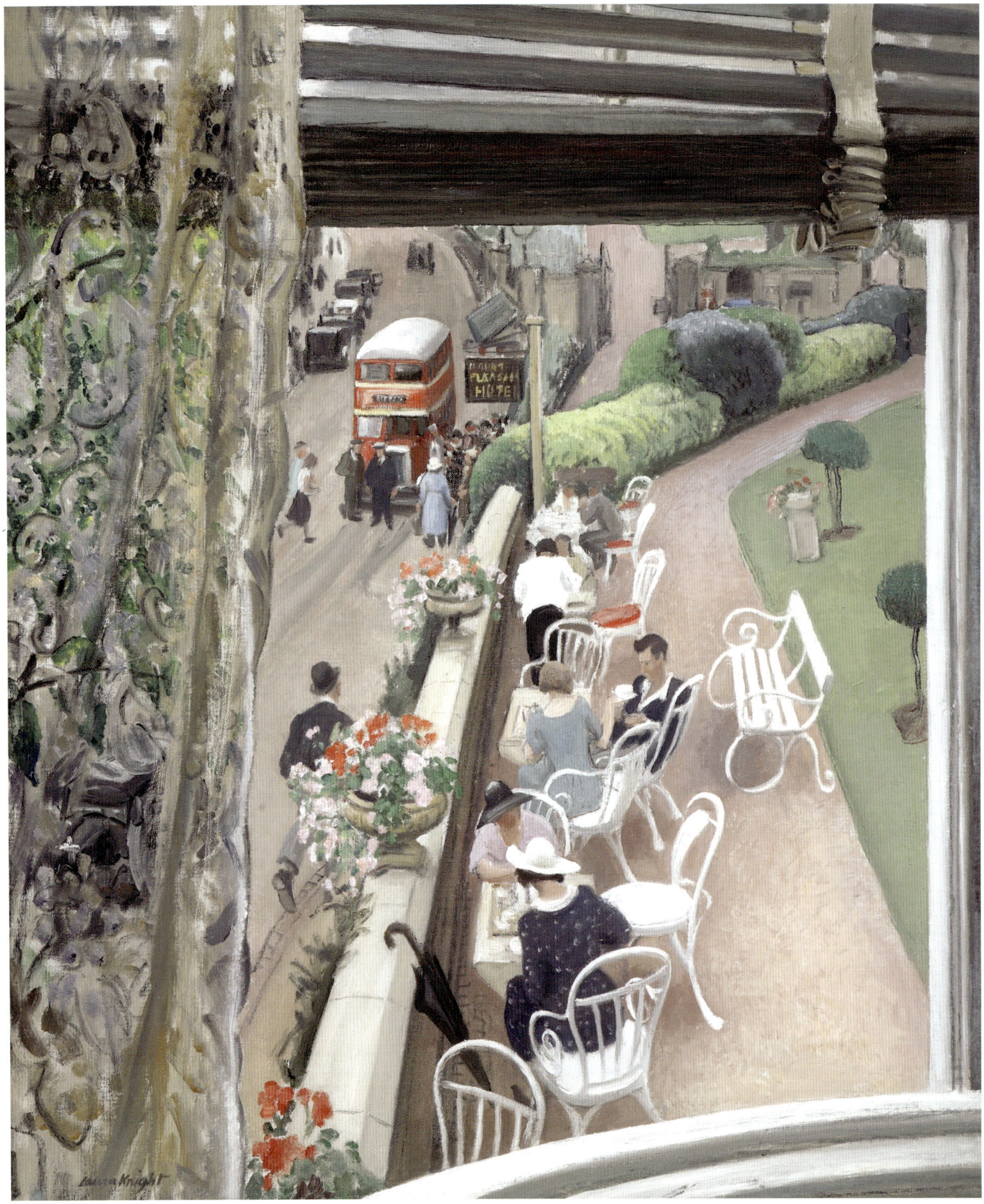

HOLIDAY TIME

*c.*1937 | oil on canvas | 75 x 62 cm

Museum of New Zealand Te Papa Tongarewa

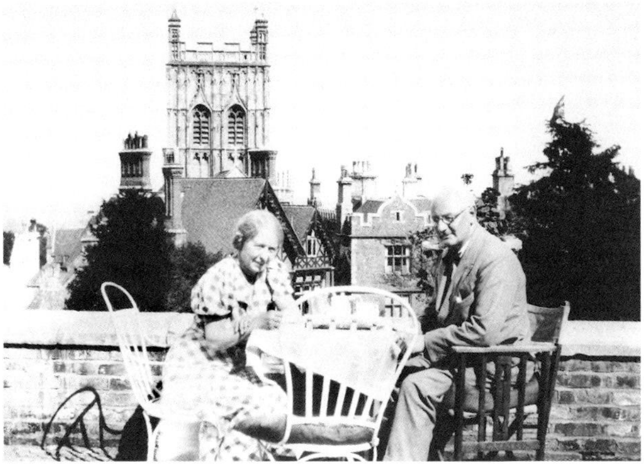

Laura and Harold, Mount Pleasant Hotel terrace, Malvern *c.*mid-1930s

private collection

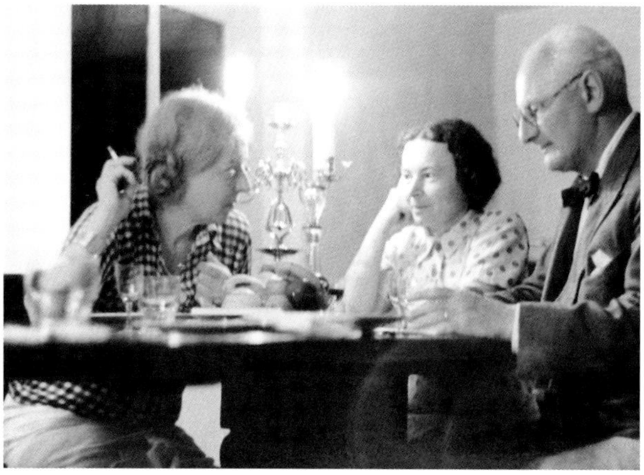

Laura and Harold with Josephine Nicoll in the Nicols' house, Windsacre, near Malvern, *c.*late 1930s

private collection

below are heard and from the Priory Gardens snatches of a Viennese waltz come in disconnected blast' and '...In panoramic view from north to south, like a half-rolled map, fertile England's beauty lies in sunlit patch of stubble, farm, copse and snug woolly tree and countless spires of churches among distant towns' blue slates. Smoke from some burning weeds billows across a distant rise and a plume in colour of watered milk rises from a tall chimney-stack. Thunderous cumuli in solemn majesty show against intensest blue, rounded mountains of glowing white modelled with both tender and heavy tones of grey, all more static and solid seeming than land itself, as in glorious game shadow chases shadow.'[5] Struggling to express her vision of a changing landscape, Laura thinks in almost cinematic terms.

In 1936 Laura Knight became a full Academician and the following year Harold also became an RA, noting proudly that now there were five Nottingham artists who were Academicians.[6] There was a great deal of press coverage for Laura when she was the first woman ever elected as an RA, and again in 1937 when Harold's election was announced, much of it re-telling stories of her early life told in her autobiography. Her reputation as a celebrity was greatly enhanced. Through the 1930s, as noted earlier, Laura Knight's subjects ranged across the circus, gypsies, the theatre and portraits. Her exhibition of recent paintings at the Leicester Galleries in April 1939 included watercolours and drawings – nearly sixty works in all and there were many landscape subjects from Cornwall and Malvern. The Knights were staying at Malvern when war was declared in 1939 and so left their London home closed up and remained, for the time being, at their base in Malvern, the Mount Pleasant Hotel. Laura describes being left there while Harold went to Scotland for what looked likely to be his last commission for some time: '...to keep myself from going crackers, I painted the nearest thing to hand: the old back garden gate belonging to the hotel...'[7]

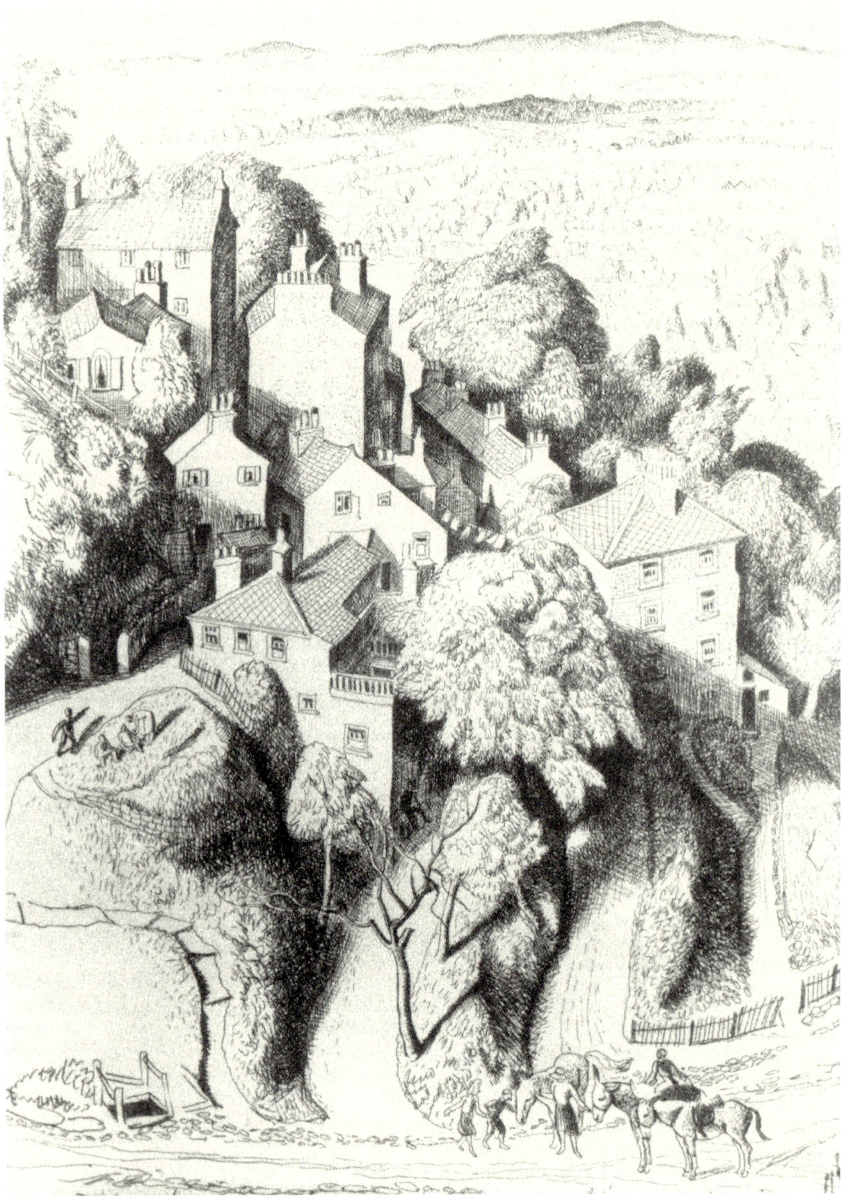

LOVE LANE (aka **AN ENGLISH HILLSIDE**)
etching | 31.4 x 22.2 cm
private collection; image courtesy Belgrave Gallery, London

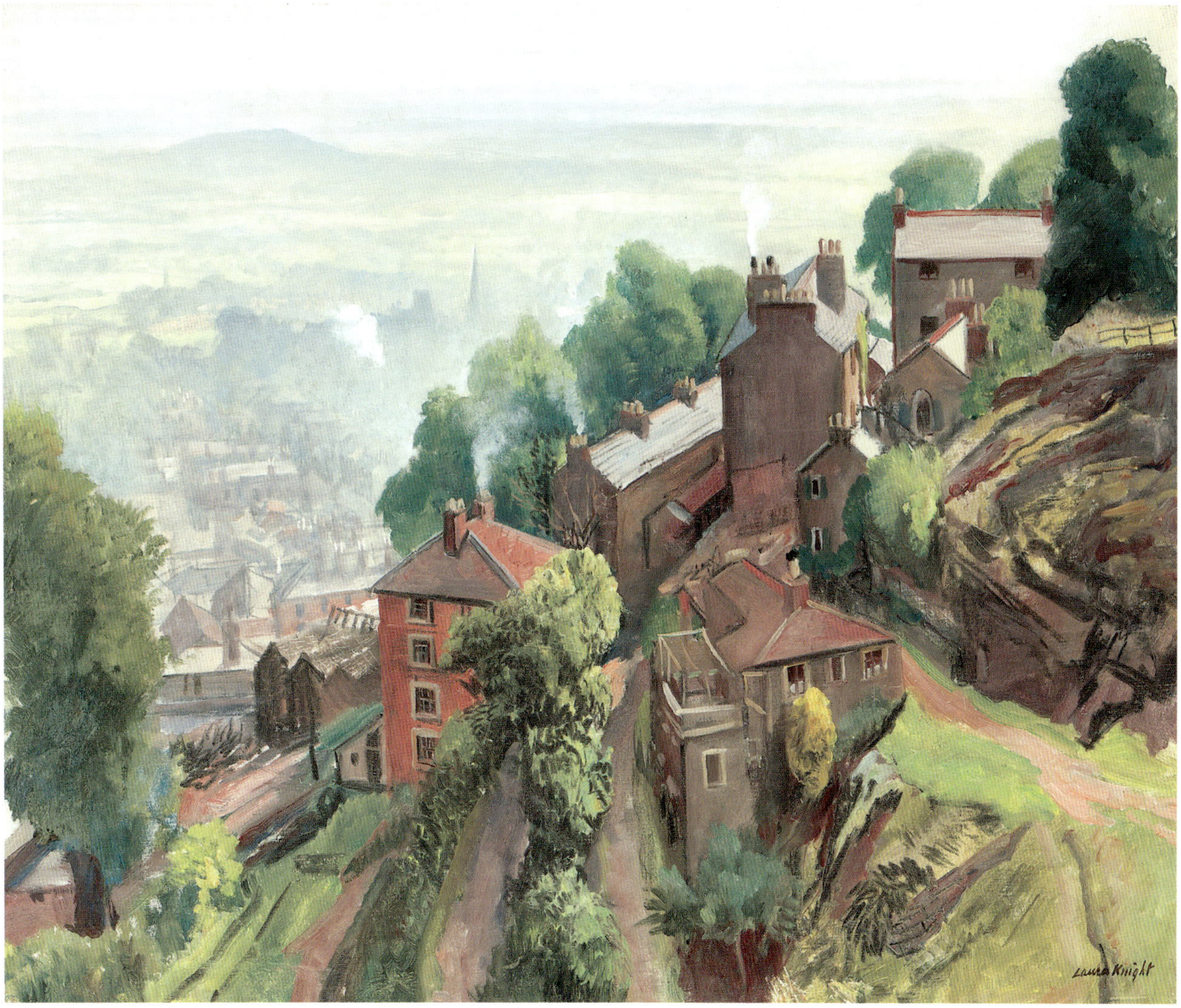

LOVE LANE

*c.*1940 | oil on canvas | 63.5 x 76 cm

private collection; courtesy Sotheby's Picture Library

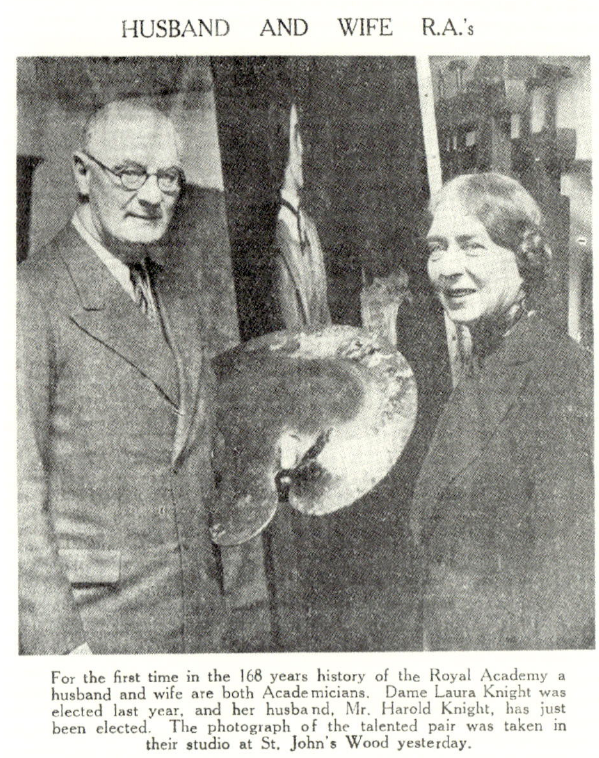

HUSBAND AND WIFE R.A.'s

For the first time in the 168 years history of the Royal Academy a husband and wife are both Academicians. Dame Laura Knight was elected last year, and her husband, Mr. Harold Knight, has just been elected. The photograph of the talented pair was taken in their studio at St. John's Wood yesterday.

Laura and Harold at the time of Harold's election from ARA to full Royal Academician in 1937

Nottinghamshire Archive (ref DD/1561/175/20)

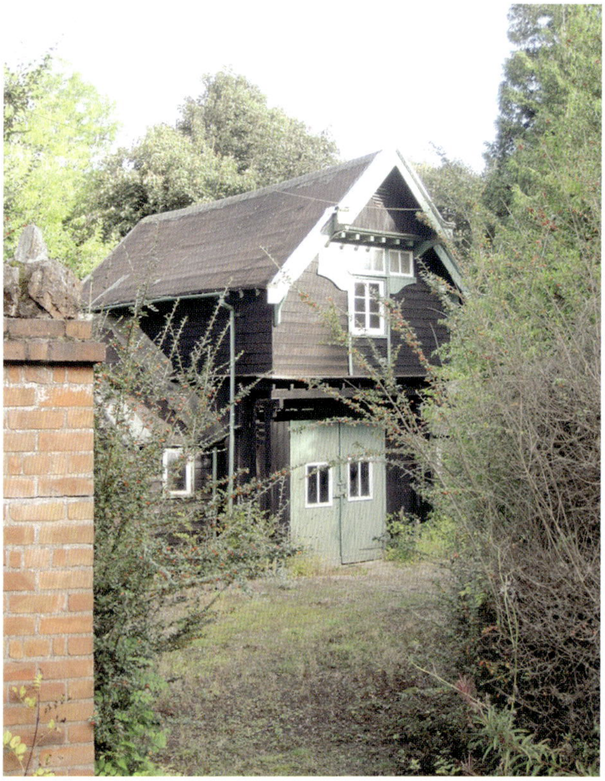

The stables, Windsacre, where Laura had a studio

photograph John Adams

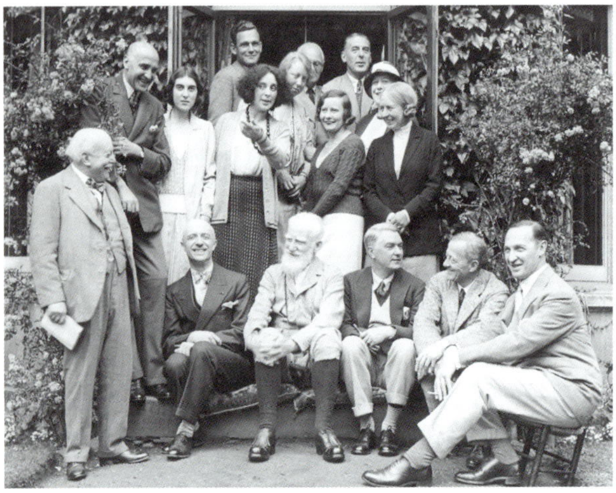

Malvern Festival guests, Lawnside School, mid-1930s

Laura standing (right), Harold standing (almost hidden, centre, back), Barry Jackson sitting (far right) and George Bernard Shaw (centre, seated)

Nottinghamshire Archives (ref DD/790/219)

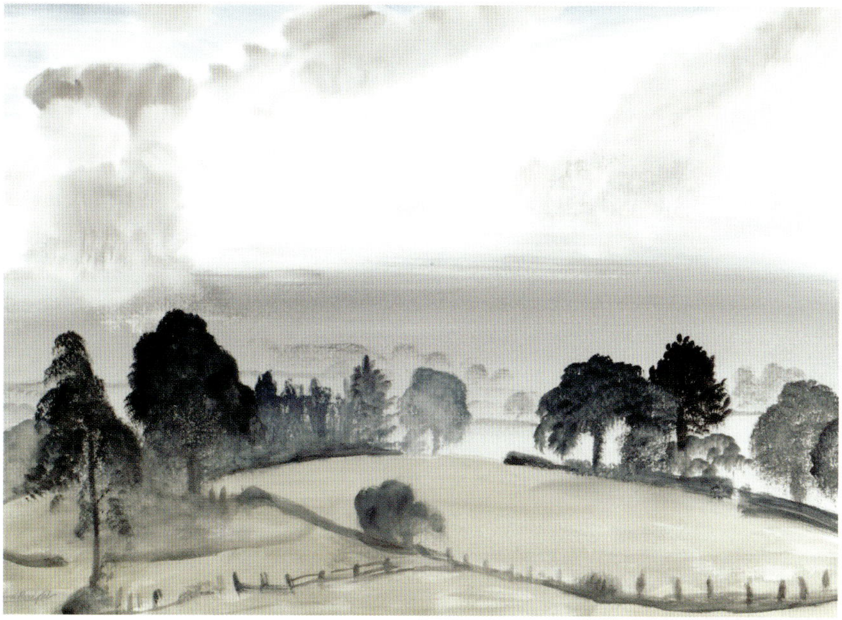

CLEARING MIST (aka **RISING MIST**)
*c.*1934 | watercolour | 35.5 x 50.8 cm
courtesy Christopher Beetles Gallery, London

By the end of 1939 or possibly early 1940 the Knights were settled a little way south of Malvern in the British Camp Hotel (now the Malvern Hills Hotel) at Wynd's Point, just below the high point of the Herefordshire Beacon and close to Barry Jackson's house, Blackhill East. From their room they could see right across Herefordshire to the Welsh mountains; Laura wrote to Ella Naper '…we are still in the midst of this grand landscape and have not tired of it despite mist and rain.'[8] They were based there until about 1943–44. Laura worked in an outbuilding of the hotel for a time but from about 1939 she was able to use studio space in a wooden outbuilding at Windsacre, a house belonging to J.R. Allardyce Nicoll, who was away in America during the war. In the mid- to late 1930s Laura had drawn portraits of Nicoll and his wife Josephine, and she used Nicoll as the pipe-smoking model for a figure in her painting *Harvest*. The Nicolls were also involved in the Festival at Malvern and their wide artistic circle included Edward Elgar as well as George Bernard Shaw and Barry Jackson. The outbuilding at Windsacre is an eccentric structure in black timber, with two studio spaces with good north light as well as windows looking out westwards over Herefordshire.

The paintings and watercolours Laura made of the farming country that lay below the Herefordshire Beacon are among the most beautiful of her landscapes. The watercolour *A Valley at Evening* of *c.*1939 shows a view looking down on Herefordshire farming country with the low light of a setting sun to the left. The same view appears in the large oil painting *Harvest* behind the old white pony Kitty, who, together with a cohort of donkeys, could be hired to carry children and the less active

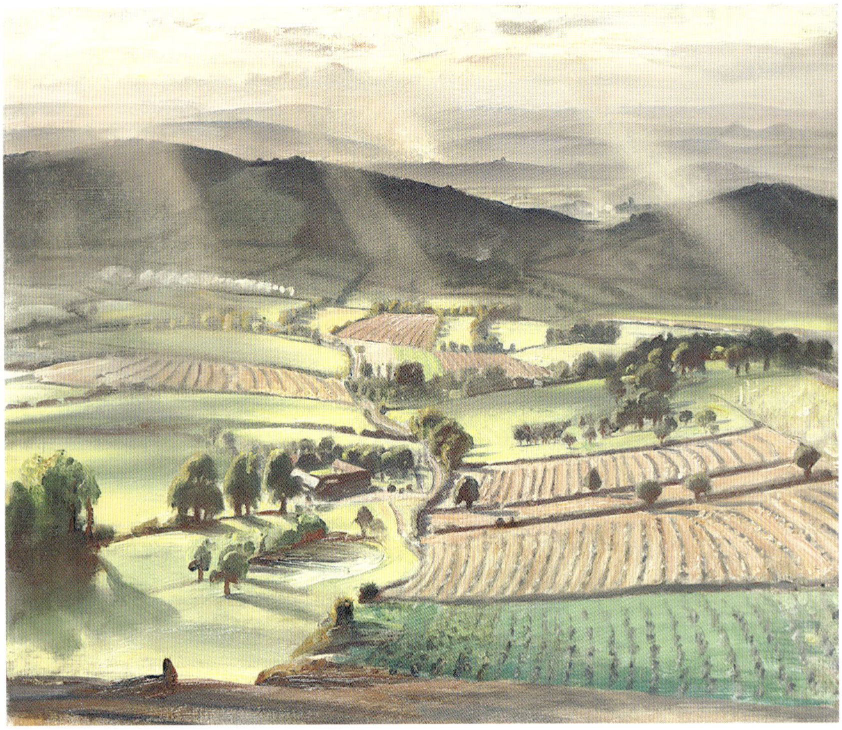

A VALLEY AT EVENING

oil on canvas | 50.8 x 60.9 cm

private collection; image Christie's Images/The Bridgeman Art Library

sight-seers up onto the Hills. The pony and donkeys were a well known feature for Malvern tourists and a motif that Laura painted several times.[9] *Harvest* was shown in the 1939 Royal Academy and must have seemed a particularly resonant image of tranquillity that summer, when the Second World War was about to be declared.

The Herefordshire countryside was the backdrop for the portrait of her daughter, commissioned by Lady Cadbury in 1942. Bryony Cadbury, then aged seven, remembers sitting for Laura with her dog Sally, in the upstairs studio at Windsacre whose big windows looked out westwards over a wide expanse of farmland with Hay Bluff and the Brecon Beacons in the far distance. In the early years of the war Laura painted a number of farming subjects including one of a man ploughing with a team of horses, making studies for it in the open in cold winter weather: 'the frozen ploughed red clay soil was partially laden with snow, and the farmer, from whom I hired two horses and a plough to pose as models, built up six stooks of straw to protect me from the bitter cold. But that barrier was not so effective as a thermos flask full of boiling bread and milk – an internal poultice.'[10] A drawing of this subject is illustrated in her second autobiography *The Magic of a Line* (p.311) where it is dated 1940. In the concluding chapter Laura writes of a painting of 'two heavy horses standing in a ploughed field in the bitter cold of 1939, and I live again in the slush and mud known when making the studies.'[11]

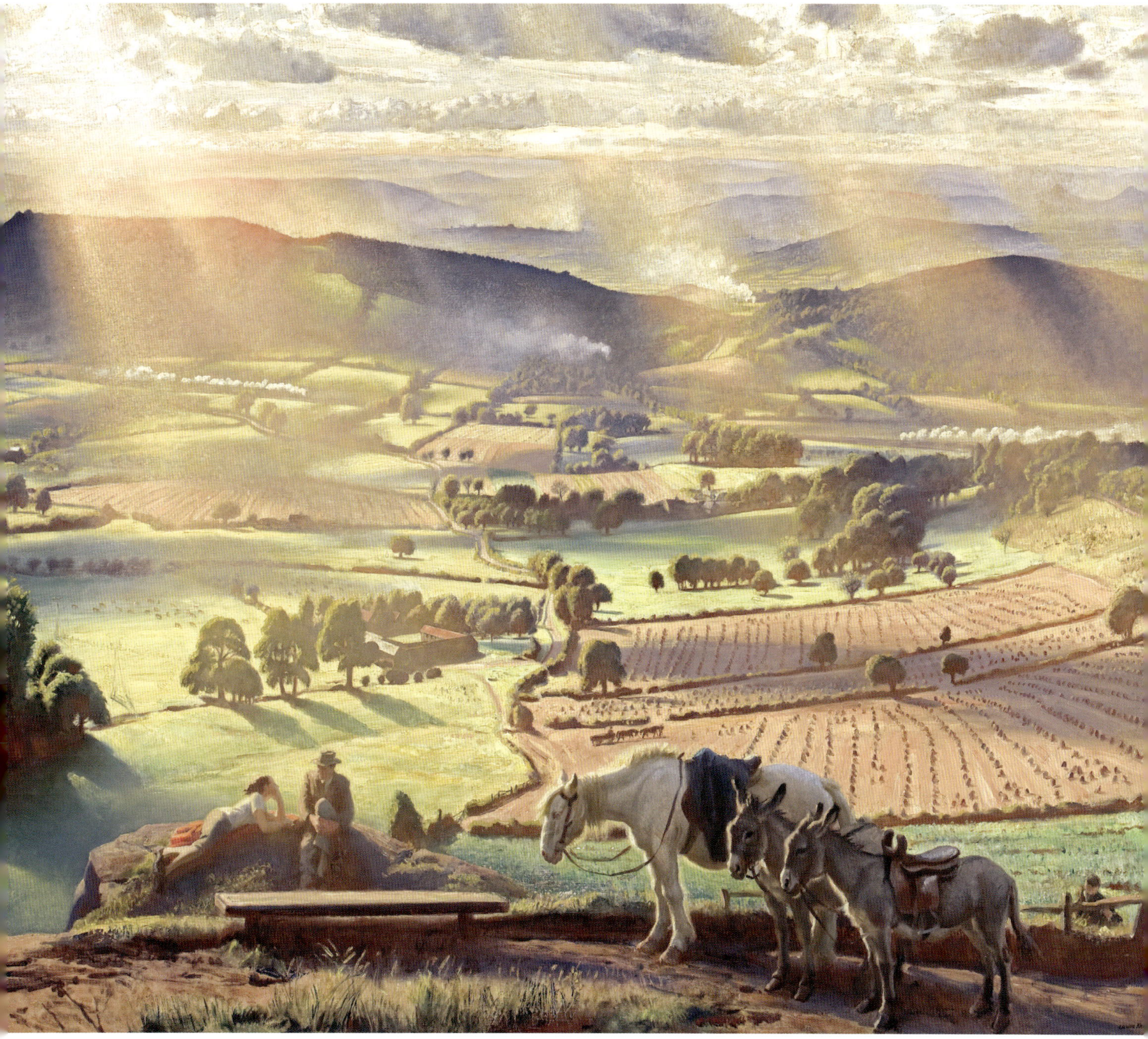

HARVEST

1939 | oil on canvas | 152.4 x 182.8 cm

Art Gallery of South Australia, Adelaide (A.R. Ragless Bequest Fund 1956)

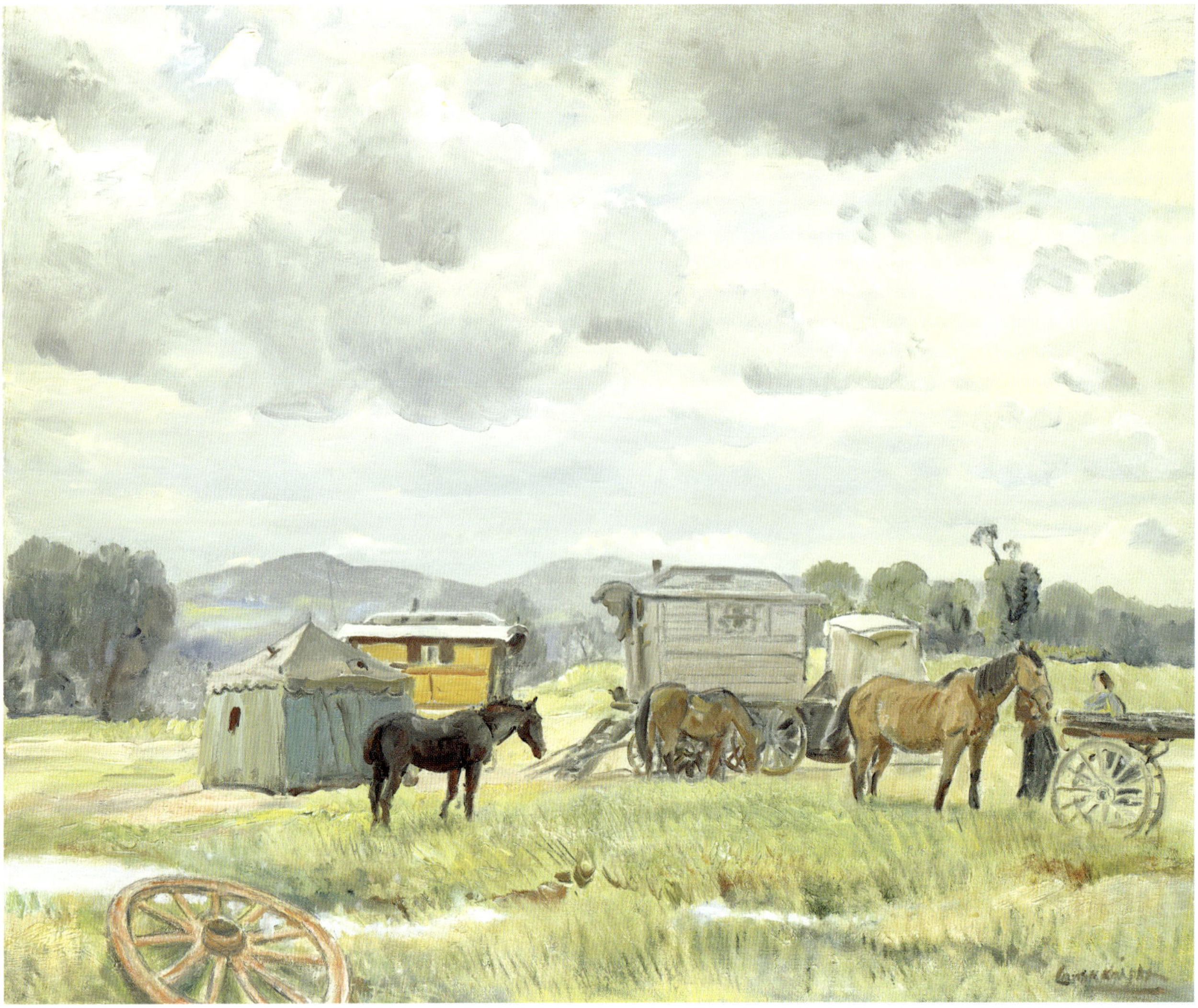

GYPSY CAMP (aka **CAMPING GROUND**)

oil on canvas | 63.5 x 76.2 cm

private collection; image Christie's Images/The Bridgeman Art Library

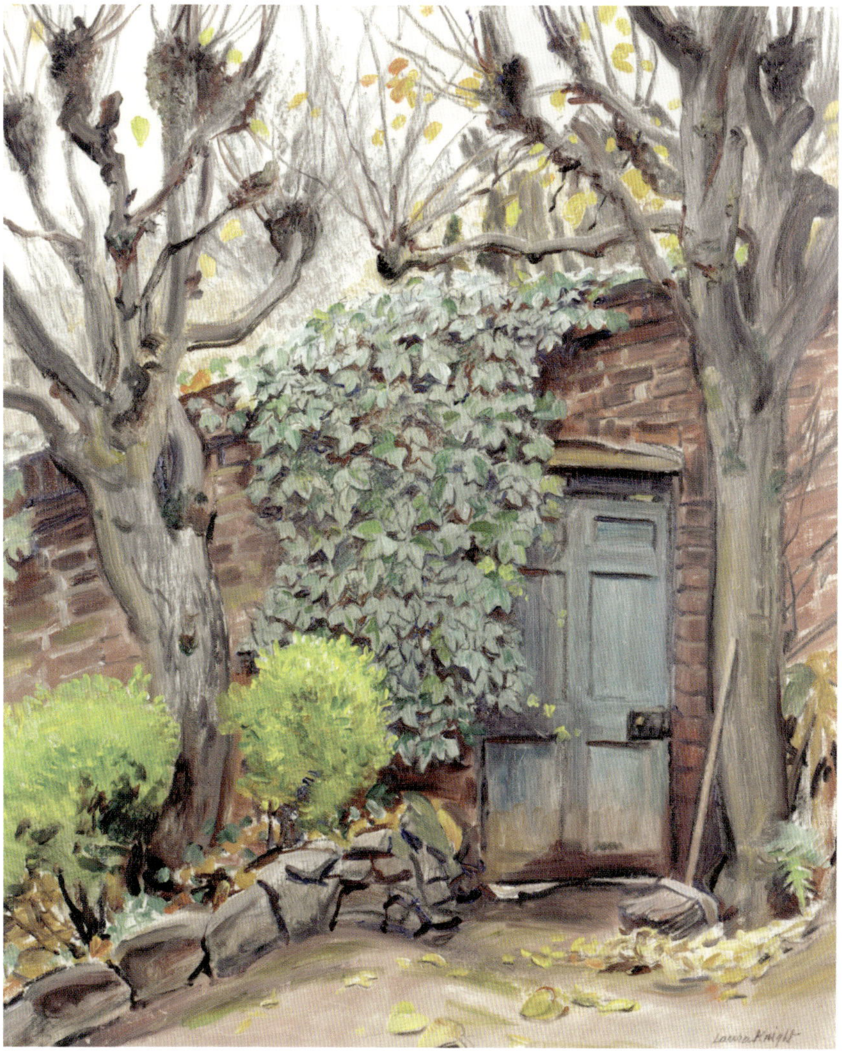

THE GARDEN DOOR
1939 | oil on canvas | 61 x 51 cm
private collection; courtesy Sotheby's Picture Library

The pressing need for increased food production during the war meant that grassland was ploughed up – including the ground between orchard trees. A work titled *The Plough* was shown at the Royal Academy in 1949 and one titled *Ploughing* was shown there in 1960.

From the hilltops at night, Laura saw waves of bombers moving towards Birmingham and Coventry, sometimes highlighted by the searchlight batteries scattered all over the Midlands. By 1943–44 Laura and Harold had moved their base to the Colwall Park Hotel, where the views were less dramatic but the food a great deal better,[12] and the proprietors arranged two studios for them. Laura contributed work to a small exhibition in aid of Army charities, held at the hotel in June 1944. The Knights seldom went to London during the war years. Laura was commissioned to paint experimental work on pre-stressed concrete,

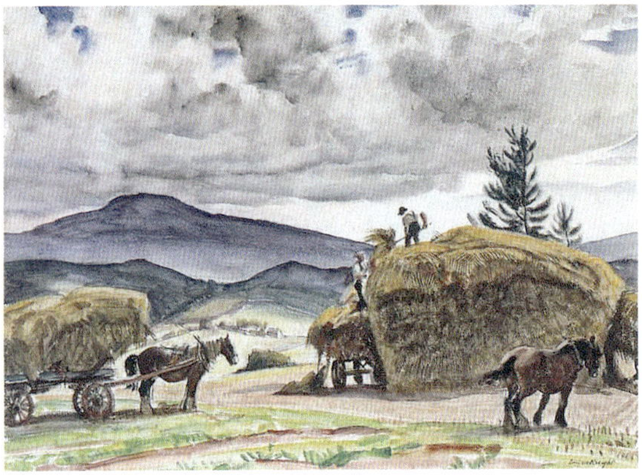

WALTER AND FRED BISHOP LOADING CORN
watercolour and gouache | 49.5 x 68.5 cm
private colection; John Martin Gallery

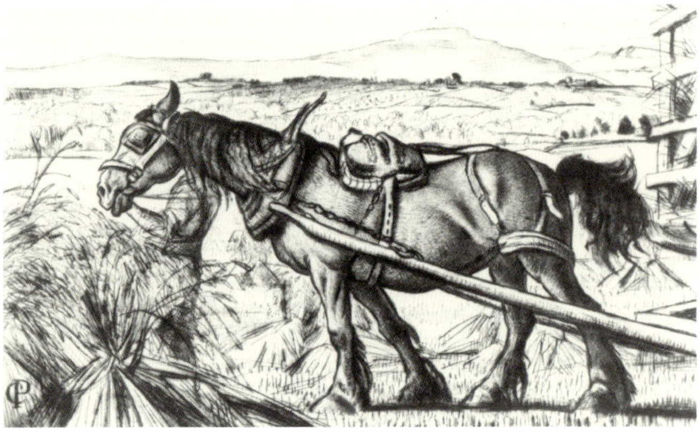

CARTING CORN (aka **A CORNFIELD**)
1943 | drypoint | 20 x 31.5 cm
private collection; image courtesy Belgrave Gallery, London

being done at the nearby racecourse (which has since disappeared); she worked out of doors in mud and cold weather '…in spite of discomfort I enjoyed painting that picture and had lots of fun using a huge plasterer's trowel in place of a paint-brush.'[13] The painting was shown at the 1945 Royal Academy exhibition.

Horses were always a favourite subject for Laura, from *March Manyweathers* of 1913–14, to circus horses, race horses and the cart horses still working on Herefordshire farms in the Second World War. In the late 1930s she was commissioned by friend and important patron Eileen Unwin, to paint her prized Suffolk Punch mare on her farm in Billingshurst, Sussex. Laura's most successful horse paintings are probably the ones of circus horses and ponies, painted from the studies she made throughout her long association with the circus. She writes, 'you can't paint circus life if you can't draw a horse. In my youth the only horses I knew were those pulling cabs and hansoms around Nottingham streets…' and she goes on to describe studying horses in Carmo's circus: 'I did not lose any opportunity to learn all I could about something I had always wished to study. How I loved those beasts. I painted them constantly; each possessed a character all its own.'[14]

There were hop-gardens on both sides of the Malvern Hills and Laura found that gypsies were employed as itinerent pickers. She went to draw and paint them at a farm at Callow End in the Severn Valley. While she was painting on the Herefordshire side, Laura naturally became friendly with the farming families and one of her paintings of this date, made on a farm at Colwall, is unequivocally titled with their names and their activity: *Walter and Fred Bishop Loading Corn*. In fact, the stretch of land where the Bishops were working (and where they tenanted their own farm) was part of a broad sweep of Herefordshire country that Laura painted successfully for many years. It appears in *A Valley at Evening* and *Harvest* and again in her later paintings.

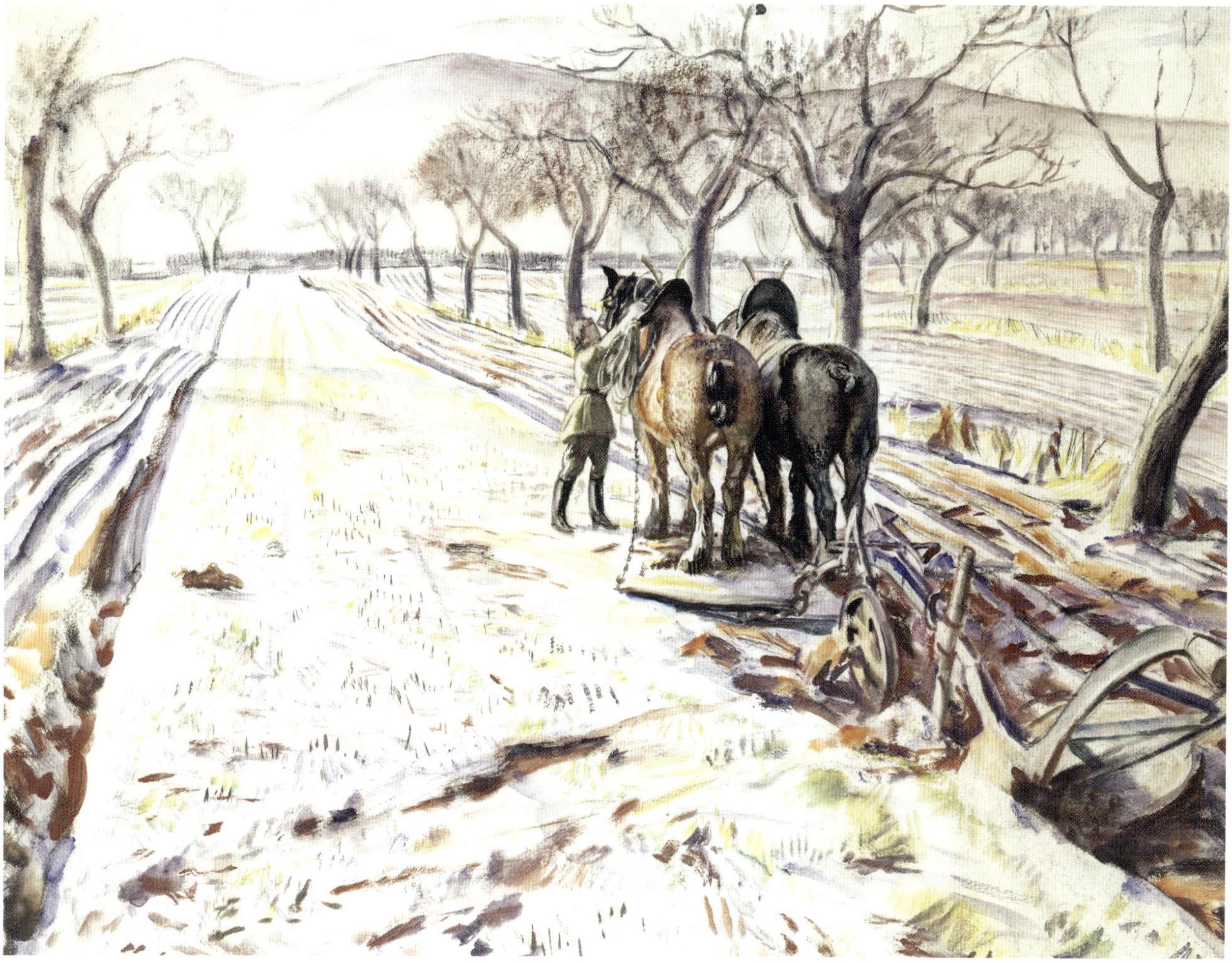

THE PLOUGH

watercolour and chalk | 63.5 x 84cm

private collection; © Christie's Images

War years and Malvern again 1942–1970

Laura Knight's wartime commissions between 1942 and 44 took her to airfields and factories all over England. Her subjects included Women's Auxiliary Air Force personnel (WAAFs) who had been decorated for outstanding service, the crew of a Stirling bomber at Mildenhall air base in Suffolk, and munitions workers at the Royal Ordnance Works in 1943 – most famously *Ruby Loftus Screwing a Breech Ring*. She also painted the production and repairs of barrage balloons, then a vital part of the nation's defences. *In for Repairs* and *A Balloon Site, Coventry* are *tours de force* of wartime endeavour, underlining the role of women working alongside the men. Laura went to the Austin works at Longbridge, where she painted a large watercolour of Stirling bombers being built: 'It was impossible to paint in oil because of the confusion of different lighting. It had to be a big picture, the fuselage of the bomber measured thirty-one feet. A paper-hanger employed in war work joined many sheets of Whatman's "hand-made" together for me and pasted them down on an enormous board. On this, supported by an easel of tubular construction, I painted.'[1] The watercolour was shown at the 1944 Royal Academy Exhibition and later hung in the Board Room at Austin Motors. Laura was commissioned to produce an image for a poster warning about the risk of fire in workshops: it '...was placed in every workshop in England and happily turned out to be such a success that I received a very handsome cheque for it.'[2] Laura wrote a stirring introduction for a book on women's contribution to the war effort, one of the series *War Pictures by British Artists* published in 1943. She writes: 'Women are with the Fighting Forces; they are in the aerodrome and the shipbuilding yard. The making and filling of shells are entrusted to them; and they convey them, driving heavy lorries...' Caroline Fox describes Laura's correspondence with the War Artists Advisory Committee[3] and implies she had a reputation for being a little difficult. Her work for them clearly made an impression, however, and at the end of the war when she herself proposed the War Trials at

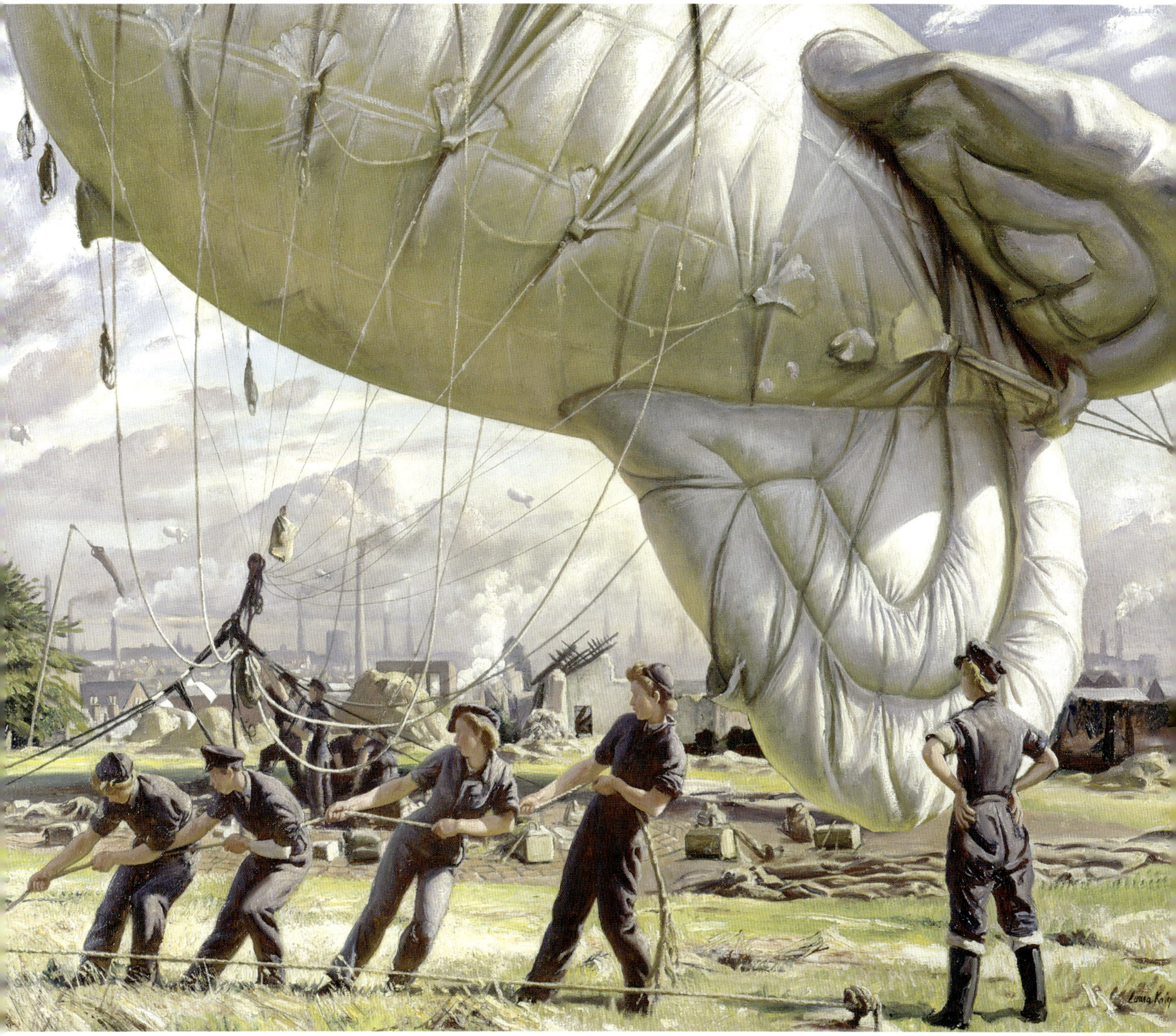

A BALLOON SITE, COVENTRY

1943 | oil on canvas | 111.6 x 127 cm

Nuremberg as a subject, they agreed. Matters were arranged by the War Office and the Ministry of Information and in January 1946 Laura was sent out to Germany with VIP status.[4]

The final painting of the high-ranking Nazis put on trial at Nuremberg is the result of many weeks of intensive work, making studies and a full-size working sketch. Laura sought and eventually found a way of expressing the devastated city that was the context of the trial, painting it as a dark and resonant passage to the left and across the top of her canvas which otherwise was a view looking directly down and along the line of defendants in the dock. The whole trip made a deep impression. Laura wrote a diary, expanded from notes she made for a broadcast, for Harold to read. In page after page of manuscript[5] she describes the men in the dock, the progress of her work, the extraordinary social life of the wide circle of people involved in the trial and the post-war administration, and the terrible bombed-out city where people were beginning to improvise life among the ruins. Later she wrote: 'it seemed to me that every corner of that city told its own poignant and terrible story.'[6]

Laura Knight flew back to London in April 1946 and was immediately involved in preparations for that year's Royal Academy exhibition. As a full Academician, it was her prerogative to participate in selection and hanging: in fact she felt obliged to give it her time and attention, describing the proceedings in some detail.[7] She remained a stalwart of the Academy from that time onwards, though not an un-critical one: there is a letter of June 1946 in the Royal Academy Archive in which she berates them for placing a table with price lists too close to her painting – 'vandalism' she says. Returning for recuperation to the Malvern landscape she was in time to see the orchards in blossom: 'how lush and green is our meadowland, how dazzling the pear orchards, then white roofed with blossom, how haphazard is our agriculture – oddly shaped, hedged in, dotted with church, cottage, pig-pen and haystack – all calm and sweet as if war had never been and sorrow never was.'[8] Laura wrote further descriptive passages about the Malvern landscapes she saw and painted again in the aftermath of the war: 'The view from my studio window was a feast in itself; red-roofed grey stone farm buildings, fields of all shapes: ploughland, golden harvest, green meadow… here a pathway leading into the far distance is outlined by a shaft of sunlight piercing blue cloud shadow. And now comes the tempestuous dark of thunderstorm and the blinding wiggle-waggle of lightning, followed by the slanting fall of a shower to curtain the great arc of a rainbow.' 'As I write I live again, basking in the first rays of the sun rising over the Bredon Hill to dry up the floating strands of mist hiding the flatter country to the west – to remember at midday tramping every inch of the hills with Harold, when from the top of Worcestershire Beacon we glimpsed a bright spark, a flick of sun on water, the entrance to the Bristol Channel. Then at sundown, looking westward, behind the tumble of little hills we watched together the extravagant glory of the sun sinking to rest in the empurpled sheets of cloud.'[9] A Herefordshire landscape of Laura's at the 1948 Royal Academy was titled *Sheep may safely graze…*

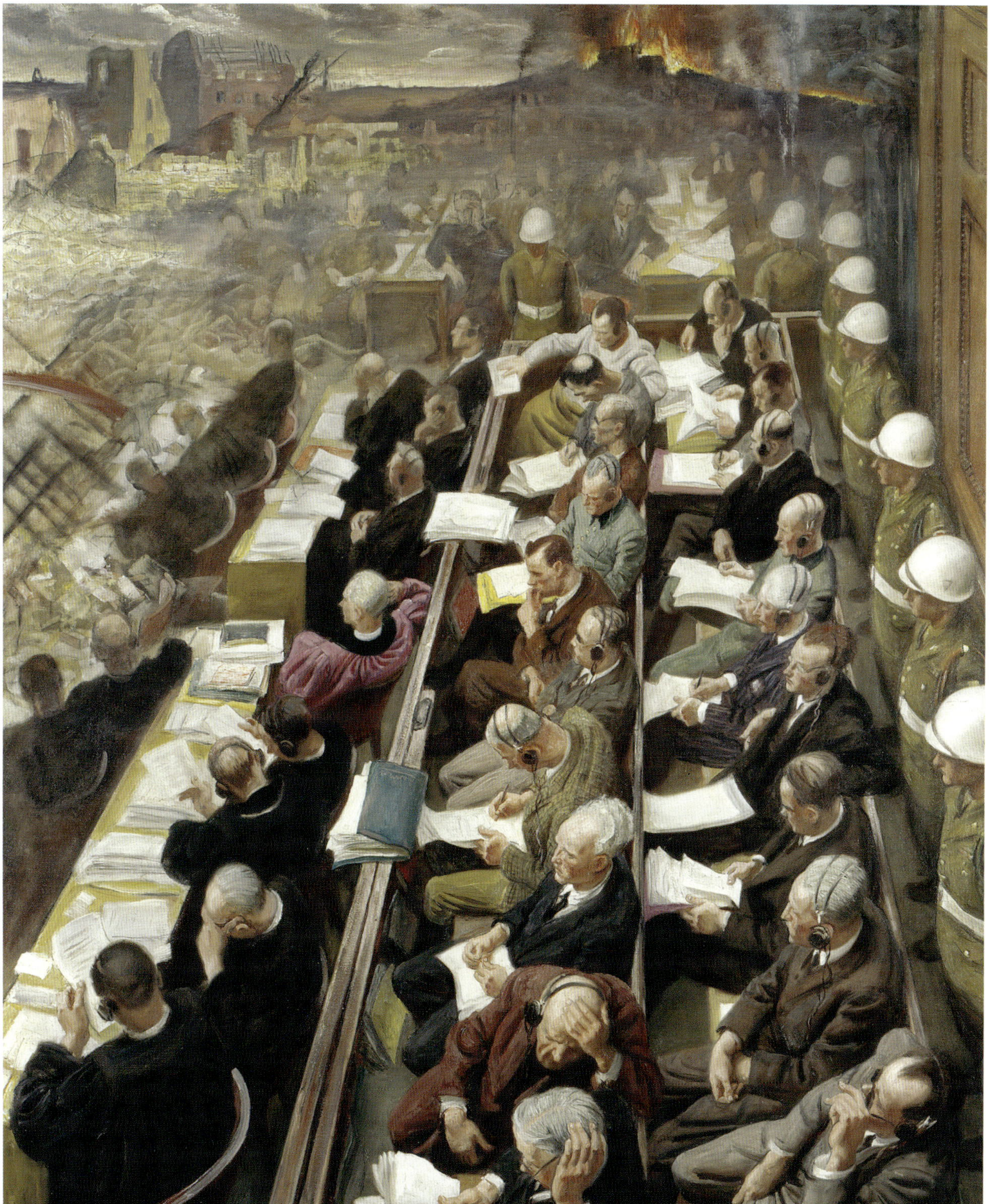

THE DOCK, NUREMBERG

1946 | oil on canvas | 177.8 x 152.4 cm

From the late 1940s and into the fifties Laura painted a number of natural effects like rainbows or thunderstorms, including the study *Rainbow and storm over a Landscape* and a painting of Malvern Priory Church in a thunderstorm with lightning and torrential rain. Besides these and the broad sweep of landscape that was evidently so important to Laura for spiritual healing and renewal, she began again to look at farming life. She made watercolour studies in the cornfields, and of women planting potatoes on a very windy day. In contrast to these, she attended the Coronation of Queen Elizabeth II in June 1953 and drew the decorations, the crowds and the procession. Laura often visited the Lake District, where a friend and patron of hers, Eileen Unwin, was the proprietor of the Rothesay Hotel. Eileen's house, the Wyke, overlooking Grasmere, contained many works by Laura, who naturally added Lake District landscapes to her repertoire. Brenda Brotherton, Eileen's cousin and later her heir, was also a friend and patron of Laura's.

All through the 1950s and into the sixties Laura continued to show landscapes at the Royal Academy Summer shows. For a time she used a studio in the garden of Hambleton, Barry Jackson's new house set among the trees a bit further down the hillside below Blackhill East, and so retained her close relationship with the steep western slopes under the Herefordshire Beacon and the farmland laid out below. She painted the old white pony Kitty and the donkeys again, against a wide westward-looking landscape. *The Hill Mokes* was shown at the 1954 Royal Academy; it was owned for many years by Morris and Marjorie Averill, who were friends and supporters of Laura's. She continued to paint effects of light and weather, particularly dawns and sunsets in watercolour, including *Misty Dawn* (also once in the Averill collection). Oils of the same subjects include a painting of sunrise through larch branches that was shown at the 1956 Royal Academy exhibition and bought for their collection; there is a drawing of the same subject and a study of a larch branch in the Fitzwilliam Museum. She also returned to earlier subjects, for example the painting *Ploughing* dated 1960 but based on earlier studies such as the drawing illustrated in *The Magic of a Line* (p.311), where it is titled *Ploughing Clayland* and dated 1940, and the large watercolour of plough horses on page 105.

Laura Knight's book *A Proper Circus Omie* was published in 1962. It is illustrated with many drawings and paintings and looks back over her long association with circus people and the way of life that she had found so attractive and so full of rich imagery for her work.

In her mid-eighties, still redoubtable but at a gentler pace, Laura continued to work in London and at Malvern. She was honoured with a large retrospective exhibition in the Diploma Galleries at the Royal Academy in the summer of 1965. Works of all periods and from a wide range of public and private collections were included. The catalogue lists a number of works that can be identified with confidence but a great many whose titles are probably not the same as when originally exhibited; there are also some whose dates may not be accurate. Many

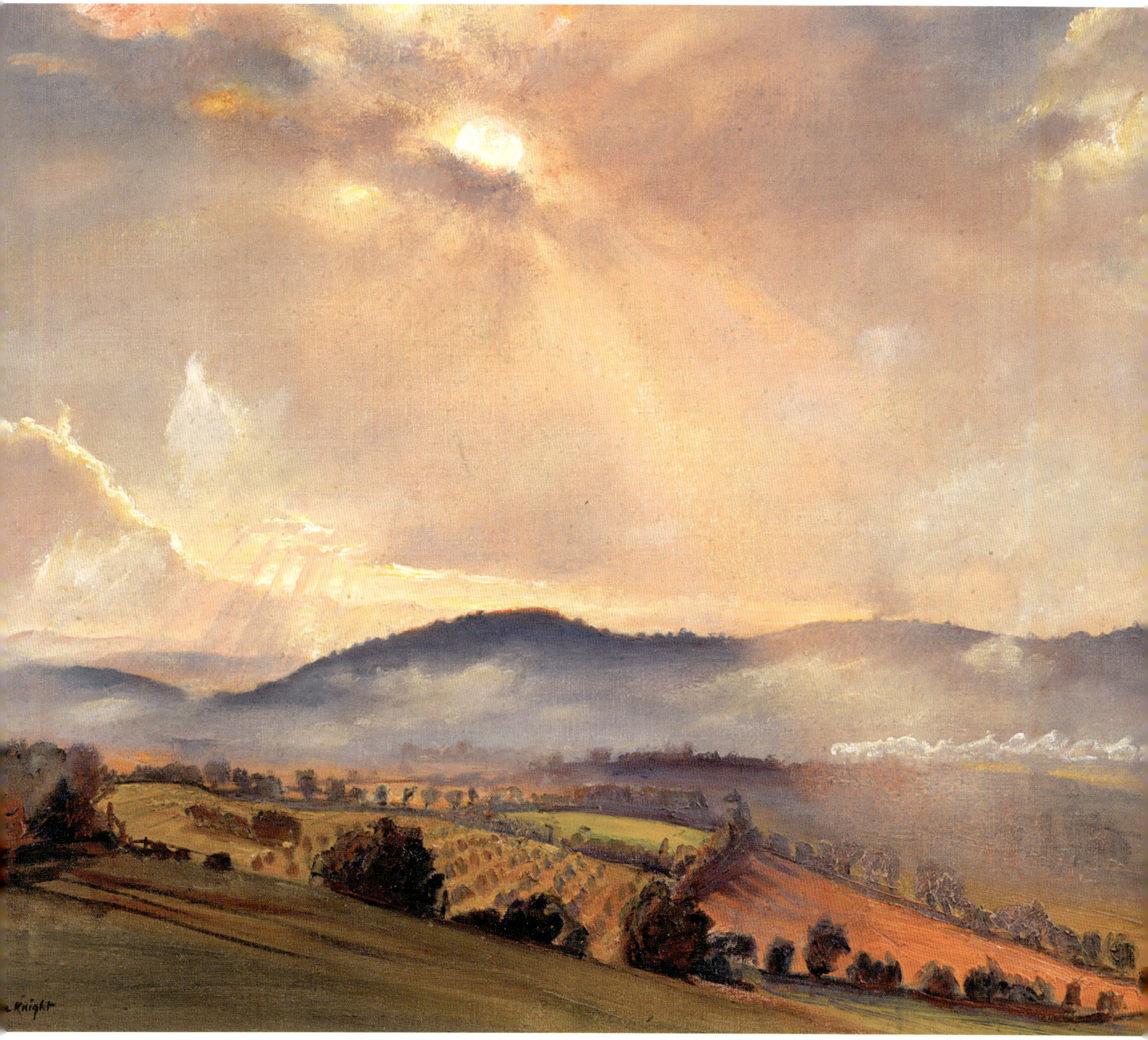

AUTUMN SUNSET
oil on canvas | 63.5 x 76 cm
private collection; courtesy the Fine Art Society

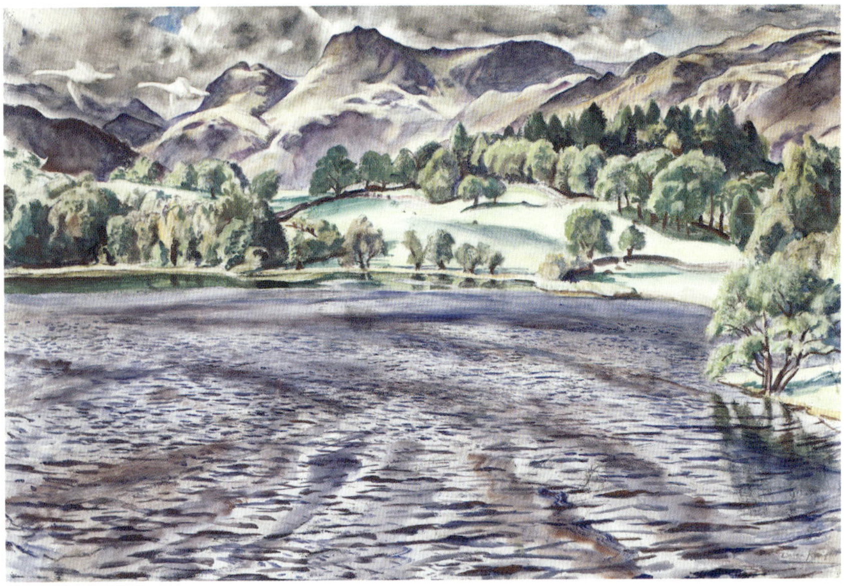

THE LANGDALE PIKES
watercolour | 67 x 102 cm
private collection; photograph Vince Bevan

works are listed as lent by the artist (and some works on paper are also listed in the catalogue of the studio sale held by Sotheby's after Laura's death). Caught up in preparations for the show she wrote to Ella and Charles Naper '...the old *Spring* has been yanked out of the Tate. Age has not wrinkled either the pain or yourselves. Charlie still makes ready to catch a trout or two for supper and Ella is still in the pink of her youthful beauty.'[10] In her exhibitions at the Grosvenor Galleries in 1963, 67 and 69 she mixed recent work with earlier paintings, drawings and watercolours. The 1969 one was titled '75 Years of Painting' and Janet Dunbar records her being interviewed by Michael Noakes for the BBC, despite having been involved in a car accident on her way to the gallery.[11] Finally, in 1970, a retrospective exhibition of her work at Nottingham Castle Museum opened just three days after her death on 7th July.

At the time of her Royal Academy retrospective, in the world of mid-1960s London, Laura Knight may have seemed an anachronism to a young generation dazzled by David Hockney, Pop Art and large-scale colour-field painting but to those who had loved her work through sixty years of prolific output it was a landmark exhibition. Her second autobiography *The Magic of a Line* was published that same year. Rather than take up where her previous book *Oil Paint and Grease Paint* left off in 1936, Laura returns to her beginnings, re-telling and adding to the stories of her family and her early years in Nottingham, meeting Harold, Staithes, Laren and Cornwall, then London and Malvern. This second life story then continues on through the late thirties, the Second World War and up to Harold's death at Colwall in 1961. She writes of their enduring marriage and how they became increasingly close again as

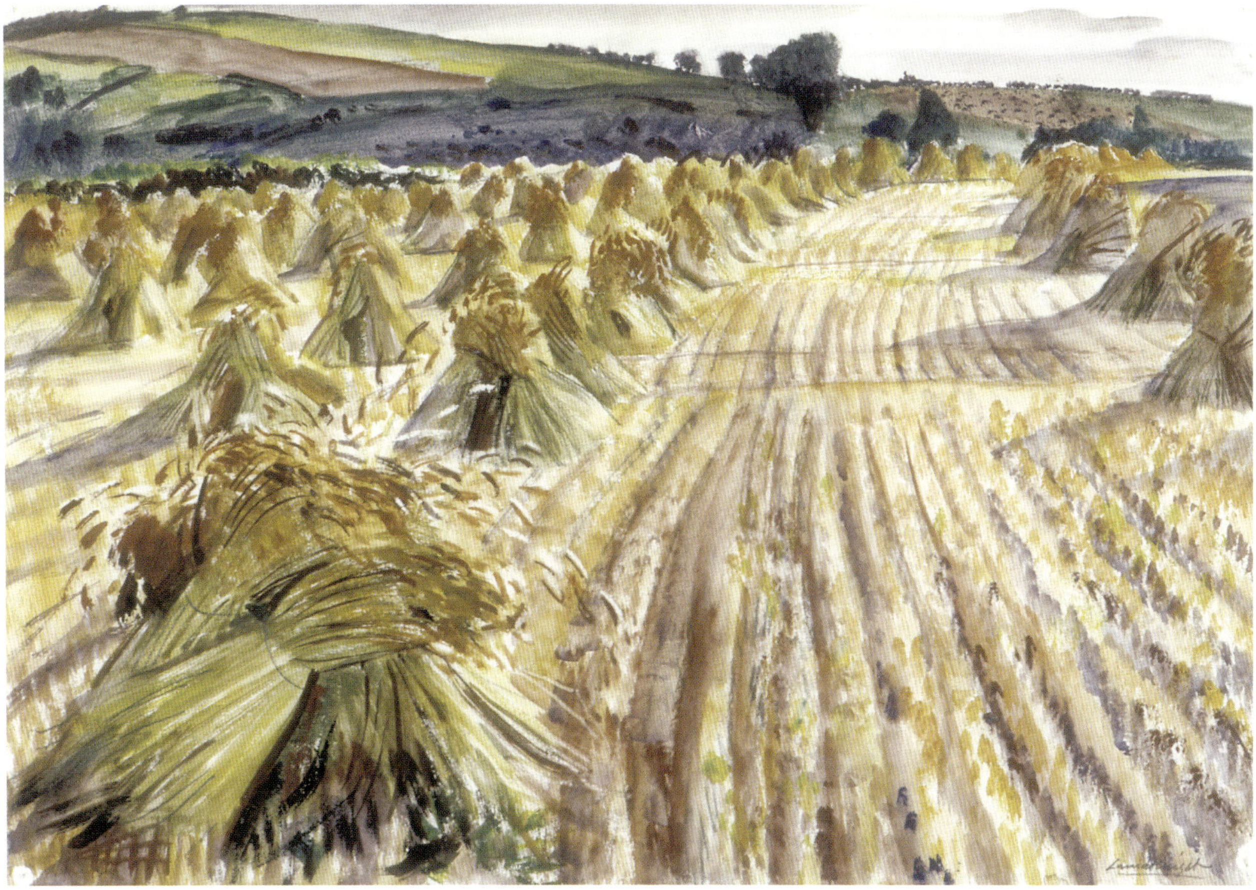

WHEATFIELD
watercolour and chalk | 40 x 57 cm
courtesy the Government Art Collection (UK)

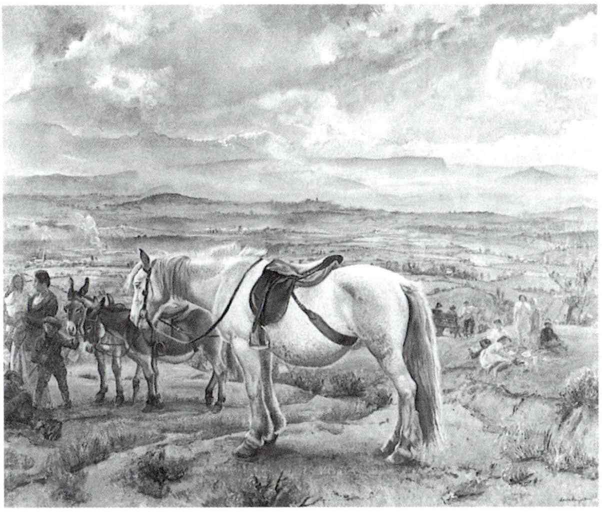

THE HILL MOKES
1954 | oil on canvas | 124.5 x 155 cm
private collection

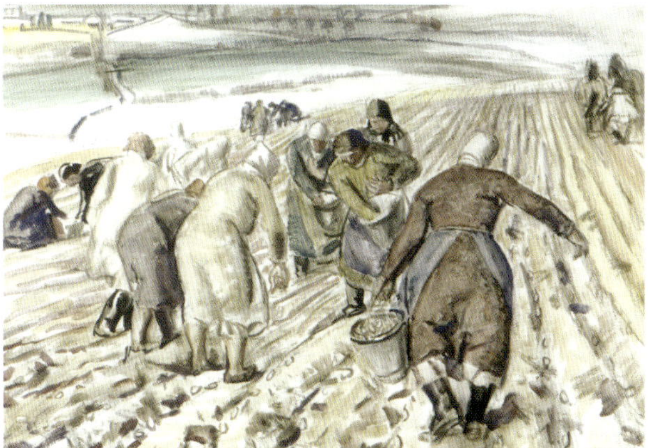

SOWING POTATOES ON A WINDY DAY
*c.*1950–51 | watercolour | 56.6 x 78.2 cm
courtesy the Government Art Collection (UK)

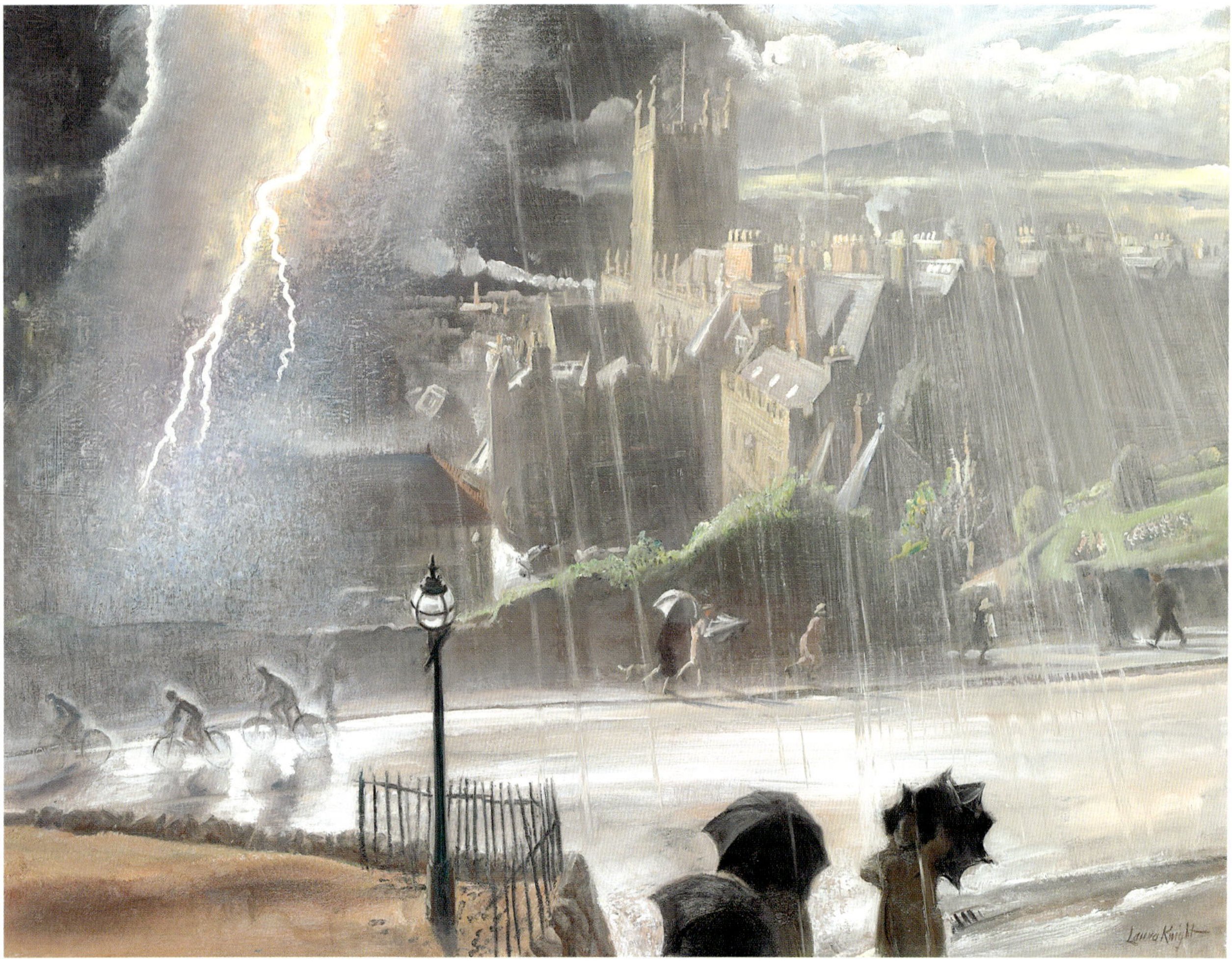

STORM OVER OUR TOWN, MALVERN

oil on canvas | 76.2 x 101.6 cm

Probably begun in the late 1930s but only completed about 1951

private collection; image © Christie's Images/The Bridgeman Art Library

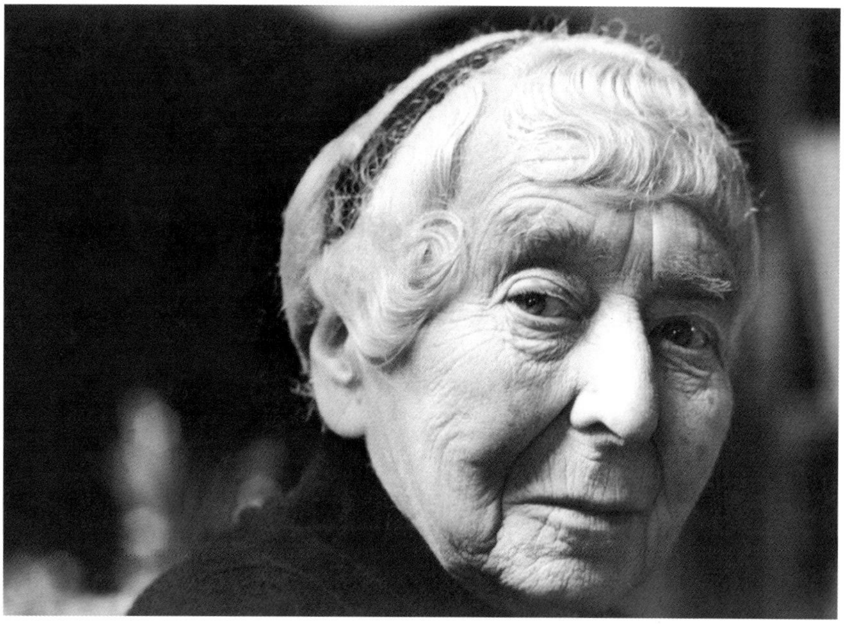

Dame Laura Knight, 1 January 1960
Hulton Archive

they spent more time together towards the end of his life. She acknowledges that '…his real nature was often hidden in darkness… nevertheless he lacked neither believers, reverence nor great love from those who truly knew him.'[12]

After 1961 Laura gave up the studio she had occupied since the late 1930s; her 'Hood' studio in Finchley Road and she moved into the studio that had been Harold's at home in 16 Langford Place. The close-up photograph from the Hulton Archive was taken in 1960, before Harold's death. Her face, in old age, shows all the personal qualities that sustained her through her long working life: quizzical enquiry, humour, energy and warmth.

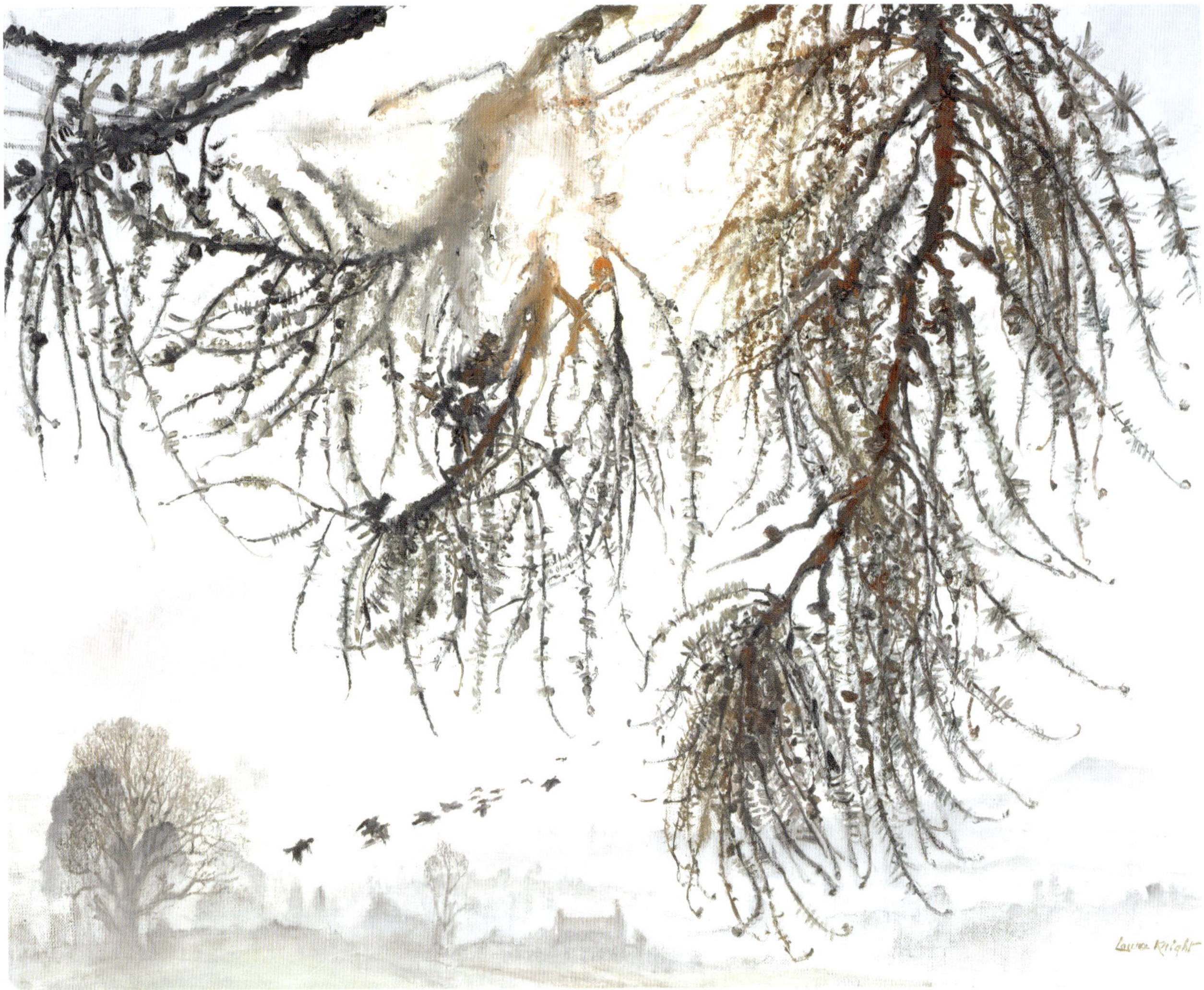

A MISTY SUNRISE

*c.*1956 | oil on canvas | 76 x 96 cm

Notes

Early days in Nottingham

1 Laura Knight's second autobiography, *The Magic of a Line*, 1965, p.137.
2 *Oil Paint and Grease Paint*, 1936, and *The Magic of a Line*.
3 *The Magic of a Line*, p.72.
4 Ibid, pp.98–99.
5 There is some doubt about this date. It may have been 1895 or 96, while in his book *The Staithes Group* Peter Phillips gives the date of the Knights' first visit as 1897.

Staithes and Laren

1 *The Magic of a Line*, p.107.
2 *Oil Paint and Grease Paint*, p.100.
3 *The Magic of a Line*, pp.74–76.
4 Ibid, p.79.
5 William Frederick Mayor (1866–1916), Henry Silkstone Hopwood (1860–1914) and Charles Hodge Mackie (1862–1920). See Peter Phillips, *The Staithes Group*, 1993.
6 See Janet Dunbar, *Laura Knight*, 1975, p.65.
7 *Oil Paint and Grease Paint*, p.103.
8 Ibid, p.117.
9 Ibid, p.108.
10 *The Magic of a Line*, p.122.
11 *Oil Paint and Grease Paint*, p.79.
12 Ibid, pp.145–6.

Cornwall

1 *Oil Paint and Grease Paint*, p.162.
2 Ibid, p.164.
3 Ibid, p.167.
4 Austin Wormleighton, *Lamorna Birch and his Circle*, Sansom & Co, 1995 pp.106–7.
5 *Oil Paint and Grease Paint*, p.167.
6 Ibid, p.169.
7 The study for the figure of Munnings reading was recently discovered behind a canvas of Laura's (*The Sunday Telegraph*, 20 September 2009, p.15).
8 Quoted in Austin Wormleighton, op.cit. p.32.
9 Ibid p.33.
10 Sir Alfred Munnings, *An Artist's Life*, p.295.
11 *Oil Paint and Grease Paint*, pp.170–71.

Cornwall and the early years of World War I

1 *The Magic of a Line*, p.139.
2 *Oil Paint and Grease Paint*, p.175.
3 Ibid, pp.184–86.
4 Austin Wormleighton, op. cit. pp.115–18, and John Branfield, *Charles and Ella Naper: Art and Life in Lamorna*, Sansom & Co., 2003 p.22–26.
5 *Oil Paint and Grease Paint*, p.186.
6 Ibid, pp.194-196.
7 Ibid, p.203.
8 Letter dated 27 August 1961 in the Royal Academy Archive; evidently the subject had been brought up by a researcher on Munnings in 1960–61.
9 See John Branfield, op.cit., p.19 and pp.27–30.
10 *Oil Paint and Grease Paint*, p.200.
11 Ibid, p.201.
12 Ibid, p.199; the painting is illustrated in the 1914 *Royal Academy Illustrated*.
13 Ibid, pp.205–7.
14 Caroline Fox, 'Painting in Newlyn 1900 to 1930' catalogue, Newlyn Art Gallery, 1985, p.100, and footnote 21, referring to a letter from Laura to Charles and Ella Naper dated 15 November 1957 quoted in the *Tate Gallery Acquisitions Catalogue*; see also John Branfield, op.cit., p.32.
15 *Oil Paint and Grease Paint*, pp.97–98.

World War I and London

1 Austin Wormleighton, op. cit.
2 Janet Dunbar, *Laura Knight*, pp.93–94.
3 *Oil Paint and Grease Paint*, pp.207–8; according to Munnings (Jean Goodman,

What a Go: The life of A.J. Munnings, pp.126–27), this was in 1915.

4 Ibid, p.227.

5 In *Oil Paint and Grease Paint* and *The Magic of a Line* Laura refers to this place as Queen's Road Studios, as do other sources including the Royal Academy's address records.

6 *The Magic of a Line*, p.152; see also *Oil Paint and Grease Paint*, p.243.

London and Cornwall

1 Jean Goodman, *What a Go: The life of A.J. Munnings*, Collins, 1988, p.145.

2 *The Magic of a Line*, p.186. The collection built by Henry and Louisine Havemeyer aided by Mary Cassatt is now in the Metropolitan Museum of Art, New York.

3 *Oil Paint and Grease Paint*, p.241.

4 Ibid, p.258.

5 Janet Dunbar (*Laura Knight*, p.119) clears up some confusion by explaining that no.9 Langford Place (the Knights' address between 1925 and 1930) was later re-numbered as no.16 (1931 to the present day).

6 Caroline Fox says the information came from E.L. Kerr (Lamorna Birch's daughter Mornie) ('Painting in Newlyn 1880–1930' catalogue, Barbican Art Gallery, 1985, cat.no.159).

7 G.F. Bolling & V.A. Withington, *The Graphic Work of Laura Knight* (with an introduction by Irving Grose and a catalogue raisonné of her prints), Scolar Press, 1993.

8 Letter from Laura to Eileen Mayo, Tate Archive.

9 *Oil Paint and Grease Paint*, pp.272–75, and Robert Austin, introduction to an exhibition of her prints and drawings, Upper Grosvenor Galleries, 1968.

10 Ibid, p.275.

11 Ibid, p.368.

12 Letter to Eileen Mayo dated 9 October 1927, Tate Archive.

13 Ibid, p.294

14 *The Magic of a Line*, pp.190–3.

15 Letter dated 3 May 1928, private collection.

16 Ibid, p.198, and *Oil Paint and Grease Paint*, pp.384–85.

17 This painting is in the keeping of the Suffolk Horse Society and shown in their Heavy Horse Museum, Woodbridge.

18 Timothy Wilcox, *Laura Knight at the Theatre*, Unicorn Press, 2008, p.75.

19 *Oil Paint and Grease Paint*, pp.386–87.

20 Ibid, p.391.

Malvern and the early years of World War II

1 *Magic of a Line*, p.252.

2 *Oil paint and Grease Paint*, p.264.

3 Article by Quex (George Nichols), *News Chronicle*, 4 August 1932.

4 *Magic of a Line*, p.270.

5 *Oil Paint and Grease Paint*, p.381.

6 Letter dated 12 March 1937, Nottinghamshire Archives.

7 *Magic of a Line*, p.273.

8 Letter dated 20 December 1942, private collection.

9 Ibid, p.244, and Rose Garrard, *Donkeys' Years on the Malvern Hills*, 2008.

10 *Magic of a Line*, p.274.

11 Ibid, p.330.

12 Letter dated 22 December 1944, private collection.

13 *Magic of a Line*, p.282.

14 Ibid, p.239.

War years and Malvern again

1 *The Magic of a Line*, p.280.

2 Ibid, p.280.

3 Caroline Fox, *Dame Laura Knight*, p.102.

4 Janet Dunbar, *Laura Knight*, pp.167–69.

5 Collection, Nottinghamshire Archives.

6 *Magic of a Line*, p.297.

7 Ibid, pp.304–5.

8 Ibid, p.302.

9 Ibid, pp.308–9.

10 Letter dated 10 June 1965, private collection.

11 Janet Dunbar, loc.cit, p.225.

12 *Magic of a Line*, p.150.

A brief chronology

1877	Laura Johnson born at Long Eaton on 4th August, third daughter of Charlotte Johnson.
c.1877–78	Charlotte moves into Nottingham, setting up house with her mother Mrs Bates, grandmother Mrs Thir and three daughters: Charlotte Ellen (Nellie), Evangeline Agnes (Sissie) and Laura.
1891	Laura is enrolled at Nottingham Art School where she meets Harold Knight, who is already a student there.
1889–95	Deaths of Charlotte, Nellie and both grandmothers.
1894	Laura's Aunt West takes Laura, Sissie and Harold to Staithes for a holiday.
1895	Laura and Sissie move to Staithes, Harold in lodgings there with other artists.
1896	Harold's first Royal Academy acceptance.
1903	Laura's *Mother and Child* accepted for the Royal Academy Exhibition. Laura and Harold get married on 14th June at Staithes.
1903–07	Laura and Harold both exhibit with the Nottingham Society of Artists.
1904	First visit to Holland, visiting Amsterdam and the art colony at Laren.
1905	Laura and Harold spend six months at Laren while still based at Staithes. Harold's *A Cup of Tea* a success at the RA.
1906	Laura's *Dressing the Children* at the RA. June: first exhibition of work by Harold and Laura Knight at Ernest Brown & Phillips' Leicester Galleries in London. Last period of working in Holland, last winter based in Yorkshire.
1907	October – second exhibition of work by Harold and Laura at the Leicester Galleries. The Knights move to Cornwall, renting rooms in Newlyn.
1907–08	Knights take rooms with Mrs Beer at Penzer House in Newlyn.
1908	Laura working on the beach at Newlyn. First circle of friends in Cornwall include S.J. Lamorna Birch and his family, Dod and Ernest Procter, A.J. Munnings, Robert and Eleanor Hughes.
1909	Laura becomes an Associate Member of the Old Watercolour Society. *The Beach* at the RA.

1910	*Flying a Kite* at the RA. Harold's *Afternoon Tea* at the RA.
1911	Knights living at Trewarveneth, Laura working at Lamorna. *Daughters of the Sun* at the RA; Laura painting nudes in the open air. *The Green Feather* shown in America and sold to Canada.
1911–15	Circle of friends of pre-war and early war years includes Charles & Ella Naper, Harold & Gertrude Harvey, Phyllis 'Pog' Yglesias, Gluck, Frank & Jessica Heath.
1912	Third joint exhibition at the Leicester Galleries including the first ballet subjects shown by Laura. *Studio* magazine article on Harold and Laura, written by Norman Garstin.
c.1912–13	The Knights move into Oakhill, Lamorna. Laura occupies large new studio at Trethinnick, a little way down the Lamorna Valley.
1913	*The Picnic* at the RA; Laura paints *Self Portrait* (aka *The Model*) and Lamorna Birch with his daughters. The Knights meet Barry Jackson in Cornwall.
1914	With Charles and Ella Naper, the Knights spend time at Dozmare Pool on Bodmin Moor.
c.1915–17	During the war, the Knights give up Oakhill tenancy but Laura retains Lamorna studio; they take lodgings for short periods, including in St Ives and Mousehole, and stay at the Napers' house, Trewoofe in 1916–17.
1915	Joint exhibition of watercolours, Laura and Lamorna Birch at the Fine Art Society.
1916	*Spring* at the RA; Laura paints *Penzance Fair.*
1916–19	Laura paints series of figures on the rocks, on the cliffs and against the sea.
1917	Commission for Canadian War Memorial: soldiers boxing at Witley Camp.
1918	Laura's exhibition at Leicester Galleries includes studies and paintings of soldiers at Witley as well as Cornwall subjects.
1919	In January the Knights leave Cornwall to live and work in London but Laura retains studio at Lamorna.
1920	Knights occupy two studios with living space off Queens Grove, St John's Wood.
1921	*Studio* magazine special edition on Laura and Harold Knight. Laura paints *Self Portrait.*
1922	Alpine Club exhibition presented by Ernest Brown & Phillips. Laura a selector for the Carnegie International Exhibition in Pittsburgh, travels to America for the first time. Knights move to a house with studio in Langford Place, St John's Wood; Harold has his studio there and Laura retains one of the Queen's Grove studios.
early 1920s	Laura begins to make etchings, printing and editioning herself.
1925	Laura becomes an exhibitor with the Royal Society of Painter-Etchers, becoming a full member in 1932.
1927	Laura elected Associate of the Royal Academy. Laura painting black American children seen in the Johns Hopkins Memorial Hospital in Baltimore.
late 1920s	Laura painting a number of female nudes including *Blue and Gold* (1927), and also begins to work on Gypsy subjects.
1928	Harold elected ARA. Exhibition at Leicester Galleries includes Cornwall and circus subjects by Laura.

1920s–30s	Laura concentrating on theatre and ballet subjects; also circus subjects from the late 1920s onwards; the Knights continue to spend time in Cornwall each summer.
1929	Laura made Dame Commander of the British Empire.
1930	Exhibition at the Alpine Club includes circus subjects and some Sennen Cove subjects.
1931	Laura's first visit to the races at Epsom Downs and the Knights' first visit to Malvern at Barry Jackson's invitation.
1932	Laura featured by *Studio* magazine as no.29 in series *Modern Masters of Etching*. Paints a portrait of George Bernard Shaw at Malvern.
1934	Laura begins her first autobiography *Oil Paint and Grease Paint*.
early 1930s	Knights begin to spend time at Malvern each year, taking rooms at a hotel in the town; Laura uses borrowed studio space and starts to paint landscape on both sides of the Malvern Hills.
mid 1930s	In London, Laura takes a studio in Finchley Road (her 'Hood' studio).
1936	Laura elected Royal Academician. *Oil Paint and Grease Paint* published.
1937	Harold also elected RA.
late 1930s	Knights based at Mount Pleasant Hotel, Malvern.
***c.*1939**	Laura begins to use studio space at Windsacre below Herefordshire Beacon.
1939	Leicester Galleries exhibition. *Harvest* shown at the RA. At outbreak of war, Knights leave their London house closed up and stay in Malvern.
1940	Knights staying at the British Camp Hotel near Herefordshire Beacon.
early 1940s	Laura painting farming subjects, hop-picking and landscape.
1942–45	War-time commissions in factories, workshops, airfields and balloon sites.
***c.*1943–44**	Knights settle at Colwall Park Hotel.
1946	Laura attends the War Trials at Nuremberg and paints the prisoners in the dock. Back in London, Laura engages with Royal Academy procedures but soon returns to Colwall Park Hotel with Harold, completes final Nuremberg canvas and resumes painting landscape and farming subjects.
1950s–60s	Laura dividing her time between London and Malvern.
1950s	For a time, Laura has the use of a studio at Barry Jackson's new house Hambleton.
1953	Laura in London to make drawings of the Coronation procession.
1961	Harold dies at Colwall. Laura gives up 'Hood' studio and moves her work into the studio at home in Langford Place.
1962	*A Proper Circus Omie* published.
1963	Upper Grosvenor Galleries exhibition, includes gypsy subjects and some earlier works.
1965	Royal Academy Diploma Galleries retrospective exhibition. Laura's second autobiography *The Magic of a Line* published.
1967	Second Upper Grosvenor Galleries exhibition.
1969	Third Upper Grosvenor Galleries exhibition.
1970	7th July, Laura dies (three days before the opening of Nottingham Castle's retrospective exhibition).

Selected bibliography

Bolling, G.F. & Withington, V.A., *The Graphic Work of Dame Laura Knight* (with an introduction by Irving Grose and a catalogue raisonné of her prints), Scolar Press, 1993.
Branfield, John, *Ella and Charles Naper: Art and Life at Lamorna*, Sansom & Co, 2003.
Dunbar, Janet, *Laura Knight*, Collins, 1975.
Fox, Caroline, 'Painting in Newlyn 1900–1930', exhibition catalogue, Newlyn Orion, 1985.
Fox, Caroline, *Dame Laura Knight*, Phaidon, 1988.
Fox, Caroline, 'Laura Knight', exhibition catalogue, Nottingham Castle Museum, 1989.
Fox, Caroline & Greenacre, Francis, 'Painting in Newlyn 1880–1930', exhibition catalogue, Barbican Art Gallery, 1985.
Garstin, Norman, an article in *Studio* magazine, December 1912.
Gerrish-Nunn, P., 'From Victorian to Modern: Innovation in the work of Gwen John, Vanessa Bell and Laura Knight', Djanogly Art Gallery, Nottingham, 2006.
Goodman, Jean, *What a Go: The life of Alfred Munnings*, Collins, 1988.
Halton, Ernest G., *Modern Painting: The work of Harold and Laura Knight*, a *Studio* special, no. 1, 1921.
Haworth, Peter, 'Painting by Members of the Staithes Group', exhibition catalogue, Fine Art Society, Whitby Museum and Bourne Art Fair, Edinburgh, 2002.
Knight, Laura, *Oil Paint and Grease Paint*, Ivor Nicholson & Watson, 1936.
Knight, Laura, 'Introduction', *War Pictures by British Artists*, second series, no. 1, Oxford University Press, 1943.
Knight, Laura, 'An Artist's Experience', *Studio*, November 1954.
Knight, Laura, *The Magic of a Line*, William Kimber, 1965.
McConkey, K., Risdon, P. & Sheppard, P., *Harold Harvey: Painter of Cornwall*, Sansom & Co, 2001.
Munnings, Sir Alfred, *An Artist's Life*, Museum Press, 1950 (also *The Second Burst* and *The Finish*, 1952).
Newton, Laura (Ed.), *Painting at the Edge: British Coastal Art Colonies 1880–1930*, Sansom & Co with Penlee House Art Gallery, 2005.
Phillips, Peter, *The Staithes Group*, Phillips & Sons, 1993.
Wallace, Catherine, 'Women Artists in Cornwall 1880–1940', exhibition catalogue, Falmouth Art Gallery, 1996.
Wallace, Catherine, *Under the Open Sky*, Truran, 2002.
Wilcox, Timothy, *Laura Knight at the Theatre*, Unicorn Press, 2008.
Wormleighton, Austin, *A Painter Laureate: Lamorna Birch and his Circle*, Sansom & Co, 1995.
Wortley, Laura & Fox, Laura, *On with the Show: Drawings by Dame Laura Knight*, David Messum /Studio Publications, 1988.

Selected exhibitions

1903–07	A few works in Nottingham Society of Artists exhibitions and Nottingham Castle annual spring exhibitions
1903	Royal Academy Summer Exhibition, first acceptance (second, 1906, third and fourth, 1909 and from 1910 onwards, regularly)
1906	Ernest Brown & Phillips' Leicester Galleries (and 1907)
1910	British Section, Venice Biennale (and 1914 and 1924)
1912	Leicester Galleries (and 1918, 1920, 1926, 1928, 1932, 1934 and 1939)
1912	Carnegie Institute/Carnegie International, Pittsburg (and 1914 and 1922)
1915	Fine Art Society
1920	Manchester City Art Gallery
1922	Alpine Club Galleries (and 1930)
1931	Usher Gallery, Lincoln
1933	Laing Art Gallery, Newcastle-Upon-Tyne
1934	Nottingham Castle Museum (and 1970)
1963	Upper Grosvenor Galleries (also 1968 and 1969)
1965	Diploma Galleries, Royal Academy
	Posthumous
1983	Editions Graphiques Gallery, London
1985	'Painting in Newlyn 1900–1930', Newlyn Art Gallery, Cornwall
1985	'Painting in Newlyn 1880–1930', Barbican Art Gallery
1988	David Messum Fine Art (also 1991)
1989	Nottingham Castle Museum
1996	'Women Artists in Cornwall 1880–1940', Falmouth Art Gallery, Cornwall
2005	'Painting at the Edge', Penlee House Gallery, Penzance and tour
2006	'From Victorian to Modern…', Djanogly Art Gallery, Nottingham and tour
2008	'Laura Knight at the Theatre', The Lowry, Salford and tour
	'The Magic of a Line', Penlee House Gallery, Penzance
2012	'Laura Knight: In the Open Air', Penlee House Gallery, Penzance and tour through 2012–13 (to Djanogly Art Gallery at the University of Nottingham and Worcester City Art Gallery)
2015	In preparation, retrospective at Dulwich Art Gallery

Author's acknowledgements

As I prepared this book, many people gave generous help with information and advice. John Croft, who is the grandson of Laura's sister Sissie and is preparing a catalogue raisonné, has been a great help. Alison Bevan and Katie Herbert at Penlee House Gallery and Museum have been patient and generous collaborators from the outset.

In addition, my thanks are due to the following people for their help and support: John Adams; Linda and Michael Averill; Peter Barnitt; Graham Bazley of W.H. Lane & Son; George Bednar; Chris Beetles; John and Diana Bishop; Bonhams Fine Art Auctioneers; Jeannie Brown; J.P. Brunas; Joanne Chamberlain, Atkinson Gallery, Southport; Christie's Fine Art Auctioneers; Simon Edsor at the Fine Art Society; Falmouth Art Gallery; Richard Green; Hilary Gresty; Irving Grose; Richard and Rosemary Harward; Amanda Hillier, Suffolk Horse Society; Andrew King of Nottingham Castle Museum; Gwynn Klee of the Dame Laura Knight Society, Malvern; Kenneth McConkey; David Messum; Alice Murray at Christies; Mim Nash; National Art Library, Victoria and Albert Museum; Nottinghamshire Archive; Jennifer Opie; Maryella Pigott; Mark Pomeroy, Royal Academy Library and Archive; Penelope Sayers; Sarah Skinner formerly of Nottingham Castle Museum; Katherine Smith; Sotheby's Fine Art Auctioneers; Tate Britain Archive and Library; Philippa Tinsley of Worcester Museum & Art Gallery; Heather Wakley of the Dame Laura Knight Society, Malvern; Sue Wolfendale.

Elizabeth Knowles

Index

Afterword

W Russell Flint wrote in 1965 that if one looks at the careers of women artists throughout the centuries, Laura Knight surpasses them all in her variety of achievement, and he questioned had any woman or how many men had successfully created such a wide variety of range of media and subject matter. Nearly fifty years later I believe that such comments are still relevant.

In my current project of compiling a catalogue raisonné of the works of the artist and her husband Harold Knight, it is noticeable that there are hundreds of Laura Knight's works that we know from exhibition catalogues but which cannot be traced today. Many are possibly lost for ever as a result of war damage, household fires and regrettably some from lack of care and maintenance.

However, a small trickle of wonderful works still emerge now and again either from sales on the market of works not seen by the public for a hundred years (ie. *In the Orchard* sold at Bonhams last year), or from members of the public contacting me having seen the website www.damelauraknight.com and wishing their picture to be included in the catalogue raisonné. Such works are emerging from not only the UK but also from many overseas countries.

It is difficult for curators not to duplicate previous exhibition works and to try and include works, if only a few, not previously seen. It is therefore a great pleasure that this year's exhibition 'Laura Knight in the Open Air' contains *Flying a Kite*, not seen in this country since 1910.

The interest in Laura Knight and her works after a long period of waning interest is now gaining momentum and this can be demonstrated in the number of recent exhibitions and planned exhibitions (see page 123), most notably the 2015 retrospective at Dulwich Art Gallery. This may tour to Nottingham with separate concurrent exhibitions devoted solely to the artist's signed prints, drawings and sketch books at locations to be agreed.

The blossoming interest in the artist is also demonstrated by the emergence of the 'Friends of Dame Laura Knight Societies', the first starting in Malvern in 2008 and the most recent in Nottingham in 2011. The Societies' aims are given on the website, their activities include talks on the artist, visits to places the artist used as a studio and lived at, plus visits to museums holding the artist's works. Those wishing to join the Society should either contact me directly or contact the local branch Society as given on the website.

Appeal for information

I would like to appeal to all collectors, admirers and those commercially involved with the works of both Laura Knight and her husband Harold Knight, to assist me in compiling the catalogue raisonné by:

- Providing me with images and information to enable the catalogue to become the recognised worldwide authority on the artists' lives and works.
- Providing documented or supportable evidence such as correspondence, invoices or other written records to corroborate events and dates within the artists' lives, to remove some current doubts and possible wrong assumptions that may have erroneously arisen.

R. John Croft FCA
great-nephew of Dame Laura Knight

Chairman
Trustees of the Estate of
Dame Laura Knight DBE RA RWS
PO Box 4710
Worthing
West Sussex BN11 9JE

info@damelauraknight.com

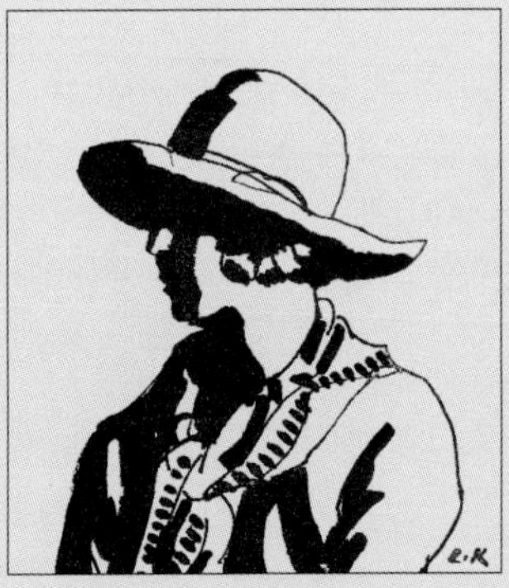